DEVELOPMENT ETHICS

About the Author

Prasenjit Maiti is a Senior Sociologist with Consulting Engineering Services (India), Kolkata. He has ealier served in various capacities in several organizations including TERI, New Delhi; Resettlement Plan Implementation Working Group of KEIP; Forum of Federations, Canada; Consumer Unity and Trust Society; Council for Development Studies; West Bengal Pollution Control Board and ActionAid. Dr Maiti has to his credit a good number of publications on development. He has also served as a reviewer for some international journals of repute. He was invited as a Guest Professor to the University of Southern Denmark, Esbjerg in 2007.

DEVELOPMENT ETHICS

Prasenjit Maiti

CONCEPT PUBLISHING COMPANY, NEW DELHI-110 059

Cataloging in Publication Data—DK
Courtesy: D.K. Agencies (P) Ltd. <docinfo@dkagencies.com>

Maiti, Prasenjit, 1971-
Development ethics / Prasenjit Maiti.
p. cm.
In Indian context.
Includes bibliographical references.
Includes index.
ISBN 13: 9788180695209
ISBN 10: 8180695204

1. Progress—Moral and ethical aspects—India. 2. Economic development projects—Moral and ethical aspects—India. 3. Social ethics—India. 4. Political ethics—India. I. Title.

DDC 170.954 22

ISBN- 13: 978-81-8069-520-9
ISBN- 10: 81-8069-520-4

First Published 2008

Published and Printed by
Ashok Kumar Mittal
Concept Publishing Company
A/15-16, Commercial Block, Mohan Garden
New Delhi 110 059 (INDIA)

Phones : 25351460, 25351794
Fax : 91-11-25357103
Email : publishing@conceptpub.com

Foreword

I am glad to recommend *Development Ethics* to both specialist as well as common readers. This is obviously a work of considerable merit and commendable scholarship whose time has definitely arrived. The author engages with the critique of development from an ethical perspective by forcefully demonstrating that moral values are inextricably a part of the ontological system that constitutes the dynamics of the development process. Values define the very standards of well-being and sustainability of primary stakeholders who happen to share the risks of development projects. The author has analyzed the different issues and concerns of development informed by ethical choices or otherwise in a most insightful and logically coherent manner. He has deployed both macro as well as micro-level contemporary analyses in order to post his arrangement of arguments and empirical evidence in a convincing style. This work by a social development expert with several years of academic training and valuable experience at both the field and policy levels working as an evaluation consultant on infrastructure projects for an international consultancy organization breaks new and exciting ground in the area of development studies. It establishes a theoretical and pragmatic framework for future research by locating the problem in its intellectual tradition and methodological lineages. I take this opportunity to wish the author well and hope that his latest work is amply rewarded by critical acclaim from readers and researchers worldwide.

Professor Michael A Peters
University of Illinois at Urbana-Champaign
United States of America

Preface

This work has steadily evolved from my everyday interactions with the concept of development in my professional capacity as a social sector expert working for an internationally acclaimed consultancy organization that specializes in infrastructure projects among other related areas. I wanted to formulate my own ideas regarding the notion of values impacting upon the dynamics of development while working on possible measures to reconcile the more often than not divergent trends of physical and human engineering. This led to a collection of writings that required a theoretical ensemble as well as a methodological defence as a justification for the kind of polemics I have occasionally tended to deploy in the logical framework of my argumentative analyses.

Development is a construct that should necessarily be predicated by at least a working arrangement of values without which one cannot possibly determine the moral standards of well-being. Benchmarks should be constantly innovated and institutionalized in order to cope with the fluid character of development that proceeds from one mode of production to the next catalyzed by the tension of changes in technology and shifts in moral priorities. It is also imperative to assess the unevenness of the playing field shared by the compulsions of market and the ethos of multiculturalism that serve either to justify the correctness of development or else to condemn its failures and limitations.

This work explores the multi-dimensional and problematic relationship between ethics and development in the context of an array of methodological tools and conceptual categories such as social capital, civil society, good governance, involuntary displacement and human rights. Especial emphasis has been laid to develop the text as a ready reference for students, research scholars, academics, activists, NGO professionals, planners, social workers, policy-makers, bureaucrats and development consultants who are professionally engaged or else intellectually interested in the dynamics of development informed by the polemics of ethical choices and polyphony of affected voices or otherwise. This work is expected to serve as a handbook that can facilitate action research or locate policy dialogues at both the global as well as the local levels.

Publication of *Development Ethics* was rather necessary on my part, as I could not quite resist the temptation of committing an academic mischief by bringing out yet another Volume in order to enhance the empathy of the academic community attuned to new ideas that I suppose would be discovered occasionally in my works on the part of posterity!

So the author is dead. I would invite you to shed your inhibitions and pre-conceived notions while studying my work, as you would come across a lot of theoretical stuff underpinned by jargons and irresistible terms of polemic discourse. But all such booby traps of activist and academic research should not ordinarily discourage you from examining this work of mine in detail.

My practitioner and scholarly points of view have more often than not clashed with one another in the course of finalizing this Volume. A lot of questions were raised in this work but I must admit that I am yet grappling with the possible strategies to arrive at sustainable answers and working solutions.

I wish to thank all those individuals who have taught me at the field level and shared their wisdom and insights with me in order to enlighten my ideas about the critical relationship shared between the larger context of ethics and the specifics of development. This work is in fact an exercise in the pursuit of memories to revisit the best practices and lessons learnt during my engagement in different development projects that were more or less identically informed by the voices and choices of beneficiaries and stakeholders as well as the ethical considerations regarding their well-being and sustainable future.

My professional colleagues in India and abroad require special mention for their valuable comments on my work in the recent past. I have also learnt considerably about the subject of this present work while editing the multi-volume book series *Development Studies* during the recent past. This was a great opportunity to interact with scholars and practitioners worldwide on the critiques and anti-critiques of development.

Several important documents from various websites have been either cited in or else appended to this work of mine. Reprint permission could not always be sought so I take this opportunity to extend my gratitude and thanks to all the domain owners and copyright holders of these websites.

My family has always been a constant source of support while I have worked impossible hours. I must also gratefully acknowledge the value addition that my most caring daughter Srabana Nandana has contributed to my limited intellectual domain. She is a most special person who has taught me countless memorable lessons in patience and understanding.

I am well aware of the limitations of my work. But I am also confident that my efforts are on to outgrow my faculties so that at a subsequent point of time I would be able to arrive at a point of reconciliation with my academic abilities and intellectual projects. May I fondly hope that Srabana Nandana would also share my faith and live my dreams.

Salt Lake City
Kolkata 2007

Prasenjit Maiti

Contents

Contents

1

Ethics of Development

Key Words

Civil Society, Civil Society Organizations, Community Participation, Community-Based Organizations, Culture Root Paradigms, Development Alternatives, Development Ethics, Empowerment, Gender, Multiculturalism, Non-Government Organizations, Pluralism, Public Sphere, Third Sector.

Executive Summary

This chapter makes an attempt to establish inter-relationships between third actor interventions and the *problematique* of human development in the context of power, culture and multiple identities. The central problem of this work has been theoretically located in this chapter (following the tradition of new theory) *i.e.* the values and preferences of development are reflections of constructed realities that tend to shift emphases in accordance with changes in the culture root paradigms of particular time and space perceptions that are scripted by the little narratives of fragmented histories.

Introduction

The problem of human development may be considered from different angles such as the civil societal approach or even the Third Sector interpretative approach that initially deliberates on the space that is located equidistant from either the State or the market. This is a critical approach that analyzes the dynamics of development from the angle of third actor capability. But the essential polemic that is disturbing intellectually in this context is predicated by the fact that developmental interventions sponsored by bilateral donor agencies in the form of loans, grants, technical assistance etc. are more often than not reflections of the trappings of uneven relationships of power. The theoretical hype and overkill associated with the concept of social capital as a methodological tool also needs to be seriously discussed in this connection.

Social Capital

The popular understanding of social capital as an embedded civil societal resource supported by networks of trust and cooperation should be analytically conceptualized here in order to locate the altogether intriguing notion of development ethics in its proper intellectual discourse. Social capital is more often than not underpinned by manufactured consent that in itself is conditioned by parallel movements of power and culture. What is trust and how can the intangible value of trust be defined by cooperation and multiple axes of social synergy that is cohered by an equally unquantifiable category called enlightened self-interest that is variously known as faith? The comparative value of trust when measured against infidelity may be quantified in order to understand why people sustain a working stock of social capital at the marketplace, in politics, public offices and the government or elsewhere where interactions and institutions come together to define various interfaces of public discourse. To disown my neighbour in his/her hour of need or crisis may not be quite a wise policy when located in a broader temporal perspective.

But the problem with rational consumers interacting at the level of the marketplace of politics is that they are not always endowed with the gift of foresight (that in itself is an asset conditioned occasionally by experience *i.e.* acquired social knowledge). Why is the notion of social capital at all relevant in our community life? Is this because it is a useful and practical idea that is mutually beneficial in utilitarian terms? You would benefit if I am truthful while I would gain if you are honest. We can translate and extend this notion into areas of good governance such as accountability and transparency. The social structure as a whole has a developmental stake rooted in the intangible yet immensely valuable resource of social capital. This argument is substantiated in the case of development ethics. Let us clarify this contention of ours in the following sections in the light of Figure 1.

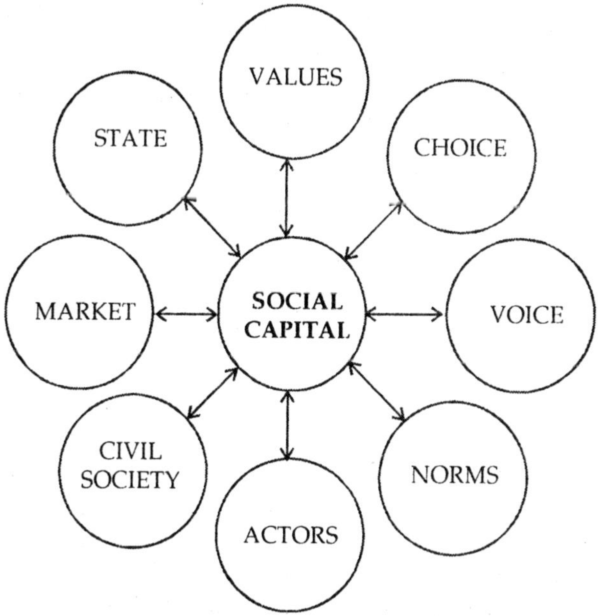

Fig. 1

This figure indicates the intricate and often equivocal interstices that may be present in the body social as well as the body politic of any common institutionalized structure of human interactions. Social capital may be located equidistant from either the state or the civil society or even the market. But this notion is nevertheless not immune from constant influences exerted by extraneous factors such as values that are actually social standards set by traditions of majoritarian behaviour and learnt reflexes.

Community Participation

Participation may be defined as purposive interaction that helps primary stakeholders at the grassroots level gain access to decision-making processes either directly or through legitimate institutionalized bodies such as Community-Based Organizations and/or Non-Government Organizations that happen to represent their interests and define their stakes in development projects. The Stakeholders' Consultative Process that emerges as a result of participatory development contends that community involvement is imperative

- to identify the needs and perceptions of primary stakeholders at the community level,
- to sustain and maintain civic amenities after withdrawal of implementing agencies,
- to monitor and evaluate the facilities and services created during the project,
- to institutionalize community-based mechanisms and
- to develop trusteeship among the community *vis-à-vis* their civic facilities.

Rapport at the community level may be achieved by organizing events that mobilize primary stakeholders to share a common platform from where their concerns may be voiced. Such events serve as an entry point to address the community psyche and streamline an interactive process, utilizing which identified representative groups may adopt a proactive role in the overall decision-making process and micro-planning of project activities and their implementation.

Rapport-building would also depend on the formal and informal groups capable of impacting the community in terms of interventions. Activities undertaken for initial rapport-building should also be gender specific, and depend on the willingness to organize such programs on the part of primary stakeholders. Follow-up of the events by way of community-level feedback would help reassess needs and reorient future intervention strategies.

Community mobilization also seeks to cohere social capital at the community level that would facilitate monitoring and evaluation of physical works undertaken during the project. Social capital would also ensure that the community continues to look after its collective assets even after completion of the project. Community participation strategies operate at

- the communitarian level where the community is brought back into developmental focus in order to sustain a proprietary sense among primary stakeholders; and
- the neoinstitutional level where actors and institutions are transformed into actors in institutions *i.e.* end-users of institutionalized civic services are mobilized to identify their personal agenda with community interests.

These are in effect utilitarian tools to motivate the community to become proactive and safeguard collective concerns at the corporate level. Community participation programs may be strategized to streamline developmental interventions and facilitate an interactive dialogue process between primary and secondary stakeholders.

Such programs serve to build empathy at the stakeholders' level and facilitate dialogic rather than pedagogic interfaces at the project implementation, monitoring and evaluation levels. Community mobilization is not an end but a means to secure rapport-building that (in its turn) ensures acceptance of interventions at the community level. This acceptance would finally serve

- to assess needs with regard to civic services/assets and physical works, vocational training programs and income-generation,
- to spread awareness with regard to health and hygiene and safe community practices, and

- to monitor and evaluate progress of physical works by the community itself.

Community mobilization and participation activities on the part of Non-Government Organizations and Civil Society Organizations seek to cohere and sustain a working stock of social capital at the community level. This is expected to facilitate monitoring and evaluation of ongoing civil works related to infrastructure development projects. Social capital may also ensure that the project beneficiaries continue to own and maintain their collective civic assets at the operation stage by mobilizing user charges.

So social capital emerges as an important dynamic in community-based initiatives to provide basic amenities, particularly for the poor. Through increased coverage, provision of more efficacious as well as affordable technology and better operation and maintenance on the part of user groups, community-owned basic service delivery systems are expected to perform better and in a more scientific manner than those built and maintained by Government Agencies.

Multi-Sectoral Dialogue

This dialogue is expected to facilitate cross-sectoral stakeholder commitment and involvement in infrastructure development projects. Such dynamic interactions may also contribute effectively to streamline timely implementation of the physical works of development projects.

Stakeholders' involvement in terms of public information and consultation exercises may extend to generation of awareness about the proposed physical works under different projects, active participation at the design stage and propagation of knowledge with regard to the timely implementation and cost-effective management of project activities. Stakeholder consultation engages primary stakeholders *i.e.* project beneficiaries in different dynamic tasks such as

- needs assessment exercises concerned with physical works, awareness-generation campaigns and training needs analyses,
- micro-planning for community-level needs in the context of finalization of proposed engineering designs and approval of user fees,
- participatory monitoring and evaluation of civil works as well as operation and maintenance of civic assets created under development projects, and
- evolution of trusteeship and expansion of networks of social capital at the civil societal level.

Needs assessment studies are important at the micro-planning stages of development projects that require involuntary resettlement of Project Affected Persons and their families. Such affected households may be entitled to compensation and benefits or otherwise may be evicted without any assistance or support mechanisms whatsoever. So their relocation at resettlement sites should be gender sensitive and ideally backed up by generation of alternative livelihood and restoration of income to ensure sustainability of the community fabric.

Resource mapping in and around proposed resettlement sites may be studied during the pre-relocation stage so that Project Affected Persons may be imparted a working idea of new sources of livelihood at the relocation sites. Local institutional and support mechanisms should also be worked out by secondary stakeholders so that primary stakeholders may either continue to or else begin to receive all sorts of humanitarian aid. This is especially crucial for the vulnerable groups who would be unevenly impacted by the process of relocation.

Stakeholder consultation utilizes crises management and sustainable development strategies by deploying different priorities for the purpose of resource and benefit mapping exercises. Participatory processes deploy public information and consultation strategies in order to reorient conventional top-down approaches to monitoring and evaluation so that beneficiaries may be empowered in terms of their community development. The participatory monitoring and evaluation model approaches individuals adversely affected by project interventions as the agencies rather than the targets of sustainable development.

So the politics of community participation is imperative in order to make development projects successful. Project beneficiaries have to be conditioned as well as deschooled so that their divergent worldviews may be adequately readjusted to participate in the carnival of developmental initiatives that are not always informed by the rhythm of everyday life at the level of grassroots actors and their institutions.

Social Impact Assessment of development projects may consider the option that development strategies, instead of being implemented from the above, can also work in tandem with participatory exercises shared by primary and secondary stakeholders and sustained by informed dialogues between them in order to establish best practices of learning from one another.

Monitoring and Evaluation

Monitoring is the systematic collection of data to provide the managers, donors and other stakeholders with an indication of project progress. Evaluation is the systematic and objective assessment of an ongoing or completed project, including its design, implementation and results. Evaluation leads to more informed decisions, allowing those involved in the project to learn from experience and to be accountable to donors and stakeholders. Both monitoring and evaluation should be used to demonstrate accountability and to understand the dynamics of the program.[1]

Willingness to pay underscores the anticipated revenue earnings of project authorities in terms of user charges/fees so far as operation and maintenance of civic assets are concerned. Better supervision of existing infrastructure indicates optimum utilization of manpower presently available *i.e.* streamlining human resources and avoiding incurrence of non-merit expenditures in this process.

Such benchmarks examine the value for money concern of good governance as a central issue of sustainable development strategies informed by stakeholders' consultation and information. Social Impact Assessment of development projects in terms of new infrastructure created is also an exercise related to physical progress measurement of engineering interventions and designs at the implementation level.

Monitoring and Evaluation indicators may be both quantitative and qualitative in order to include process indicators, progress indicators and qualitative indicators. These indicators will provide data inputs to monitor the project, evaluate progress of engineering works and guide the Project Authority to ensure and safeguard efficient use of valuable resources. Monitoring and Evaluation indicators may also determine the magnitude of project impacts on the quality of life of beneficiaries before and after implementation of civil works. Such indicators can also examine the increased level of civil societal participation and awareness-generation in terms of project interventions.

Social Interactionism

Popular institutions serve as indices to assess the quality of grassroots activism. Such institutions, moreover, have a proclivity to become somewhat indispensable as their networks expand and become increasingly detailed in terms of organization. Their levels of encompassment and embeddedness in the everyday politics at the grassroots rise accordingly. The role of social trust and networks of cooperation in the context of such decentralized governance is rather vital. Trust leads to social bonds and intra-as well as inter-institutional connectedness. Trust sustains institutions.

For what are institutions but formal agencies and domains of human interaction? And is not the problem of governance really a problem of interaction in its primary sense, a problem of interface involving both the State and its civil society/ societies? If rules are the accepted and expected (modes) of behaviour, then institutions are the facilitating channels that help socialize such behaviour. Neoinstitutionalism-in order to understand this baffling phenomenon of good governance-deals with actors *and* institutions as well as actors *in* institutions. Governance derives from an able handling of institutions.

Actors who function through institutions tend to make a lot of difference as to how such institutions perform. The kind of legitimacy and politics of development that we have in mind here would ideally emerge from real life, indigenous knowledge and intimate culture root paradigms of everyday life. We cannot deny the fact that institutions are necessary. But what are social institutions other than interactive arrangements of power that are best evolved indigenously?

This neoinstitutional argument is also supported by rational choice analysis that suggests that any democratic régime would legitimately prefer entrenchment[s] of its own power and authority rather than problems of governance. This, however, prompts an essential cost-benefit analysis *i.e.* what magnitude of political investment to establish pro-people and responsive institutions at the grassroots would yield good governance?

Development Ethics

The issue of human values conjoined to the discourses of development is more often than not predicated by the choices and priorities of infrastructure augmentation and enhancement of physical assets for a public purpose. The priorities of ethical choices applied to the sanctity of human development emerges as a critical policy imperative in the larger context of moral emancipation. This leads us to the larger and more problematic question of human rights when considered from the angle of civil societal liberties. How ethical can development ultimately become when analyzed in the light of assumptions informed by hegemony and the power/knowledge discourse. Development often appears to be a panoptican construct that is cohered by a gaze that is transnational and transcommunal in its scope and purpose.

People are at the centre of concerns for sustainable development. The international community has therefore pledged to eradicate poverty, to promote full and productive employment, and to foster social integration to achieve stable, safe and just societies for all. The rights-based definition of development in the Declaration on the Right to Development sees it as a comprehensive economic, social, cultural and political process.

A rights-based approach to development is a conceptual framework for the process of human development that is normatively based on international human rights standards and operationally directed to promoting and protecting human rights. There is no single, universally agreed rights-based approach, although there may be an emerging consensus on the basic constituent elements.

While it has recently received unprecedented attention, the idea of rights-based approaches is not a new concept. Many of its elements have been tried and tested for years. Rights-based approaches bring the promise of more effective, more sustainable, more rational and more genuine development processes.[2]

The architecture of dominant knowledge and the specificity of its impacts should be interpreted in a spatio-temporal manner that is conducive with the tenets of practical reason. But the most uncomfortable question remains: what is the cost of ethical development that takes into account angularities of politics and considers the dynamics of progress judged by objective parameters? This is a most difficult proposition that is underpinned by the politics of definitions and the multiplicity of identities.

Sustainable development can never emerge as a value-free project that is not conditioned by the microphysics of power or even the archaeology of knowledge. The semantic of learning is an ontologic exercise that cannot be unduly coerced by the versatility of multicultural complexities or pluralist politics.

We have to appreciate the fact that the overall dynamic of ethical definitions cannot be undermined irrespective of whatever value connotations development may subsume at different stages of infrastructure augmentation projects that happen to impact different categories of stakeholders in variant magnitudes and qualities.

Public Sphere

The concept of public sphere is especially important in this respect. According to Jürgen Habermas, the public sphere is "a realm of our social life in which something approaching public opinion can be formed. Access is guaranteed to all citizens. A portion of the public sphere comes into being in every conversation in which private individuals assemble to form a public body". A rhetorical theory of the public sphere emphasizes that "sphere" is a metaphor.

The public does not exist prior to the conversations that bring it into being. Its shape, boundaries and agents are all the products of discourse, although not divorced from their material aspect as well.[3] A concept in continental philosophy and critical theory, the public sphere contrasts with the private sphere, and is the part of life in which one is interacting with others and with society at large. Much of the thought about the public sphere relates to the concept of identity and identity politics.[4]

Poverty and Well-Being

Redefining entitlements is a process that intrinsically challenges predominant assumptions in the context of growing pressure of population and fragmentation of urban resources. New material conditions of life are redefined and differently influenced in this process. Lesser mileage in terms of minimum tangible benefits to primary stakeholders may result as a direct spin-off of the multipliers of poverty reduction programs. This is somewhat similar to the diminishing marginal utilities of consumption and over-utilization of resources that finally lead to satiety.

Poverty alleviation initiatives and income-generation measures may lead to gender empowerment for a certain section of the community. This may or may not result in formation or facilitation or even enhancement of the available stock of social capital so far as the target groups among the community are concerned. New culture dynamics may get entrenched in this critical process as functions of new societal arrangements and perceived specifics of realigned identities and different matrices of power. Such may be the case when new local markets are sought to be explored in the face of established global markets.

Such a state of affairs would require new institutional networks that may work in a milieu of change management predicated by development alternatives. This necessitates a new regime of discourse where the terms beget different signifiers and alternating signifieds. Voices and choices of the people would become confused otherwise in a cacophony generated by the multitude or the Tower of Babel of policy alternatives. Such an overwhelming otherness would provoke dystopic and dysfunctional social pathologies that would be without any incipient tenets of hospitality whatsoever.

Systemic compulsions of the New International Economic Order ushered in by the World Trade Organization and the General Agreement on Trade and Tariff may be viewed as in-built disruptions that only add background noise to disturb channels of communication between the market and the consumer who is prepared to utilize significant and limited resources in order to access utilities. Depleted capacities of primary stakeholders occur as a result of the systemic imperatives of globalization. So Government Schemes generally may not sound workable in theory but are more often than not ineffective in practice due to this fact.

Populism is another disabling factor that plagues liberal democracies such as the Indian political system. We come across policy decisions that are not commercially tenable in the market but are implemented nevertheless due to the compulsions of so-called pro-people and pro-poor politics. Local actors may be able to reorient a new brand of politics in their favour by manipulating primary resources available at the grassroots. But we have to deal with local as well as macro-level politics simultaneously in order to coordinate between the compulsions of subalternist and elitist power approaches.

This communitarian approach to social realities may ultimately serve to restore the community at the center of our developmental focus but at a significant cost. This cost is the one incurred during informed exercises pertaining to social choice. So it appears that the incidence of poverty and the eradication of poverty are often to be studied in a context of change management.

Obtainable social realities would suggest that poverty becomes institutionalized as a phenomenon in the interest of powerful social actors who are able to obtain the maximum mileage from the sense of relative deprivation that afflicts civil society. Poverty is also a function of social asymmetry. Inflation and stagnation of the currency may adversely affect the population in uneven ways.

This is due to the fact that social clusters are located along the economic hierarchy in different degrees of embeddedness. Public action and civic engagement in an enabling environment may or may not entrench channels of cooperation among primary stakeholders. Such vertical divisions among society are caused by differing axes of participation and priorities conditioned by dynamic variables such as knowledge, attitude and perception. This contention is established by Figure 2.

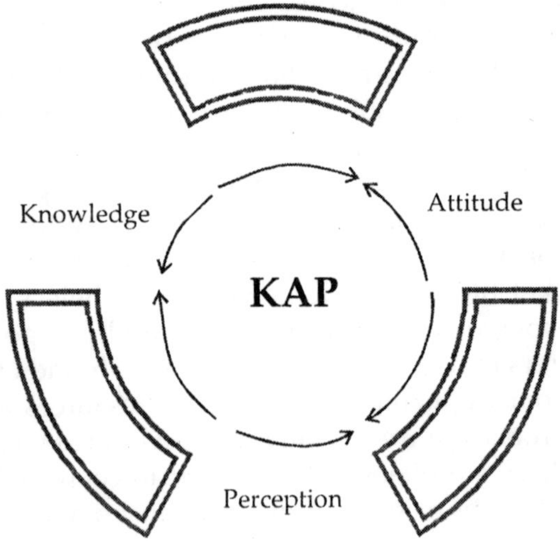

Fig. 2

Community Initiatives

Efforts may be made at the initial stage to involve Community-Based Organizations as well as Civil Society Organizations during training needs assessment and local market surveys for their logistic support and field-level inputs. Non-Government Organizations may assess the level of community preparedness to avail vocational training in slums where the community has already undergone such training in the recent past.

NGOs may also concentrate on slums where the level of community preparedness is not so high. Development Agencies may lay emphasis on motivating the community in order to sensitize slum residents with regard to the likely future impact of vocational training programs and formation as well as facilitation of Self-Help Groups.

Community mobilization and participation events organized in consultation with local-level Resource Persons and/or Key Informants may be planned at this critical stage as rapport-building exercises in order to gain acceptance at the community level. Entry points may constitute youth clubs and similar institutions. Such events may act as a forum where the local women can extensively interact with NGOs to plan and implement poverty alleviation programs.

NGOs may subsequently organize a series of joint meetings with community members interested to form SHGs. The concept, future impact and objectives of SHGs may be explained to such members during meetings and/or Focus Group Discussions where the community's mindset with regard to poverty alleviation initiatives may be assessed by professionals trained in Participatory Poverty Assessment techniques.

A basket of Participatory Rapid Appraisal tools such as the problem tree analysis, matrix scoring, priority ranking and resource and benefit mapping exercises may be utilized at this juncture in order to derive a clear picture of the community's felt needs and perceptions. NGOs may next form and/or facilitate SHGs to obtain institutional financial support for community development activities.

The level of community preparedness needs to be high in order to accept the rules and regulations of the group. Attitudes of group members need to be assessed in a scientific manner before any SHG is developed as a thrift and credit group. A series of workshops may be organized after a few months of SHG formation and/or facilitation in order to reflect upon the lessons learnt and the way forward.

Poverty Alleviation

Poverty alleviation initiatives may focus on training needs assessment and local market surveys in order to assess existing demand and supply forces with regard to domestic commodities or handicraft items. Such commodities should have an effective demand supported by purchasing capacities. Their nature should also be such so that they can be produced at low skills levels. Poverty alleviation programs may next concentrate on upgradation of existing skills or even creation of new skill sets *vis-à-vis* the community.

Need-based skills may be assessed among community members, existing infrastructural lacunae identified and vocational training courses accordingly planned and implemented to facilitate income-generation activities. A community-level coordination committee may be formed to monitor the demand for raw materials required in connection with production-related activities. Representative Groups working in association with this committee may also be constituted for marketing purposes.

Such groups may be trained to monitor changing market trends so that they can reorient trained community members accordingly. This is imperative in order to continuously upgrade the dynamic database of market-related information to be shared among Self-Help Group members for best product-wise results in terms of total sales and the annual business turnover of concerned SHGs. Representative Groups may also act as User Groups for operation and maintenance of civic assets.

Benefit mapping of poverty alleviation initiatives will sustain the long-term goals and objectives of Development

Agencies due to the fact that such exercises extend credibility to such community-level interventions. Such interventions may continue to be process driven rather than being progress-driven, as this works out to be more viable at the grassroots level in the long run. This neoinstitutional approach to alleviate urban poverty may also facilitate good urban governance practices in terms of better accountability, better transparency and more efficacious service delivery mechanisms *vis-à-vis* the municipal authorities. Any intervention designed by secondary stakeholders may be implemented in consultation with primary stakeholders. Such informative dialogue sessions may begin during the stage of planning for physical works for the urban poor as mandated by developmental projects.

Either the community as a whole or its representatives may be required to attend Focus Group Discussions where urban planners, civil engineers and social entrepreneurs are present to represent the secondary stakeholders. Problems of lack of access to or availability of water supply and sanitation services may be discussed in such platforms. It is to be understood that lack of access to basic facilities constitutes a measurable poverty indicator. Such service delivery lacunae existing at the grassroots may be identified by the secondary stakeholders in association with the primary stakeholders in order to formulate workable micro plans that evolve from participatory exercises.

Micro plans are informed by ground realities: so these have a higher rate of probability to succeed when implemented. Minute details of urban planning may be factored in micro plans by the community if decided on the basis of consensus. Priority ranking of available and required resources is essential in this regard. Poverty is predicated by intrinsic problems that are defined by local anatomies and social pathologies. Either distribution channels do not function or else the initiative to consume more is absent due to lesser income levels and rising inflation rates. The poor are rendered increasingly vulnerable either way in terms of entitlements and/or capabilities.

Such a state of affairs leads to marginalization of the poor in more critical ways than ever before. So we conclude that empowerment can subsequently be translated into development if the voices of the community are reflected in an able manner *vis-à-vis* realities of the market. Demand and supply forces will ultimately decide whether defined pockets of urban poverty are able to transform themselves into economically embedded zones of well-being sustained by resolute voices among the open-ended carnival of choices.

Locating the Global

We may increasingly appreciate nowadays that globalization is not only about processes but also about mechanisms that impact our daily lives and the manner in which we would prefer our lives to be impacted upon. This contention may appear to be somewhat irreverent but is nevertheless supported by a certain level of objectivity as well. So the nuances and criticalities of existence become all the more difficult to negotiate while rooted in one single destiny conditioned by one given and preordained order of values. We require more values and non-values in order to cohabit with more meanings and non-meanings. It is merely all about conjoining abstract signifiers with concrete signifieds as the fashionable global way of life.

So the contemporary processes of globalization do not only happen to constitute polemic engagements with *laissez-faire* utopianism because of the political specifics available in the First as well as in the Third Worlds but that most of the benefits of globalization also accrue to the First World because of its dominant policy to resist *laissez-faire* market arrangements in the movement of goods and services and labour forces around the world, especially into its domain, and its sustained opposition to the norms laid down by the Washington Consensus.

Rich countries religiously maintain their immigration barriers and discourage agricultural imports while most poor countries have not been quite successful to attract much Foreign Direct Investment due to misgovernance on the part of their national governments. Rich countries, however, may as well concede that politics is a fundamental informant of economic inequality since they are not likely to lower their agricultural and immigration barriers in the near future in order to facilitate protectionism at home. Rich countries may also review the performance of the Washington Consensus, which assumes that free markets necessarily promote economic convergence and underscore important issues [like the rule of law, property rights and transparent banking systems] to sustain dialogues between the North and the South.

The dynamics of globalization are more often than not perverted by the First World's studied reluctance to apply identical standards of *laissez-faire* to its borders and imports that it tries, with varying degrees of success, to impose on the Third World's legal structures and political arrangements. New global bodies such as the World Social Forum have also emerged in the recent years to meaningfully negotiate with the World Economic Forum and its politics of hegemony that extends to identities, cultures, languages, material conditions of life, ethnicity, social baggages, epistemology and ontology.

Personal is Political

May we now shift our stance somewhat to reflect that development may not always lead to freedom? Basic human rights [if guaranteed by the state apparatuses] may lead to capacities on the part of citizens. But what about capacities that do not sell at the globalized marketplace? If globalization, on the one hand, facilitates decentralization then, on the other, it also helps develop pockets of dynamic Free Trade Areas in large developing countries like China and India by reorganizing their economic geography, Foreign Direct Investments and global commodity chains.

This process, however, creates large hinterlands of economic backwardness and entrenches economic inequality *within* the developing South. Globalization, therefore, intensifies regional disparities in the Third World. The so-called Internet Revolution is indicative of the hegemonistic battles waged on a daily basis around the world with reference to critical discourses of production, consumption, distribution and exchange. But the World Wide Web was originally designed as a virtual space to permit efficacious and intuitive transfer of data across an array of proprietary networks.

Conclusion

Development, it may be appreciated at this point, is not anything extrinsic like politics imposed from the above without any regard whatsoever to the end-users of limited political resources. Actors who are supposed to interface with their own institutions are nearly always more comfortable if left alone with the material conditions of daily life that cohere organic ethos of community existence. This is where the colonial masters went wrong in Asia, Africa and South America when they bled the colonies white and left behind a legacy of comprador bourgeoisie and crony capitalism that, in turn, fostered a Repressive State Apparatus and a perverted anti-people bureaucratic managerial state system that was not only anti-people but was also occasionally anti-progress.

NOTES

1. Source: UNDP Handbook on Monitoring and Evaluating for Results.
2. http://www.unhchr.ch/development/approaches.html
3. http://www.wfu.edu/~zulick/MovementTheory/glossary.html
4. http://en.wikipedia.org/wiki/Public_sphere

REFERENCES

Bakhtin, Mikhail. "Author and Hero in Aesthetic Activity." *Art and Answerability: Early Philosophical Essays*. Trans. Vadim Liapunov. Ed. Michael Holquist and Vadim Liapunov. University of Texas Press Slavic Series, 9. Austin: University of Texas Press, 1990. 4-256.

—. "Discourse in the Novel." *The Dialogic Imagination*. Trans. Caryl Emerson and Michael Holquist. Ed. Michael Holquist. University of Texas Press Slavic Series, 1. Austin: University of Texas Press, 1984. 259-422.

—. "The Problem of Speech Genres." *Speech Genres and Other Late Essays*. Trans. Vern W. McGee. Ed. Caryl Emerson and Michael Holquist. University of Texas Press Slavic Series 8. Austin: University of Texas Press, 1986. 60-102.

Bitzer, Lloyd F. "The Rhetorical Situation." *Philosophy and Rhetoric* 1 (1968): 1-14.

Bormann, Ernest G. *The Force of Fantasy: Restoring the American Dream*. Carbondale: Southern Illinois UP, 1985. Bosmajian, Haig A. *Dissent, Symbolic Behaviour and Rhetorical Strategies*. Westport, CT: Greenwood P., 1980.

Burke, Kenneth. "Interaction III: Dramatism." *International Encyclopedia of the Social Sciences*. Ed. David L. Sills. New York: Crowell, Collier and Macmillan, 1968. 7: 445-452.

Cathcart, Robert S. "Movements: Confrontation as Rhetorical Form." *Southern Speech Communication Journal* 43 (1977): 233-247.

Charland, Maurice. "Constitutive Rhetoric: The Case of the *Peuple Quebecois. Quarterly Journal of Speech* 73 (1987): 133-150.

DeCaro, Peter A. *Rhetoric of Revolt: Ho Chi Minh's Discourse for Revolution*. Westport, CT: Praeger, 2003.

Giddens, Anthony. *The Constitution of Society: Outline of the Theory of Structuration*. Berkeley: U of California P, 1984.

Griffin, Leland M. "The Rhetoric of Historical Movements." *Methods of Rhetorical Criticism: A Twentieth Century Perspective*. Ed. Robert L. Scott and Bernard L. Brock. New York: Harper and Row, 1972.

—. "The Rhetorical Structure of the 'New Left' Movement: Part I." *Quarterly Journal of Speech* 50 (1964): 113-135.

—. "On Studying Movements." *Central States Speech Journal* 31 (1980): 225-232.

Habermas, Jürgen. "The Public Sphere: An Encyclopedia Article." *New German Critique* 1 (1974): 49-55.

Hilbruner, Anthony. "The Theory of the Avant-Garde: Some *Topoi* for the Study of Movements." *Central States Speech Journal* 29 (1978): 251-262.

Houston, Marsha, and Chris Kramarae "Speaking from Silence: Methods of Silencing and of Resistance." *Discourse and Society* 2 (1991): 387-399.

Jamieson, Kathleen Hall. "Antecedent Genre as Rhetorical Constraint." *Quarterly Journal of Speech* 61 (1975): 406-415.

"Generic Constraints and the Rhetorical Situation." *Philosophy and Rhetoric* 6 (1973): 162-170.

Jamieson, Kathleen Hall, and Karlyn Kohrs Campbell. "Rhetorical Hybrids: Fusions of Generic Elements." *Quarterly Journal of Speech* 68 (1982): 146-157.

Lake, Randall A. "Between Myth and History: Enacting Time in Native American Protest Rhetoric." *Quarterly Journal of Speech* 77 (1991): 123-151.

—. "Enacting Red Power: The Consummatory Function in Native American Protest Rhetoric." *Quarterly Journal of Speech* 69 (1983): 127-142.

Leff, Michael C. "Topical Invention and Metaphoric Interaction." *Southern Journal of Speech Communication* 48 (1983): 214-229.

Leff, Michael, and Andrew Sachs. "Words the Most Like Things: Iconicity and the Rhetorical Text." *Western Journal of Speech Communication* 54 (1990): 252-273.

Osborn, Michael M. "Archetypal Metaphor in Rhetoric: The Light-Dark Family." *Quarterly Journal of Speech* 53 (1967): 115-126.

Scott, Robert L. "The Conservative Voice in Radical Rhetoric: A Common Response to Division." *Communication Monographs* 40 (1973): 125-135.

Smith, Craig R. "Zeal as a Function of Danger." *Today's Speech* 16 (1968): 29-31. Smith, Jonathan Z. *Map is not Territory: Studies in the History of Religions*. Chicago: U of Chicago P, 1978.

Stewart, Charles J. "Championing the Rights of Others and Challenging Evil: The Ego-Function in the Rhetoric of Other-Directed Social Movements." *Southern Communication Journal* 64 (1999): 91-105.

Tucker, Kenneth H. "How New are the New Social Movements?" *Theory, Culture and Society* 8 (1991): 75-98.

Warnick, Barbara. "The Rhetoric of Conservative Resistance." *Southern Speech Communication Journal* 42 (1977): 256-273.

West, Thomas. "Beyond Dissensus: Exploring the Heuristic Value of Conflict." *Rhetoric Review* 116 (1996): 142-155.

Zarefsky, David. "President Johnson's War on Poverty: The Rhetoric of Three 'Establishment' Movements." *Communication Monographs* 44 (1977): 352-373.

—. "A Skeptical View of Movement Studies." *Central States Speech Journal* 31 (1980): 245-254.

Zulick, Margaret D. "Generative Rhetoric and Public Argument: A Classical Approach." *Argumentation and Advocacy* 33 (1997): 109-119.

Zulick, Margaret D., and E. Anne Laffoon. "Enclaved Publics as Inventional Resources: An Essay in Generative Rhetoric." *Argument in Controversy: Proceedings of the Seventh SCA/AFA Conference on Argumentation*. Ed. Donn W. Parson. Annandale, VA: Speech Communication Association, 1991. 249-255.

2

Ethics of Displacement

Key Words

Corridor of Impact, Entitlement Matrix, Land Acquisition, Livelihood Restoration, Monitoring and Evaluation, Non-Government Organizations, Project Affected Persons, Resettlement Action Plan, Resettlement and Rehabilitation, Right of Way, Social Development.

Executive Summary

This chapter summarizes the different issues and concerns of involuntary resettlement that is induced by infrastructure development projects such as roads, flyovers, dams, airports etc. The various conceptual categories and methodological tools involved in these critical human engineering exercises are discussed in this chapter.

Introduction

One of the most crucial aspects of implementing infrastructure development projects is acquisition of land and/or properties and resettlement thereof of Project Affected Persons and their families/households.

Context

Resettlement of Project Affected Persons and rehabilitation of their lost assets (land and/or structures) and livelihood are critical yet imperative social development exercises of linear road projects that require displacement of individuals and groups in order to either upgrade/widen existing road networks or else to construct new road systems for better transport facilities and streamlined movement of vehicular traffic essential for economies undergoing reforms. Involuntary resettlement caused by road projects should be informed by comprehensive mitigation measures in order to reduce adverse impacts on the existing social fabric of Project Affected Persons. This framework makes an attempt to reconcile the concepts of development and displacement in the context of the Indian liberal democratic political system presently committed to undergo sectoral reforms in order to institutionalize structures of good governance *vis-à-vis* the civil society.

National Policy Guidelines

The Government of India has prepared a R&R Policy that strives to standardize the good practices related to involuntary resettlement of persons and their assets in the national context. State Governments as well as Central Government Agencies more or less adhere to this policy in the case of infrastructure development projects. This is evident from the review of different Entitlement Matrices of road projects spread across the country. It is imperative that best practices and lessons learnt continuously evolve during the preparatory and operational phases of development projects so that change management in difficult situations may be efficaciously handled by the concerned Project Authorities. So information dissemination and knowledge-sharing exercises have to be constantly upgraded with regard to the problems as well as the solutions in the context of projects involving R&R.

The National Policy on Resettlement and Rehabilitation for Project Affected Families (2003) prepared by the Ministry of Rural Development (Department of Land Resources) of the Government of India states that "Compulsory acquisition of land for public purpose including infrastructure projects displaces people, forcing them to give up their home, assets and means of livelihood. Apart from depriving them of their lands, livelihoods and resource-base, displacement has other traumatic psychological and socio-cultural consequences. The Government of India recognizes the need to minimize large scale displacement to the extent possible and, where displacement is inevitable, the need to handle with utmost care and forethought issues relating to Resettlement and Rehabilitation of Project Affected Families. Such an approach is especially necessary in respect of tribals, small and marginal farmers and women."

The National R&R Policy displays concern for the more vulnerable sections of society that may be unevenly impacted by project interventions. It is to be realized that R&R is centrally about securing justice in nearly all its forms to Project Affected Persons. The unique feature that sets R&R apart is its attempt to explore new institutional mechanisms outside the scope of the conventional legal framework.

"The system of extending cash compensation does not, by itself, in most cases enable the affected families to obtain cultivable agricultural land, homestead and other resources which they have to surrender to the State. The difficulties are more acute for persons who are critically dependent on the acquired assets for their subsistence/livelihoods such as landless agricultural workers, forest dwellers, tenants and artisans, as their distress and destitution is more severe, and yet they are not eligible for cash compensation."

This is a limitation of the National R&R Policy. The primary stakeholders who are not entitled to any cash compensation from the project can subsequently become a social problem in terms of their relative deprivation.

". . . The Policy essentially addresses the need to provide succor to the assetless rural poor, support the rehabilitation efforts of the resource poor sections, namely, small and marginal farmers, SCs/STs and women who have been displaced. Besides, it seeks to provide a broad canvas for an effective dialogue between the Project Affected Families and the Administration for Resettlement and Rehabilitation. Such a dialogue is expected to enable timely completion of projects with a sense of definiteness as regards costs and adequate attention to the needs of the displaced persons, especially the resource poor sections. The intention is to impart greater flexibility for interaction and negotiation so that the resultant (compensation/support/assistance) package gains all-round acceptability in the shape of a workable instrument providing satisfaction to all stakeholders/requiring bodies."

Dialogues in the context of involuntary resettlement of Project Affected Persons is essential in order to provide the necessary interactive space within the framework of entitlements and benefits designed for PAPs. This dialogue must continue throughout and even beyond the project cycle in order to ensure that PAPs have secured adequate representation during the policy formulation stage and comprehensive participation during the project implementation stage.

This policy further states that "In case of projects relating to railway lines, highways, transmission lines and laying pipelines wherein only a narrow stretch of land extending over several kilometers is being acquired, the Project Affected Families will be offered an ex gratia amount of Rs. 10,000 per family, and *no other Resettlement and Rehabilitation benefits shall be available to them*" (emphases added). This contradicts the long-term income/livelihood restoration objective of development projects that induce displacement as per the World Bank's policy guidelines. "The National Policy on the Resettlement and Rehabilitation of Project Affected Families will be in the form of broad guidelines and executive instructions for guidance of all concerned and will be applicable to Projects *displacing 500 families or more en masse* in plain areas and *250 families en masse* in hilly areas, Desert Development Programme (DDP) blocks, areas mentioned in Schedule V and Schedule VI of the Constitution of India" (emphases added).

This is another limitation of the National R&R Policy due to its mentioning of the specific number of Project Affected Families. It implies that development projects displacing lesser number of families would not be covered by this policy. This shortcoming may be corrected in the future to ensure social safeguards. It is essential to impart social and economic justice to Project Affected Persons. It is also imperative to ensure that their community fabric and kinship ties and cultural identities are not destroyed due to project interventions.

World Bank Policy Guidelines

The World Bank has extended different categories of bilateral support to facilitate implementation of infrastructure development projects since its inception. It also simultaneously ensures that Structural Adjustment Programs are duly implemented by the countries receiving monetary support (loans/grants) as a condition attached to such financial assistance. So adherence to the World Bank's R&R Policy Guidelines on the part of National and/or State Governments is imperative in order to be eligible for any project support. "The World Bank's involuntary resettlement policy states that project planning must avoid and minimize involuntary resettlement, and that if people lose their homes or livelihoods as a result of Bank-financed projects, they should have their standard of living improved, or at least restored."[1]

Project implementing authorities who seek World Bank funding must ensure proper adherence to the Bank's policy guidelines in order to qualify for long-term financial support and assistance. Comprehensive R&R policy frameworks must be prepared in this connection as one of the preliminary tasks during the project preparatory phase. "Involuntary resettlement may cause severe long-term hardship, impoverishment and environmental damage unless appropriate measures are carefully planned and carried out. For these reasons, the overall objectives of the (World) Bank's policy on involuntary resettlement are the following:

1. Involuntary resettlement should be avoided where feasible, or minimized, exploring all viable alternative project designs.
2. Where it is not feasible to avoid resettlement, resettlement activities should be conceived and executed as sustainable development programs,

providing sufficient investment resources to enable the persons displaced by the project to share in project benefits. Displaced persons should be meaningfully consulted and should have opportunities to participate in planning and implementing resettlement programs.

3. Displaced persons should be assisted in their efforts to improve their livelihoods and standards of living or at least to restore them, in real terms, to pre-displacement levels or to levels prevailing prior to the beginning of project implementation, whichever is higher."[2]

It is evident that the World Bank intends to maintain all possible social safeguards in order to mitigate/reduce negative impacts caused by development project interventions. So policy planners of the concerned implementing agencies who accept World Bank funding should prepare their R&R guidelines in accordance with the Bank' social and environmental prescriptions. Such guidelines must also be in tune with the national context and ground realities of specific projects.

World Bank Funded Road Projects

Several State Governments in India such as Andhra Pradesh, Gujarat, Karnataka, Kerala, Uttar Pradesh, Mizoram and Tamil Nadu and Government Agencies like the National Highways Authority of India have in recent times undertaken road improvement projects funded by the World Bank. R&R Policy Guidelines were prepared by the concerned implementing agencies in accordance with the World Bank's Operational Directive 4.30/Operational Policy 4.12 related to involuntary resettlement. A few road projects can be cited in this regard such as:

1. Third National Highway Project (TNHP)
2. Grand Trunk Road Improvement Project (GTRIP)
3. Allahabad Bypass Project (NHAI Project)
4. Lucknow-Muzaffarpur National Highway Project (NHAI Project)

5. Andhra Pradesh State Highways Project (APSHP)
6. Karnataka State Highways Improvement Project (KSHIP)
7. Tamil Nadu Road Sector Project; and
8. Uttar Pradesh State Roads Project.

Certain changes have taken place over time in the policy formulation stage of different road projects funded by the World Bank. Such moderate policy shifts indicate that road or any other development projects require streamlining in accordance with the local-level situation and ground realities although the general policy framework with regard to involuntary resettlement of Project Affected Persons remains almost the same.

This is a lesson learnt *i.e.* specific projects require specific planning attuned to the ground realities in order to ensure that R&R policy guidelines are properly followed as mandated by the World Bank. Lacunae identified in earlier road projects can be addressed in subsequent projects (especially with regard to the entitlements of PAPs) in this process that strategizes continuous knowledge upgradation underpinned by change management mechanisms.

Case Studies

For instance: the Entitlement Matrix of the Allahabad Bypass Project mentions that "PAPs will be explained the process (of acquisition of land and assets and compensation against such acquisition at replacement cost or actual market value) and their views will be taken into consideration while determining the market value."

This concern was not reflected in similar terms in the Entitlement Matrix of the Lucknow-Muzaffarpur National Highway Project. But it was duly reflected in the case of the Kerala State Highways Project. The National Highways Authority of India's Detailed Entitlement Matrix for the National Highway Corridor (Public-Private Partnership Project) also includes this people's participation factor in its design (2002).

The provision of verification of mortgage clearance by the Project Authority is included in the Allahabad Bypass Project while it is not included in the Lucknow-Muzaffarpur Project. Categories of land loss were included in the Entitlement Matrix of the Andhra Pradesh State Highways Project (1996). This was a novel approach to identify the types of land loss in terms of magnitude (>25% and <25%).

The provision of "Unforeseen impacts shall be documented and mitigated based on the principles agreed upon in this policy framework" was absent in the Andhra Pradesh State Highways Project. This provision is essential to address new factors that may emerge at different points of the project cycle.

The Kerala State Highways Project (2000) provided "For those who choose self-relocation, the Project Displaced Persons will be entitled to plots ... even if they do not opt for resettlement sites." This was a unique effort to incorporate an adequate social space required for Project Affected Persons in their pursuit of alternative places of residence and/or work.

This project also mentioned that "Easily replaced resources such as cultural properties will be conserved (by means of special protection, relocation, replacement etc) in consultation with the community." This provision respects the cultural identities of Project Affected Persons and ensures that participatory development is safeguarded under the project so that the primary stakeholders duly benefit from the positive impacts of the civil works undertaken in connection with the project. It is also reflected in the Entitlement Matrix of the Uttar Pradesh State Roads Project Phase I (2002).

The Tamil Nadu Road Sector Project (2003) remarked in its Detailed Entitlement Matrix that "The land (agricultural or otherwise) purchase grant will be available if alternative land is purchased and registered within one year of receiving the compensation amount. The grant will be released on the submission of copy of registered sale deed".

This provision (available to those Project Affected Persons who lost more than 25 per cent of their land holdings and were left with less than the minimum economic land holding) is a good practice, as it considerably streamlined the land compensation mechanism and ensured social safeguard for PAPs. This project also included the option of built houses depending on the size of houses lost. This may be replicated elsewhere if practicable.

The Karnataka State Highways Improvement Project (Raichur and Bijapur Bypasses) pinpointed the budgetary provisions for implementation of the Resettlement Action Plan by mentioning that "All the costs calculated will be pegged to the inflation costs after 2 years from the Cut-Off Date". It also proposed in its Entitlement Matrix that "The maintenance of common property resources and infrastructure will be handed to the Local Authority." This provision ensures that the benefits of the project percolate to the grassroots as a result of decentralization of power and devolution of resources. The project also included a "Scope for making amendments in the R&R Policy." This is critical in order to accommodate any factor(s) not conceived during the project preparatory stage.

The Detailed Entitlement Matrix of the Gujarat State Highways Project (Phase IIB) included the institutional arrangement of an Independent Committee entrusted to decide the replacement cost or actual market price of agricultural land and assets of private property owners. This was a good practice and can be emulated elsewhere. This provision made the assessment procedure of land and assets transparent and also made this committee accountable to the Project Affected Persons.

The organizational structure of the R&R Cell has been mentioned in the Assam State Roads Resettlement and Rehabilitation Policy (2004). This is important because such organizational structures and institutional arrangements ultimately help implement the Resettlement Action Plan and facilitate entrenchment of good practices as per World Bank guidelines.

Review of different project policies reveal that a uniform set of guidelines apply to the Detailed Entitlement Matrices with minor inclusion and exclusion of certain provisions. The key beneficiaries have already been identified and the principal entitlements have been decided upon. Such policy continuity is essential for the long-term sustainability of benefits accruing from road projects funded by the World Bank.

The civil society[3] should be involved increasingly during site visits and physical examination of land in order to build a sustainable stock of social capital at the grassroots. Social capital refers to networks of trust and cooperation that are important to facilitate intra as well as inter-group dialogues:

"Social capital refers to the internal social and cultural coherence of society, the norms and values that govern interactions among people and the institutions in which they are embedded. Social capital is the glue that holds societies together and without which there can be no economic growth or human well-being."[4]

Such project-people dialogue may subsequently ensure decentralized good governance during the implementation stage of the project by ruling out the possibility of violation of human rights (in terms of coercive evictions). Gender representation may be accommodated during negotiations for purchase of land by the Government Agencies in order to ensure that women's voices and choices are duly recognized in this process.[5]

It is to be noted that physical works designed under the project cannot begin until the issue of land acquisition has been amicably settled on a mutual basis. Protracted official procedures may be avoided as far as practicable and the project-landowner dialogue should be facilitated under the relevant laws in order to acquire the land necessary for the project in a time-bound manner.

It is imperative that a multi-stakeholder and multi-sectoral dialogue is institutionalized by utilizing suitable mechanisms in order to ensure long-term sustainability of the benefits of the project. Project Affected Persons should always be consulted by the project planning and implementing agencies prior to design of compensation and assistance packages intended to restore land holdings and assets and re-establish livelihood and levels of income of PAPs.

Such norms of participatory development are required by the World Bank and delegate the accountability related to the implementation aspects of the project among the different categories of stakeholders:

"Participation is a process through which stakeholders influence and share control over development initiatives and the decisions and resources which affect them."[6]

It is to be remembered that individuals are always at the center of development projects and no project implementation can be considered to be a good practice until the issues and concerns perceived by individuals and their groups are thoroughly addressed.

Development projects that induce displacement in democratic political systems should always try to ensure that the cultural as well as social networks and economic viability of Project Affected Persons are not negatively impacted as far as practicable.

PAPs should always have both viable options and effective representation (in general and specific terms) in the overall process of development. The social security aspects of development projects (as implied by the World Bank's R&R policy guidelines) would otherwise be subverted.

Support Principles for Different Categories of Impact

Loss of Assets (Including Lands and Houses)

The project may cause affected persons to lose agricultural land, residential plots, residential/commercial structures, civic assets (wells, stand posts, latrines etc), cow sheds, boundary walls, trees and other assets. The project would compensate lost assets as per the current land acquisition practices. The entitlement unit for such assistance would be the Project Affected Household. The entitlement should cover loss of land and structures (and other assets such as standing crops) depending on the types of assets lost and the legal status of such land holdings. The project may provide the options of compensation in cash or in kind and other support mechanisms to vulnerable groups. Persons may be assisted to move back and away from the Corridor of Impact without disrupting existing facilities and support mechanisms. Squatters and encroachers would not be provided any compensation for the land they have occupied. They may be assisted to move back and restore their livelihood elsewhere. Targeted support would be extended to vulnerable group members among squatters and encroachers.

Loss of Livelihood or Income Opportunity

The displacement caused by the project in some cases may lead to loss of livelihood or income opportunities in either a temporary or permanent manner. Assistance in such cases should be provided to the Project Affected Persons to restore their livelihood and levels of income to existing or better status and to replace temporary losses. The project should provide support and assistance through alternative employment strategies if its negative impacts compel Project Affected Persons to discontinue their previous occupation. Project Affected Persons would be accorded preference (by way of relevant provisions in the contract documents) in employment opportunities created by the project such as labour mobilization at the construction sites or assignments related to maintenance of assets created under the project. Long-term earning opportunities should be provided through strategies such as vocational training programs, employment counselling, inclusion in government-sponsored income-generating schemes [such as the Swaranjayanti Gram Swarozgar Yojana (1999)], Swaranjayanti Shahri Rozgar Yojana, Sampooran Gramin Rozgar Yojana (2001) and National Food for Work Programme (2004)[7]] and access to microcredit through nationalized banks.

Collective Impacts on Groups

The project would have indirect negative impacts on the persons living in the vicinity of the road corridor in addition to the direct losses of their assets or livelihood. Such negative impacts should be mitigated as far as practicable. Negative impacts can be anticipated in areas such as traffic safety, access to water supply and sanitation and other existing facilities, access to Common Property Resources[8] and non-motorized transport such as pedestrians and bullock carts etc. Collective assets such as schools and places of religious worship may also be adversely affected by the project. Impacts related to a population's cultural heritage should be addressed with especial care in accordance with the World Bank's guidelines related to preservation of cultural heritage.[9] The project would replace lost assets and minimize any negative impact on groups (particularly groups that are considered vulnerable) through engineering designs, provision of infrastructure and other support mechanisms.

Targeted Support to Vulnerable Groups

Different impacts would affect vulnerable groups differently due to the different categories of vulnerability *i.e.*, children may be particularly at risk in terms of traffic safety, women-headed households[10] or persons belonging to households below the poverty line may be at a greater risk from losing their livelihood while small and marginal farmers may be at risk of suffering in terms of economic viability if they happen to lose their agricultural land holdings. Those considered as poor should be members of any household earning at or below the official poverty level. Special attention would be paid (on a case by case basis) to their habitats, livelihood, educational opportunities, vocational training etc. They would be provided with more options and support mechanisms than those not considered vulnerable by the project. This would be done in order to institutionalize social safeguard as a good practice under the project.

Engineering Design

Engineering design of civil works (for road upgradation purpose) should consider social and resettlement issues as an integrated approach in order to minimize displacement and mitigate negative impacts that would be caused by the project. Provision for roadside amenities, safety measures, restoration of Common Property Resources such as water hand pumps and stand posts, sanitation facilities, social forestry programs, bus shelters, rehabilitation of ponds, wells and water bodies, landscaping etc should be incorporated in civil works design as far as practicable. The necessary costs in this regard would have to be included in the project's Bill of Quantities.

Value Addition

The Design Consultant should follow the standard design for bus shelters that is available with the State Government. The contractor would involve local labour to construct these bus shelters and would complete construction before dismantling the existing ones for the purpose of upgradation of roads. These civil works would relate to the value addition aspect of the project roads. Bus shelters on both sides of the roads would be equipped with small roadside shops, drinking water sources (hand pumps) and public toilets. Medical and first aid facilities, consumer goods and public telephone booths would be provided along with these shops that would be allotted on lien to local-level Project Affected Persons belonging to vulnerable groups. A suitable methodology would be evolved by the Project Authority and the public representatives of the villages concerned in order to decide on the allotment of these shops. This arrangement would (to a limited extent) address the livelihood concerns of the vulnerable categories of Project Affected Persons.

Payment for the shops may commence after a year or so and this money can be used for the Operation and Maintenance of the bus shelters. This money can be kept in a joint bank account to be operated by the shop owner, the Sarpanch of the area and a Public Works Department staff member. The concerned Panchayat(s) along with the shop owners and a PWD official would be entrusted with the maintenance of bus shelters and public toilets. These shops would be maintained by the shop owners themselves.

This would ensure that benefits of the project ultimately accrue to the end-users of the roads and the stakeholders residing in the immediate vicinity of the project area. Proper security measures would be adopted at the construction sites to prevent accidents and loss of life as well as theft of raw materials. Group life insurance policies of the labourers may be arranged and paid for by the project. Water supply and sanitary measures have to be maintained so that the labourers can work in a healthy and hygienic environment. Pollution caused as a result of construction activities should be mitigated as far as possible.

Alternative Livelihood

The Resettlement Action Plan should include suitable provisions for deployment of local-level unskilled labour by the contractor agencies during the construction phase of the project. This clause can be incorporated in the contract documents to ensure due compliance.

This short-term employment provision can be utilized by Project Affected Persons as a temporary reprieve to compensate loss of their earlier modes of livelihood. The contractors should make regular payments in accordance with the Minimum Wages Act 1948.[11] Representative groups comprising labourers, labour contractors and project staff members (site supervisors) can be set up to monitor payments to workers on a continuous basis.

Middlemen should not be allowed to exploit the labourers. All payments should be recorded by the contractors and made in a public place to maintain transparency. Women labourers would receive their payments separately. Workers would be encouraged to form Self-Help Groups. Thrift and Credit societies (having access to nationalized bank accounts) facilitated by the Non-Government Organization(s) contracted by the project can follow as the logical next step. Child labour would not be deployed at construction sites. Sexual harassment of women labourers and their children should be prevented by the NGO(s).

Gender Security

Women (labourers) and children should be protected both at the construction and resettlement sites in order to prevent cases of gender violence and child abuse. Children and adolescent girls are especially vulnerable in this regard. The support mechanisms of the project should deal at length with the issue of gender empowerment so that the restoration of livelihood of Project Affected Persons can be carried out in a meaningful manner.

Support Systems

The NGO(s) recruited by the project for the purpose of public consultation and participation should ensure that gender mainstreaming[12] continues during and after the project cycle, public awareness is spread about the hazards of HIV/AIDS[13] (this is especially relevant in the case of road projects where high-risk target groups constitute truck drivers and commercial sex workers), minimum standards of public health and community hygiene are maintained to prevent the outbreak of water-borne diseases and literacy drives as well as vocational training programs are duly undertaken.[14] All the necessary support services required to protect the vulnerable groups among the Project Affected Persons should be explored and implemented as far as practicable.[15]

Resettlement Sites and Rehabilitation Measures

Agricultural land compensation would be provided to vulnerable persons and would be allotted jointly to the husband and the wife. New resettlement sites and/or sites for shopping complexes should be developed if so opted for by 25 or more number of Project Displaced Families or displaced shop owners (as the case may be) at a single locality (preferably in the neighbourhood). Adequate assistance should be provided by the project if Project Displaced Persons do not opt for such sites and prefer cash compensation instead.

At the relocation sites civic amenities like drinking water, link roads, medical facilities, schools, electricity etc would be provided along with any other facilities that the Project Displaced Persons had access to at their earlier place(s) of residence. Any facility provided by the Government and Common Property Resources being availed of by the Project

Displaced Persons prior to their resettlement should be provided by the project (as far as practicable).

Plots for houses and shops at the new resettlement sites would be provided to the Project Displaced Persons on a payment basis (excepting the vulnerable group members). The costs shall not exceed replacement value paid as compensation by the project. The allotment of plots for houses and shops would be made jointly to the husband and the wife in a public place in order to maintain transparency. All payments would be made by cheques. The cost of registration of land would be borne by the Project Authority.

Transitional allowance, shifting allowance, rent, assistance for loss of income etc shall be provided to the Project Affected Persons. Training for upgradation of skills related to income-generation activities would be provided as a rehabilitation assistance by the project. Such vocational training programs shall be linked with employment opportunities for income restoration purpose and re-establishment of livelihood. This measure for capacity-building of the PAPs would be integrated in the project design.

Entitlements

The different types of entitlements to be provided by the Project Authority for Project Affected Persons would vary according to their legal status. Such entitlements are as follows:

Entitlements for Project Affected Households

These entitlements would cover loss of land, structures and other assets (such as crops) and would include shifting allowance, right to salvage building materials, advance notice to harvest non-perennial crops, compensation for lost standing crops and counselling on alternative assistance. Those not eligible for legal compensation for loss of their structures and assets would be assisted by other support mechanisms. Entitled Persons would be extended the option of voluntary relocation to a site they have chosen themselves or (wherever possible) to a site chosen by the Project Authority. Whichever option the Entitled Person chooses he/she would receive support from the project to resettle and subsequently rehabilitate his/her household.

Entitlements for Project Affected Persons

Each household member over the age of 18 at the time of displacement is eligible for assistance for loss of livelihood. So there may be more than one person eligible for assistance in each household. The project would provide rehabilitation and assistance for lost or diminished livelihood for individuals impacted by the project. Additional support mechanisms would be made available to vulnerable groups to restore or enhance their livelihood through existing government employment programs and by giving them preference in employment opportunities created by the project.

Entitlements for Project Affected Groups

These group entitlements are targeted for additional support in order to ensure the sustainable development aspect of the project. Social safeguards at all levels must be maintained by the project. This is done by designing appropriate entitlements. Community-based entitlements for vulnerable groups would include:

1. Restoration and improvement of Common Property Resources such as water hand pumps and stand posts, sanitation and drainage facilities.
2. Provision to meet the needs of women, especially related to location of sources of water and firewood.
3. Provision of safe space and access to the same for business purpose, local transport and public use.
4. Safety measures for pedestrians (especially children) and other non-motorised transport.
5. Landscaping of community common areas in urban environments.
6. Provision of roadside amenities.

Entitlement Actions

General compensation and/or assistance actions for Project Affected Persons to be implemented by the Project Authority would be as follows:

Consultation and counselling regarding alternatives and assistance in identifying new sites and opportunities: PAPs are eligible to receive consultation and counselling assistance with regard to their entitlements and compensation alternatives. They would receive assistance to identify new sites for relocation and would be guided on what options are available to them for vocational and training opportunities for income/livelihood restoration purpose.

Compensation for land, structures and other assets at replacement cost plus allowances for fees or other charges: Only legal titleholders would be eligible for compensation under the Land Acquisition Act. Certain titleholders may be vulnerable group members and would thus be eligible for other support mechanisms. Squatters, encroachers and tenants would not be eligible for land compensation. All fees, taxes and other charges incurred in connection with the relocation of Entitled Persons would be compensated by the project. The unit of compensation shall be the Project Affected Household. Compensation shall be in conformity with the Land Acquisition Act and shall be at actual market value of land (replacement cost). The compensation shall include damage (if any) sustained by the Entitled Person due to severing his land (acquired by the project) from his adjacent land holdings, damage (if any) sustained due to adverse impacts on his/her other property (movable or immovable) or his income, reasonable expenses (if any) incidental to change of residence or place of business in case the Entitled Person is compelled to change his residence or place of business and loss of income in consequence of the acquisition of land when earning was derived directly from such land. Replacement cost shall be equivalent to an amount required to acquire substitute land of equal productive value as well as to replace any structures or other assets. Replacement cost shall be determined by an Independent Committee to be headed by the concerned District Collectors. The additional sum of money would be paid by the project in case of any difference between the actual market value as per the Land Acquisition Act and the replacement cost. Options of compensation and assistance shall be given to the Entitled Persons if residual plots are not viable so that they are appropriately compensated for their non-viable plots of land. An additional grant of 10 per cent of the amount paid for land acquisition shall be given in case of severance of agricultural land.

Advance notice to harvest non-perennial crops or compensation for lost standing crops: PAPs would be informed well in advance that the land on which their crops are planted would be acquired by the project in the near future and that they must harvest their crops in time. Entitled Persons would be compensated for their loss if standing crops cannot be harvested in time. Compensation for crops lost before harvest shall be equal to market value of crops lost plus cost of replacement of seeds for the next season's harvest. The unit of entitlement shall be the Project Affected Household. This provision is required in order to safeguard the PAPs from losses in terms of their subsistence/sustenance.

Compensation for perennial crops and trees would be calculated as the annual average net produce value for the crop in question times average number of years for a similar crop to reach production age: Only titleholders would be eligible for appropriate compensation for perennial crops. The unit of entitlement in this case shall be the Project Affected Household.

Replacement or compensation for structures or other non-land assets: Entitled Persons are eligible for replacement or compensation against structures and other non-land-related assets that are impacted by the project. An Independent Committee to be headed by the concerned District Collectors shall determine the replacement cost. Priority in Government Housing Programs would be extended to the Entitled Persons wherever possible.[16] The tenants would receive the following in the form of cash assistance:

1. The amount of deposit or advance made by the tenant to the landlord prorated on the basis of months remaining at the time of expropriation (this would be deducted from the payment to be made to the landlord).
2. A sum equal to six months' rental in consideration of the disruption caused by project interventions.
3. Compensation for any essential structure erected by the tenant on the landlord's property.
4. Absentee landlords would receive only the compensation at replacement cost or actual market value.
5. The owner occupier would receive 5% more than the absentee landlord. This is a fairness clause that recognizes the land owner's period of occupation *vis-à-vis* his/her plot(s) of land to be acquired by the project.

Right to salvage materials from existing structures: Entitled Persons are eligible to salvage materials from their existing structures and settlement sites (with the exception of trees).

Inclusion in existing governmental housing schemes: Only those Entitled Persons belonging to vulnerable groups (as defined by the project) are eligible for inclusion in the existing governmental housing schemes intended for the weaker sections of society.

Shifting assistance: Entitled Persons are entitled to a shifting allowance of Rs 500.00 to move their belongings. The amount of shifting allowance would be reviewed in each financial year. The unit of entitlement shall be the Project Affected Household.

Assistance for self-relocation to alternative sites: Entitled Persons would be given the option of voluntary relocation to a site they have chosen themselves or (wherever possible) to a site chosen by the project. Whichever option the Entitled Person chooses he/she would receive the required support from the project to resettle and rehabilitate his/her household. The resettlement sites shall be identified and finalised prior to relocation of Project Affected Persons.

Rehabilitation and assistance for lost or diminished livelihood: Entitled Persons would be eligible for support to regain their original levels of economic well-being. Vulnerable groups would receive the maximum targeted support. All Entitled Persons would be counselled on options to improve their standard of life. A grant equal to six months' lost income would be given to:

1. Persons indirectly affected due to their employers being displaced (on a case by case basis); and
2. Squatters carrying out self-employed business from structures within the public Right of Way (who are unable to move back at the original location).

Project Affected Households losing perennial crops such as fruit trees would be compensated at market value calculated as equal to capitalised value that is the net present value of production of such crops at a discount rate of 12 per cent per annum.

The encroachers would receive no compensation in general. They would be notified a deadline within which to remove their assets (except trees) and harvest their crops. Encroachers would be assisted (on a case by case basis) according to their household income and existing assets in the event of fulfilling both the following criteria:

1. Not owning the land adjacent to the land upon which he/she is presently encroaching; and
2. Being a vulnerable group member.

The unit of entitlement in the case of the above assistance to encroachers shall be the Project Affected Household.

Additional support mechanisms for vulnerable group members in restoring or enhancing their livelihood: Vulnerable group members who are Entitled Persons would receive targeted support from the project over and above the entitlements in their respective category as well as counselling service. Counselling on alternatives, guidance on appropriate training programs and advice on marketing new products would be provided. The unit of entitlement shall be the Project Affected Household. Additional assistance in the form of inclusion in income-generating schemes and/or vocational training programs of the Entitled Persons' choice shall be equivalent to a lump sum grant of Rs 2000.00 per annum for 3 years. Entitled Persons who would lose their places of residence would be entitled to cash assistance (based on status and eligibility) for the purpose of construction of their new houses.

Compensation or assistance for disruption of location of shifting business: Owners of kiosks who would suffer business disruption during the construction period of the project would be entitled to cash assistance. The amount of this assistance would be arrived at by considering such disruption to last for three months. Mobile vendors would not be eligible for compensation or assistance. Ambulatory vendors licensed for fixed locations would be considered as kiosks. Provision for vendors' markets would be made if suitable sites for shopping areas are available in those cases where 50 or more vendors would be displaced. The market would be rent-free for the first six months. Thereafter displaced vendors would be encouraged to purchase the market site collectively.

Employment opportunities created by the project: Local persons whose livelihood would be adversely impacted by the project would get preference in jobs and training programs associated with the project. Such employment prospects would be additional opportunities that would not be limited to the entitlements required to restore the livelihood of Entitled Persons. These opportunities would not be necessarily limited to vulnerable groups. Such groups must be targeted nevertheless. The project would require labour for construction as well as Operation and Maintenance of assets. The jobs in the semi-skilled and unskilled categories shall be offered to Entitled Persons and Project Affected Persons in preference to other persons. A clause would be incorporated in the contract agreement requiring contractors to extend employment opportunities to local-level Project Affected Persons in preference to other persons. Community-based facilities would also be provided with particular attention to the vulnerable and weaker groups besides the above mentioned compensation and/or assistance to Project Affected Persons and their Households.

Options and Choices

The project would provide options and choices among different entitlements to the Project Affected Persons. PAPs would be informed and consulted about the project and its impacts as well as their entitlements and options under the public consultation and participation mechanism of the project. PAPs would be duly counselled so that they are able to make informed choices from among the options provided. The project would undertake a risk and benefit analysis of each of the options and support mechanisms and explain the benefits and potential risks to the Project Affected Persons, Households and Groups. This would be done particularly in the case of vulnerable individuals and groups. They would be encouraged to choose the options that entail the minimum risk. The project would seek to make PAPs active participants in the development process and to achieve greater acceptance of the resettlement and rehabilitation efforts by allowing PAPs to choose among the different available options.

Collaboration with External Agencies

The Project Authority would collaborate with agencies experienced in Resettlement and Rehabilitation since most of the work related to R&R involves social development and community participation. External agencies such as Non-

Government Organizations/Civil Society Organizations/ Community-Based Organizations with adequate R&R project experience would be consulted by the project to ensure amicable resettlement of the Project Affected Persons and rehabilitation of their livelihood.

Coordination with Government Agencies

Various Government Agencies/Departments would have an important role to play in order to ensure streamlined implementation of the Resettlement Action Plan. Implementation of the Resettlement and Rehabilitation program of the project would be carried out in close coordination with these Agencies and Departments and also with the concerned District Magistrates, Sub-Divisional Officers, Land Acquisition and Land Revenue Officers and local-level representative bodies such as Municipalities and Panchayats.

Knowledge Building

An important objective is to develop local-level capacity to plan and implement Resettlement and Rehabilitation programs. The project would be required to document how capacity-building at different levels is achieved and how implementation of the Resettlement Action Plan contributes to good R&R practices and policies at the State and National levels.

This is required for information dissemination and knowledge sharing practices as encouraged by the World Bank.[17] The public disclosure aspect of this project should focus on accountability and transparency in order to ensure facilitation of social capital at the grassroots and observance of good governance procedures.[18]

Grievance Redress

It is expected that chances of acceptance of the project on the part of the Project Affected Persons would be enhanced (and complaints reduced) by ensuring a participatory Stakeholders'

Consultation Process underpinned by adequate compensation and support mechanisms. There may nevertheless be individuals or groups who feel that they have not been extended adequate support or that their needs have not been properly addressed by the project.

So the project would establish a Grievance Redress Cell comprising local-level representative committees that would hear complaints lodged by Project Affected Persons and facilitate solutions. This grievance redress process would be utilized to settle disputes through mediation and to reduce the volume of protracted litigation. The NGO(s) contracted by the project would be primarily responsible for running this Grievance Redress Cell.

Land Acquisition Act 1984

The Land Acquisition Act I of 1984 (along with its modifications) usually forms the basis of the land acquisition process in India. [The National Highways (Amendment) Act 1997 may be applied if the project road is declared as a National Highway.] The value of land depends upon its area and location along with its type that is classified as residential, agricultural, ponds, barren etc besides Government Land being used for railways, roads, canals, public utilities etc.

Legal Framework

The Land Acquisition Act I of 1984 allows Government Agencies to expropriate any private land for a public purpose (by exercising Eminent Domain), provided the owners in possession of legal titles to occupy the land and structures are duly compensated. Current land acquisition compensation packages include the following:

1. Market value of the land.
2. A solatium of 30 per cent on the market value of land.
3. An interest of 12 per cent on the market value of land from the Date of Notification to the Date of Declaration of Award.

4. Additional compensation is also allowed for loss of trees, crops, houses and other immovable assets.
5. The compensation for loss of earning to the sharecropper would be not more than six times of net average annual income derived during the three years immediately preceding the Date of Acquisition.
6. Damage due to severing of the land holding from adjoining land.
7. Damage due to land acquisition leading to change of residence or place of business.

Whenever it appears to the appropriate Government that the land in any locality (is needed or) is likely to be needed for any public purpose (or for a Company), a Notification to that effect shall be published in the Official Gazette (and in two daily newspapers circulating in that locality of which at least one shall be in the regional language), and the District Collector shall cause public notice of the substance of such Notification to be given at convenient places in the said locality.[19]

Where land acquisition is required the practice is to refer to the Date of Notification under law as the Cut-Off Date. Compensation is paid on the basis of value of the land at the time of Notification. The District Collector would issue a Notification announcing the public purpose for which the land or property is to be acquired. This would be followed by a period of one month during which objections may be filed by concerned persons with an interest in the land/property to be acquired.

Hearing of objections and the award of compensation by the District Collector would follow subsequently. All legal procedures would be meticulously followed while awarding compensation packages to Project Affected Persons in possession of legal titles to the land and (residential/ commercial) structures to be acquired for the project.[20]

Resettlement and Rehabilitation Guidelines

Every conceivable effort should be made during the project design and preparation stages to minimize acquisition of land

and other assets in order to reduce adverse socio-economic impacts. The structures/assets falling outside the Right of Way/ Corridor of Impact should be left undisturbed as far as practicable. Road and/or flyover projects may have to deal with Project Affected Persons who fall under the following categories:

1. Legal owners and/or tenants getting adversely affected due to the acquisition of their land and assets or due to the fact that such land or assets so acquired are their sources of livelihood; and
2. Encroachers and/or squatters who are the illegal occupants/users of public property/land/structures falling within the Right of Way and accordingly live and/or earn their livelihood by operating within the Right of Way.[21]

The Project Authority would take final decision with regard to compensation and/or Resettlement and Rehabilitation assistance. No compensation for land may be provided to the encroachers and squatters keeping in mind their illegal status. R&R assistance may be provided to encroachers and squatters who belong to the disadvantaged and vulnerable groups. Compensation for structures and other lost assets (required for the project) may be paid at the replacement value[22] to encroachers/squatters who belong to the vulnerable groups.[23] The Project Authority would take final decision in this regard.

R&R Compensation

Legal owners of land and property shall be entitled to compensation. Squatters and encroachers who are not ordinarily entitled for compensation may receive certain benefits as per their respective entitlements if they belong to vulnerable groups. The compensation for land and buildings shall be provided within the ambit of the Land Acquisition Act 1894 and assistance would be provided to meet the replacement value. All losses, including loss of income, should be compensated within the overall Resettlement and

Rehabilitation package as per the (proposed) Entitlement Framework. The Project Authority shall take the final decision in this regard.

Compensation and assistance would be extended to Project Affected Persons who were identified on or prior to the Cut-Off Date. Where land acquisition is required the practice is to refer to the Date of Notification under law as the Cut-Off Date. Compensation is paid on the basis of value of the land during Notification.

The Project Authority would ensure that a Notification is issued by announcing the public purpose for which private land and/or property are to be acquired. This would be followed by a period of one month during which concerned persons may file objections with an interest in the land/property to be acquired. The Grievance Redress Committee would deal with claims regarding assistance.

Payment of compensation against land acquired by the Project Authority may be made on the basis of updated official records and ground-level information. Land records of title/classification/current land use may be updated to ensure adequate cost compensation and allotment of land to the Entitled Persons/Project Displaced Persons. Official records as they are on the Cut-Off Date may be consulted in order to determine the classification and current use of land.

If seventy five per cent or more land holding of a Project Affected Person/Project Displaced Person is acquired or when the part of a plot of land remaining after acquisition becomes economically unviable after acquisition, the owner of such land/property shall have the right to seek acquisition of his/her entire contiguous land holding/property provided the residual land is less than the Minimum Economic Holding.[24]

The compensation amount for the land and properties to be acquired by the Project Authority shall be paid according to the provisions of the Land Acquisition Act. The Project Authority shall pay the difference as assistance if the provisions are less than the replacement value. The Project Authority may decide on the magnitude of loss to structures (in terms of percentage of the existing area or otherwise) in order to consider the owners of such affected structures to be Project Displaced Persons.

The Project Authority shall determine the possible replacement cost of land and assets to be acquired. Land rate surveys may be carried out by the Project Authority for this purpose in association with representatives of Project Affected Persons and external assessment agencies. The Project Authority may utilize the following systems of assessment while determining the replacement cost of land:

1. Taking into account such prescribed rates or the average of the actual transaction rates of similar lands for contemporary years for which sale deeds are registered.
2. Taking into consideration twenty times of the annual value of gross production of the concerned land averaged over the preceding five years.
3. Fixing up market value of land equal to the minimum land value if so prescribed by the State Government under the Indian Stamp Act for the purpose of registration of sale deeds under the Indian Registration Act of 1908.

The replacement cost of land to be fixed by the Project Authority would be the amount that shall be the highest among the three amounts arrived at by the aforesaid three alternative methods. The difference shall be paid in the form of assistance in case the replacement cost is higher than the market value determined by the Project Authority. The value of the houses, buildings and other immovable properties of the Project Affected Persons (including the Project Displaced Persons) shall be determined for the purpose of payment of compensation without depreciation.

Compensation for properties belonging to the Project Affected Community or for common places of religious worship that would be acquired for the project shall be provided to enable construction of the same at the relocation site(s) (if any) through the offices of the concerned local self-governing bodies in accordance with the modalities determined by such bodies to ensure proper utilization of the compensation amount.[25] Persons (belonging to the vulnerable groups) who derive their livelihood from the common places of religious worship may be supported by the project's special assistance scheme (if any). Compensation for trees would be based on their market value in case of timber bearing trees and replacement cost in case of fruit bearing trees as per the rates decided by the Project Authority in consultation with the concerned Government Departments. Loss of income may also be considered when assessing the compensation amount.

Compensation shall be paid and efforts would be made to complete the Resettlement and Rehabilitation of Project Affected Persons/Project Displaced Persons before taking possession of their land and/or properties. The Project Affected Persons/Project Displaced Persons shall hand over their land and properties to the Project Authority free from all encumbrances such as mortgage, debt etc for the purpose of acquisition.

In the case of any loan on such acquired land and properties extended to the Project Affected Persons by any Government Agency remaining unadjusted as per the information furnished by the Project Affected Persons or by the loaner agency such amounts shall be deducted from their total compensation. All transaction costs (including transportation costs/wages lost due to the project) shall be assessed and compensated for.

The payment of this amount shall be made in accordance with the relevant clauses of the Land Acquisition Act. All payments shall be made into the joint bank accounts of the husband and the wife while all new titles issued shall be in the joint names of the husband and the wife. All payments shall be made in public to ensure transparency. Disposal of acquired properties shall be carried out as follows:

- The acquired land and properties shall vest in the Government Department(s) paying compensation for such land and properties.
- Project Displaced Persons shall be allowed to collect the materials salvaged from their houses and shops

etc acquired by the project even after payment of compensation. The Government would levy no charges upon them for the same. A notice to that effect would be issued to take away the materials so salvaged within 48 hours of demolition of structures. If not collected then the Project Authority without giving any further notice shall dispose of the same.

- The Project Displaced Persons receiving compensation for trees shall be allowed to take away timber from their trees (acquired by the project) for domestic use. Trees standing on Government Land shall be sold by public auction to be organized by the concerned Government Department(s).

The Project Authority can take appropriate action to demolish structures within the project's Corridor of Impact after the expiry of the notified deadline. The Project Authority can also dismantle structures and evict individuals within the Corridor of Impact of the project if it is established that such structures and individuals occupied the public Right of Way after the duly notified Cut-Off Date. Any grievances and objections in this connection would be referred to the Grievance Redress Committee.

Information Dissemination Campaign

Information dissemination exercises for Project Affected Persons may be carried out prior to implementation of the Resettlement Action Plan. This campaign may be facilitated by the Project Authority and executed by the Partner Non-Government Organization(s) that would be appointed to implement the Resettlement Action Plan.

Impact Categories

Project-induced displacement may lead to loss of income or reduced income for Project Affected Persons. The main categories of impact expected as a result of the project include the following types of loss:

1. Loss of commercial establishments,
2. Loss of commercial space,
3. Loss of residential (dwelling) units,
4. Loss of livelihood and
5. Loss of Common Property Resources.[26]

Loss of temporary commercial structures is a complex problem since the issue of retaining the present customer base must be considered in this regard. Another problem pertains to the tenants and owners. Mitigation measures delivered under the Resettlement Action Plan may include reconstructing demolished commercial structures in an adjacent area so that the present customer base is retained. The Project Authority should duly consider the means of accomplishing this and addressing ownership of the new structures. The Project Authority would make final decision with regard to all aspects of this matter. There is also the need to respond to more generalized impacts of disturbance in the lives and livelihood of Project Affected Persons. Such adverse impacts may be mitigated by payment of Maintenance Allowance. A Rehabilitation Grant (for vulnerable groups) may be considered in the event income restoration cannot be entirely achieved by utilizing the compensation provided. Project Affected Persons may be assisted by the Project Authority to improve or regain their former status of living at no cost to themselves.

Institutional Arrangements

Implementation of the Resettlement Action Plan requires staff, resources and close coordination with different agencies and organizations working in the project area. The Resettlement Action Plan seeks to provide a strategy for developing the required implementation capacity on the part of the Project Authority. Capacity-building and training may be coordinated with the project implementation schedule in order to ensure that skilled staff members are available to implement the Resettlement Action Plan without any delay in civil works. Orientation workshops may be organised by the Project

Authority (Project Implementation Unit) and Partner Non-Government Organizations. A R&R Cell may be established within the Project Implementation Unit. Partner NGOs would be engaged to support the Project Authority and counterparted with PIU personnel to foster transfer of social development expertise. An independent external agency may provide professional services for monitoring and evaluating the R&R process. The Project Authority may initiate high priority actions to establish institutional linkages necessary for time-bound delivery of the Project Affected Persons' entitlements and assure coordination across agencies as well as between the various social and economic mitigation measures outlined in the Resettlement Action Plan.

Institutional Context

Effective implementation of the Resettlement Action Plan would require institutional relationships and responsibilities, rapid organizational development and collaborative efforts on the part of the Project Authority, State Government, Partner NGO(s) and Project Affected Persons.

R&R Coordination

The Project Implementation Unit would be responsible for coordinating with different Government Agencies. The R&R Cell would establish operational links to facilitate the critical process of project-induced resettlement. It may establish an effective process of dialogue between the Project Authority and the Project Affected Persons/Communities. The R&R Cell would have to provide the means and mechanisms for coordinating the efficacious delivery of compensation and assistance entitlements to those adversely affected due to implementation of the project. The R&R Cell would have to contribute social development perspectives and field-level inputs to ongoing project design and implementation by working closely with project planners, contractors and construction supervision consultants.

The R&R Cell would link the project with the concerned Government Agencies, provide liaison with Affected Communities, establish decentralized (grassroots) committees to coordinate social development and resettlement operations in the field, mobilize Partner NGO(s) and motivate local-level Community-Based Organizations to represent and safeguard the interests of Project Affected Persons. It would also engage training services, oversee a grievance redress process, actively monitor Resettlement Action Plan implementation and cooperate with project evaluation exercises. The R&R Cell would be responsible for disseminating project-related information to the public and providing additional opportunities for civil societal feedback.

Inter-Departmental Coordination

Resettlement Action Plan entitlements for Income Restoration Programs and Project Affected Groups are exclusively the responsibility of the Project Authority (apart from the land acquisition and compensation components in which the Revenue Department and the Project Authority would jointly provide entitlements). Several entitlements comprise services and benefits ordinarily provided by other government-sponsored social development programs such as the vulnerable groups' housing schemes. The R&R Cell may establish liaison with these ongoing programs to facilitate access of the Project Affected Persons and take advantage of services and programs already in place. It may negotiate cost-sharing arrangements wherever feasible. Restoration of community assets would require coordination with the Public Health Engineering Department. The R&R Cell's coordination with the Education Department would be required in the event schools are adversely impacted. A variety of State and Central Government programs addressing women's needs may be associated with other group entitlements, including those responding to potential transmission of Sexually Transmitted Diseases as well as Reproductive and Child Health.

Grievance Redress Mechanism

The Resettlement Action Plan's participatory processes as well as its compensation and support mechanisms are expected to enhance acceptance of the resettlement program and reduce complaints. There may nevertheless be individuals or groups who perceive that they have not received adequate support or that their needs have not been properly addressed.

The Project Authority would, therefore, establish a Grievance Redress Committee. This Committee would have representation from Project Affected Persons, NGO(s)/CBO(s)/ CSO(s) involved in the Resettlement Action Plan implementation, local-level Government Officials and the Project Authority.

This Committee would hear complaints and facilitate solutions. This process is expected to promote settlement of disputes through mediation in order to reduce the volume of time-consuming litigation. The Project Authority would take final decision on different aspects related to grievance redress of Project Affected Persons.

Monitoring and Evaluation

Monitoring and Evaluation are critical activities in the process of involuntary resettlement. Monitoring involves periodic checking to ascertain whether R&R activities are going according to the Resettlement Action Plan. It provides required feedback to the Project Authority to ensure that the Resettlement Action Plan implementation program runs on schedule. Evaluation is basically the post-project assessment of whether the implementation program was finally able to achieve its stated objectives. An independent external agency may be engaged by the Project Authority to carry out the (impact) monitoring and evaluation of the project with regard to implementation of the Resettlement Action Plan. M&E would measure project performance against project objectives. Long-term impact indicators may be examined during the project evaluation stage. The Project Authority may contract an external agency (such as an academic institution) that would undertake independent evaluation studies at least twice during the lifetime of the project. These evaluations would provide inputs to the mid-term review and the post-project report. Independent evaluation exercises may focus on assessing whether the overall objectives of the project are being met and would utilize the impact indicators as a basis for evaluation. The Project Authority would take final decisions on all M&E (and related) aspects of the project. Monitoring of involuntary resettlement operations require an application of general project monitoring procedures to the processes occurring in resettlement with particular attention to the specific high risks intrinsic in such operations. This means that monitoring of R&R requires certain specialized skills. To meet this requirement a sub-unit within the R&R Cell may be established.

An external agency may be appointed to monitor and evaluate the R&R program on a periodic basis. This additional perspective in Resettlement Action Plan implementation is critical because conventional M&E exercises carried out by Government Agencies may not adequately focus on certain aspects of importance to the implementing agencies. This external agency would be required to streamline the R&R process. External M&E studies may synchronize with the implementation of the Resettlement Action Plan. The external agency may submit periodic reports on the progress of Resettlement Action Plan implementation to the Project Authority. It may also identify the issues and concerns that require attention and subsequent action on the part of the Project Authority.

Conclusions

- Implementation of the Resettlement Action Plan on the part of Non-Government Organization(s) appointed by the Project Authority would require sensitive handling of the critical issue of involuntary resettlement that is a necessary result of infrastructural development projects involving roads and highways, bridges, flyovers and interchanges etc.

- Legal owners of land and structures would suffer in terms of loss of immovable assets while their tenants would suffer losses either in terms of residence or livelihood or both.
- Resettlement of affected persons and rehabilitation of their lost assets (land and/or structures) and livelihood are critical yet imperative social development exercises of infrastructure development projects that require displacement of individuals and groups.

Recommendations

- The Project Authority may set up a dedicated office in order to provide information with regard to the R&R guidelines and the Resettlement Action Plan.
- Fixation of compensation to the legal owners of affected land and structures should be based on the present market rate.
- The Grievance Redress Committee may expedite the process of redress of grievances. Project Affected Persons may be counselled by Partner Non-Government Organization(s) as and when required.
- Unauthorized encroachers and squatters as such do not have any legal rights to their occupied land and structures but the vulnerable groups among such illegal occupants may be considered by the Project Authority for R&R support/assistance.
- Illegal encroachers and squatters may be allowed to salvage the dismantled materials. The Project Authority may consider appointing such persons (belonging to vulnerable groups) as casual workers during the construction stage of the project in order to provide livelihood at least on a short-term basis in order to mitigate the adverse impacts of involuntary resettlement.
- Representatives from the local bodies such as Municipalities/Panchayats, officials from the local administration and police, local Community-Based Organizations/Non-Government Organizations/Civil

Society Organizations may be consulted on a periodic basis to ensure efficacious implementation of the Resettlement Action Plan.

- Involuntary resettlement caused by infrastructure development projects should be informed by comprehensive mitigation measures in order to reduce adverse impacts on the existing social fabric of Project Affected Persons.

NOTES

1. http://www.ciel.org/Ifi/wbinvolresettle.html
2. http://wbln0018.worldbank.org/Institutional/ManualsOp Manual.nsf/toc2 CA2D01A4D1BDF58085256B19008197F6? OpenDocument#foot
3. *Ibid.*
4. http://povlibrary.worldbank.org/library/topic/4294/5050/
5. "Research from around the world has shown that gender inequality tends to slow economic growth and make the rise from poverty more difficult." http://web.worldbank.org/WBSITE/EXTERNAL/TOPICS/ EXTGENDER/0,,menuPK:336874~pagePK:149018~piPK: 149093~theSitePK:336868,00.html
6. http://www.worldbank.org/wbi/sourcebook/sb0003.htm
7. http://punjabgovt.nic.in/ECONOMY/Poverty%20Alleviation. htm
8. "The common property resource management approach integrates perspectives, data, and ways of working from the environmental sciences, economics, and anthropology. From the point of view of the overriding goals of the (World) Bank's work—poverty reduction and sustainable development—it represents a broad and holistic approach. Common property resource management complements the emphasis on private property, eases analysis and understanding of the interaction of different resource management systems on various levels, allows a more culturally sensitive approach to project preparation and implementation, and contributes to increasing environmental and social sustainability." http://www.worldbank.org/html/dec/Publications/Abstracts 97/ 03esd/esd25.html
9. "The integration of culture in its mandate has become inevitable for the World Bank as its programs inevitably affect the cultural heritage of country clients and as these countries demand for Bank's assistance. But it has impelled the Bank to carry out this mandate sensitively and effectively. Interventions have been designed identifying and exploiting the comparative advantage which

distinguishes the World Bank from other specialized organizations with better technical expertise and triggers the clients ' demand." http://web.worldbank.org/WBSITE/EXTERNAL/TOPICS/EXTURBANDEVELOPMENT/EXTCHD/0,,menuPK:430438~pagePK:162100~piPK:159310~theSitePK:430430,00.html

10. "There is considerable variation in the nature and extent of gender inequality across countries, making it difficult to generalize that disparities between women and men are systematically larger below the poverty line. The evidence surrounding the incidence of poverty in female-headed households is also found to be country and case specific ... The evidence indicates that a more nuanced approach to understanding the relationship between headship and poverty is needed."
http://siteresources.worldbank.org/INTGENDER/Resources/11abstract.htm
11. "This Act is of interest to women workers, as it sets minimum wages for employees, which include those working on a temporary basis, piece rate workers and workers paid daily wages. In addition, no employee can be asked to work more than 9 hours a day without additional wages being paid and the normal hours of work must be fixed."
http://www.ilo.org/public/english/employment/gems/eeo/law/india/mwa.htm
12. http://web.worldbank.org/WBSITE/EXTERNAL/COUNTRIES/EASTASIAPACIFICEXT/EXTEAPREGTOPSOCDEV/0,,contentMDK:20327365~menuPK:746810~pagePK:34004173~piPK:34003707~theSitePK:502940,00.html
13. The HIV prevalence level of Punjab (2004) was 1.09%.
http://www.nacoonline.org/facts_statewise.htm
14. "It is felt that the involvement of voluntary organisations/Non-Government Organisations can effectively help in reducing the delivery costs of welfare programmes and in identification of beneficiaries because of the flexibility and simplicity in their approach for implementing the schemes at the grassroots level."
Source: Tenth Five Year Plan 2002-207 and Annual Plan 2002-03 (Department of Planning, Government of Punjab), p. 7.
15. The external (independent) monitoring and evaluation agency should incorporate the benchmarks necessary to measure project progress in terms of community development in its overall framework of indicators.
16. "The Punjab Area and Urban Development Authority launched a statewide scheme under the title of 'farmer friendly land policy scheme ' in 1996 ... For pooling more resources, the housing schemes like Valmiki Ambedkar Awaas Yojana and other such programmes can be exploited to meet out the requirement of the poor."

http://64.233.161.104/search?q=cache:FYoAf96xVSwJ: naredco.org/11_policiesandprojectsforlandandshelterdevelopmentfordelhi-implementationmechanisms_hhgill.doc+punjab+vambay+ &hl=en

17. "Knowledge sharing at the World Bank has evolved over time. From an early emphasis on capturing and organizing knowledge, its focus now is on adopting, adapting, and applying knowledge in a way that helps World Bank staff, clients, and partners work more effectively to reduce global poverty." http://web.worldbank.org/WBSITE/EXTERNAL/WBI/0,,contentMDK:20251495~menuPK:204788~pagePK:209023~piPK:207535~theSitePK:213799,00.html
18. "The World Bank views good governance and anti-corruption as central to its poverty alleviation mission." http://www.worldbank.org/wbi/governance/
19. http://www.indiahousing.com/general/acquisition.asp
20. Public sector organizations have in certain cases directly purchased land/property through negotiations due to project exigencies.
21. Identification of encroachers and squatters may be sought from the voters' lists or from any other legal documents or information from the community (in the absence of ration cards/photo identity cards).
22. Replacement cost shall be equivalent to an amount required to acquire substitute land of equal productive value as well as to replace any structures or other assets. The difference is to be paid by the project in the form of assistance in case the replacement cost is more than the compensation at market price as determined by the Project Authority.
23. Vulnerable categories include Women Headed Households, Landless Agricultural Workers, Scheduled Castes, Scheduled Tribes, Persons from households with income less than 20% above the Poverty Line, Elderly Persons (above 65 years of age) who are the single earning members of their respective households, Persons with Disability and Orphan Children.
24. The Minimum Economic Holding is equivalent to 2 Hectares of non-irrigated or 1 Hectare of irrigated land.
25. This provision would be applicable in those cases where relocation site(s) may be developed for Project Affected Persons/Project Displaced Persons.
26. Common Property Resources may include playgrounds, community meeting platforms, bus bays, public stand posts, hand pumps, wells, vats, cattle grazing areas, solid waste disposal sites, sewerage and drainage systems, water supply and sanitation systems, electrical infrastructure, educational institutions, primary health centres, local markets etc that are utilized by the affected community members for their everyday civic requirements.

APPENDIX-I

Key Definitions

Corridor of Impact

The Corridor of Impact is defined as the construction width or the operational width plus a safety zone on either side of the road. Within the Corridor of Impact there should not be any structure or other hindrances. The Corridor of Impact would vary depending on site requirement.

Compensation and Assistance

Compensation refers to restitution made to legal property owners in possession of title deeds under the Land Acquisition Act. Compensation is payment made by the Government to legal owners when Eminent Domain is exercised to transfer ownership of private property/land to the State. Assistance refers to all other support mechanisms such as grants, assets, services etc provided to Entitled Persons (or their groups).

Project Affected Persons

Project Affected Persons are individuals who would be adversely impacted by implementation of the civil works of the project. They would lose land/property/livelihood in this process. So a Project Affected Person is an individual who (as a direct consequence of the project) sustains damages

1. due to severance of his/her land,
2. due to negative impacts on his/her immovable properties in any manner or
3. due to adverse effects on his/her livelihood calculated on the basis of an objective assessment.

Project Affected Persons include Project Displaced Persons. These are individuals who are compelled to change their place of residence/work/business due to implementation of the project. Project Affected Persons are categorized as follows:

1. Private Property Owners,
2. Tenants,
3. Sharecroppers,
4. Squatters and
5. Encroachers.

Depending upon their category, Project Affected Persons would be entitled to either compensation or assistance or both. Each category is described as follows:

Private Property Owners have legal titles to land, structures and/or other assets. They are entitled to compensation under the Land Acquisition Act. They are also entitled to shifting (relocation) assistance. They may also be facilitated for voluntary relocation to alternative site(s) (if any).

Tenants have bona fide tenancy agreements with private property owners to occupy a structure or land for residence, business or cultivation purposes. They are eligible for certain compensation/assistance as per existing norms.

Sharecroppers are those individuals who have formally or informally entered into an agreement with private property owners to cultivate their land.

Squatters have illegally occupied Government Land for residential, commercial and/or other purposes. They are not eligible for compensation but would qualify for certain assistance and targeted support if they belong to vulnerable groups (defined subsequently). They would be entitled to shifting assistance. They would also be assisted for voluntary relocation to alternative sites.

Encroachers have extended their buildings, land holdings, business premises or work places illegally into Government Land. They are not eligible for either compensation or assistance. Vulnerable groups among encroachers would be entitled for project support.

Persons Losing Their Livelihood

Persons losing their livelihood are Project Affected Persons who are at least 18 years of age at the time of displacement and who stand to lose their primary occupation or primary source of income as a result of project interventions. Such persons are eligible for support extended by the Project Authority on the basis of their contributions to household income.

Vulnerable Groups

Vulnerable groups may receive special targeted support and assistance under the project because they would be unevenly impacted by developmental interventions. It is desirable that such groups receive special support from the project in order to ensure social safeguards. The human face of the project would be duly maintained if adequate attention is paid to these vulnerable groups. The following categories may be considered vulnerable:

1. Women Headed Households,
2. Landless Agricultural Workers,
3. Scheduled Castes,
4. Scheduled Tribes,
5. Persons from households with income less than 20 per cent above the Poverty Line,
6. Elderly Persons (above 65 years of age) who are the single earning members of their respective households,
7. Persons with Disability and
8. Orphan Children.

Project Affected Households

Project Affected Households are those that would be adversely affected by implementation of the civil works. Project Affected Households are entitled to certain benefits as a household unit.

Project Affected Groups

Project Affected Groups are communities (with a focus on the more vulnerable and weaker sections) that may be adversely/ disproportionately affected by the project.

Entitled Persons

Entitled Persons are Project Affected Persons who qualify for (or are entitled to) assistance/compensation since they would be resettled or otherwise be negatively impacted by the project. Entitled Persons include Project Affected Households and Project Affected Groups.

Cut-Off Date

The Cut-Off Date would be announced in consultation with the concerned District Magistrates in order to ensure that squatter settlements do not proliferate in the affected area due to lack of proper information. A Project Affected Person not identified at the Cut-Off Date may be considered for support if he/she can produce the necessary documentary evidence of his/her residential proof (of not less than three years) before declaration of the Cut-Off Date. The Cut-Off Date identifies Project Affected Persons (within the existing/proposed Right of Way) who are entitled to compensation and/or assistance. Persons occupying the Right of Way after the Cut-Off Date would not be considered as Project Affected Persons under the project. Such persons would not be entitled to any assistance. The list of Project Affected Persons may be made public to ensure that Entitled Persons are duly covered under the project. Project Affected Persons may be allowed to lodge complaints (if any). Appropriate measures may be taken by the Project Authority to avoid any further encroachment(s) or squatter settlement(s) in the project area after announcement of the Cut-Off Date. Information dissemination exercises are critical to make the Cut-Off Date credible *vis-à-vis* the general public. The Project Authority may ensure that the Cut-Off Date is suitably publicized in the project area. Public Notifications in this regard should be prominently displayed in government offices, post offices, market places, telephone booths, shop windows and public notice boards in the local language. Word of mouth may also be spread by deploying public address systems.

Household Unit

The Household Unit is defined as all persons living and eating together as a single unit. The household as a collective entity shall be entitled to compensation and assistance in certain cases.

Family

A family shall mean the husband, wife and their minor children. Every son or unmarried daughter who has attained 18 years of age on or before the Cut-Off Date would be treated as a separate family. Every divorced or widowed daughter living separately or with the family on or prior to the Cut-Off Date would be treated as a separate family. Orphans in one single household would be clubbed together as one single family. Mentally handicapped persons irrespective of age and sex would be treated as one single family.

Landless Agricultural Worker

A landless agricultural worker is a person who does not hold any agricultural land and who has been deriving his/her principal income by working on the lands of others as a sub-tenant or as an agricultural labourer prior to the Cut-Off Date.

Small Farmer

A farmer holding 2 Hectares of non-irrigated or 1 Hectare of irrigated land shall be treated as a small farmer.

Marginal Farmer

A farmer holding 1 Hectare of non-irrigated or ½ Hectare of irrigated land shall be treated as a marginal farmer.

Minimum Economic Holding

The Minimum Economic Holding is equivalent to 2 Hectares of non-irrigated or 1 Hectare of irrigated land.

Income

The Income of a Project Affected Person shall mean the amount of income as shown in his/her Income Tax Return prior to the Cut-Off Date. His/her income shall be calculated (in the absence of any Income Tax Return) by an objective assessment applying the same method as adopted by the Government Agencies to identify Below Poverty Line families.

APPENDIX-II

Recruitment of Partner NGO(s)

Objectives

Objectives of the Non-Government Organization(s)' consultancy services are to facilitate the Resettlement and Rehabilitation program of the project by

1. educating the Project Affected Persons about their rights, entitlements and obligations in the context of the Resettlement Action Plan;
2. ensuring that the Project Affected Persons obtain their full entitlements under the Resettlement Action Plan. The Non-Government Organization(s) shall advise the Project Affected Persons with regard to the relative benefits of each option in those cases where such options are available;
3. assisting the Project Affected Persons to redress their grievances by utilizing the Stakeholders' Consultation process laid out in the Resettlement Action Plan; and
4. supporting the Project Authority to monitor and evaluate implementation of the Resettlement Action Plan based on participatory processes.

Tasks

The Non-Government Organization(s) would serve as a link between the Project Authority (represented by the R&R Cell) and the affected community. The Non-Government Organization(s) would be responsible for assisting the Project Affected Persons during their Resettlement and Rehabilitation process. The Non-Government Organization(s) shall ensure that the provisions of the Resettlement Action Plan with regard to the well-being of the Project Affected Person(s) are duly implemented. The Non-Government Organization(s) would specifically focus on the following tasks:

1. Develop rapport between the Project Affected Persons and the Project Authority (especially the R&R Cell). This would be achieved by regular interactive dialogue sessions between the Non-Government Organization(s), Project Affected Persons and Project Authority. All meeting minutes and resolutions taken are to be properly documented.
2. Assist the R&R Cell to undertake regular public information dissemination campaigns at the commencement of the project to inform the affected communities about the following (and facilitate the following tasks):

    - The need for Land Acquisition.
    - The need for eviction of squatters and encroachers.

3. Analyze the likely consequences of the project on the economic livelihood of affected communities.
4. Identify the Project Affected Persons and facilitate distribution of their photo identity cards (if required).
5. Assess the R&R entitlement packages.
6. Assist the Project Affected Persons to receive compensation for their land and properties to be acquired for the project.
7. Assist the Project Affected Persons to pursue their disputes (if any) through the grievance redress mechanism.
8. Assist the Project Affected Persons to identify suitable sites for their relocation and agricultural purpose (if required). The Non-Government Organization(s) would identify such relocation sites (Government Land) in association with the Project Authority and Government Agencies and assist in negotiating transfer of land to the Project Affected Persons. The NGO(s) would assist in negotiating the purchase price of private

land in the event suitable government land is not available for resettlement of Project Affected Persons.

9. Ensure that the R&R benefits due to the Project Affected Persons under the Resettlement Action Plan are duly provided. The NGO(s) would determine the entitlements of the Project Affected Persons from the Resettlement Action Plan and compare such entitlements to the offer(s) being made by the R&R Cell. The NGO(s) would be responsible for assisting the Project Affected Persons to reach an agreement with the R&R Cell if there are discrepancies in terms of entitlements laid down in the Resettlement Action Plan and entitlements being actually offered by the R&R Cell. The NGO(s) would have to pursue any such dispute(s) through the grievance redress mechanism of the project (if required).
10. Assist the Project Authority to streamline participatory processes and make suitable arrangements for the efficacious resettlement of the Project Affected Persons and rehabilitation of their livelihood. This task would involve continuous consultation with the Project Affected Persons in order to ensure that the arrangements made by the Project Authority are acceptable to them.
11. Ensure proper utilization by the Project Affected Persons of various grants available under the R&R package. The NGO(s) would be responsible for advising the Project Affected Persons about how best to utilize any cash compensation that may be awarded by the Project Authority. Special emphasis may be placed on using such funds in a sustainable manner *e.g.* purchasing replacement land against acquired land.
12. Assist Project Affected Persons to receive benefits from various government-sponsored social development programs (especially for the purpose of house construction). There are quite a few government housing schemes and livelihood restoration programs (vocational training schemes to facilitate income-generation and self-employment programs) that may

be availed of by the Project Affected Persons. The Non-Government Organization(s) would analyze the comparative advantages of these programs and shall inform the Project Affected Persons about the available social development opportunities and their relative merits.

13. The Non-Government Organization(s) would coordinate the training programs for livelihood restoration in a sustainable manner and assist Project Affected Persons to develop the required vocational skills for income-generation and self-employment programs. The Non-Government Organization(s) shall constantly coordinate with different Government Departments and Community-Based Organizations/ Civil Society Organizations working in the vicinity of the project area to ensure that all the options available to the Project Affected Persons are properly communicated to them.
14. The Non-Government Organization(s) would develop micro-level plans for relocation in consultation with the Project Affected Persons and the R&R Cell. Such plans shall include the following items:

    - List of options available to the Project Affected Persons. The Non-Government Organization(s) would explain to the Project Affected Persons the options available to them for the R&R program of the project and assist them to make their informed choices.
    - Alternative sites for relocation (if required).
    - A list of benefits due to the Project Affected Persons.
    - Arrangements for shifting of the Project Affected Persons.
    - Proposed utilization of any grant (cash compensation) due to the Project Affected Persons.
    - Modalities of involvement of Project Affected Persons in the existing government-sponsored social development programs.

15. The Non-Government Organization(s) would update the data available with regard to Project Affected Persons and collect any new information.
16. The Non-Government Organization(s) would assist the Project Authority to monitor input-output and impact indicators.
17. The Non-Government Organization(s) would undertake any other responsibility as may be assigned by the R&R Cell for the welfare of the affected community. Such actions would be situation-specific.

Methodology

The NGO(s)' staff members are to be stationed in the project area in order to carry out the above tasks. The NGO(s) would conduct Focus Group Discussions with Project Affected Persons and community meetings with affected groups on a regular basis. The frequency of such meetings would depend on the requirements of the Project Affected Persons. Regular interactive dialogue sessions would enable the Project Affected Persons to update themselves about project developments. The NGO(s) would encourage participation of individual Project Affected Persons in such meetings by discussing their problems regarding land acquisition, involuntary resettlement and related aspects focused on their socio-economic conditions. Such participatory processes are examples of good practices and would facilitate exploration of viable solutions.

Reporting/Documentation

1. The NGO(s) shall submit an Inception Report that would focus on the Plan of Action, manpower deployment, time schedule and detailed methodology within 21 days/3 weeks from the commencement of the assignment. The NGO(s) should also submit fortnightly progress reports on the activities carried out during that fortnight and the proposed activities for the coming month. The fortnightly progress reports would include

data on input and output indicators as required by the R&R Cell.

2. Updated data on the Project Affected Persons and data on the additional Project Affected Persons (if any) would be submitted within two months of the commencement of the assignment.
3. Data on the Project Affected Persons for monitoring of impact indicators would be submitted to the R&R Cell on an as and when required basis.
4. Micro-level plans for Project Affected Persons would be submitted to the R&R Cell for information within 3 months of commencement of the NGO consultancy services. The NGO(s) would update the relevant plans and resubmit the same to the R&R Cell whenever changes occur during the project (requiring changes to the micro-level plans).
5. At the completion of the assignment the NGO(s) shall submit a final report summarising all the actions taken during the project, the methodology and manpower used to carry out the work and a summary of assistance given to the Project Affected Persons by the Project Authority.

APPENDIX-III

National Policy on Resettlement and Rehabilitation for Project Affected Families 2003 [Ministry of Rural Development (Department of Land Resources)]

Published in the Gazette of India, Extraordinary Part-I, Section 1, No. 46, dated 17 February 2004.

Preamble

Compulsory acquisition of land for public purpose including infrastructure projects displaces people, forcing them to give up their home, assets and means of livelihood. Apart from depriving them of their lands, livelihoods and resource-base, displacement has other traumatic psychological and socio-cultural consequences. The Government of India recognizes the need to minimize large scale displacement to the extent possible and, where displacement is inevitable, the need to handle with utmost care and forethought issues relating to Resettlement and Rehabilitation of Project Affected Families. Such an approach is especially necessary in respect of tribals, small and marginal farmers and women.

The system of extending cash compensation does not, by itself, in most cases, enable the affected families to obtain cultivable agricultural land, homestead and other resources which they have to surrender to the State. The difficulties are more acute for persons who are critically dependent on the acquired assets for their subsistence/livelihoods, such as landless agricultural workers, forest dwellers, tenants and artisans, as their distress and destitution is more severe, and, yet they are not eligible for cash compensation.

Some States and Central Ministries/Departments have their own Policies and Guidelines for Resettlement and Rehabilitation. However, a National Policy on Resettlement and Rehabilitation of Project Affected Families (PAFs) has not so far been enunciated. This Document aims at laying down basic norms and packages in the shape of a Policy which would henceforth be referred to as the National Policy on the Resettlement and Rehabilitation of Project Affected Families-2003 (NPRR-2003).

The Policy essentially addresses the need to provide succour to the assetless rural poor, support the rehabilitation efforts of the resource poor sections, namely, small and marginal farmers, SCs/STs and women, who have been displaced. Besides, it seeks to provide a broad canvas for an effective dialogue between the Project Affected Families and the Administration for Resettlement and Rehabilitation. Such a dialogue is expected to enable timely completion of projects with a sense of definiteness as regards costs and adequate attention to the needs of the displaced persons, especially the resource poor sections. The intention is to impart greater flexibility for interaction and negotiation so that the resultant Package gains all-round acceptability in the shape of a workable instrument providing satisfaction to all stake-holders/Requiring Bodies.

The National Policy on the Resettlement and Rehabilitation of Project Affected Families will be in the form of broad guidelines and executive instructions for guidance of all concerned and will be applicable to Projects displacing 500 families or more en masse in plain areas and 250 families en masse in hilly areas, Desert Development Programme (DDP) blocks and areas mentioned in Schedule V and Schedule VI of the Constitution of India. It is expected that the appropriate Government and Administrator for R&R shall implement this Policy in letter and spirit in order to ensure that the benefits envisaged under the Policy reaches the Project Affected Families, especially resource poor sections, including SCs/STs.

The rehabilitation grants and other monetary benefits proposed in the Policy would be minimum and applicable to all Project Affected Families whether belonging to BPL or non-BPL families. States where R&R packages are higher than proposed in the Policy are free to adopt their own packages.

Objectives of the Policy

The objectives of the Policy are as follows:

1. To minimize displacement and to identify non-displacing or least-displacing alternatives;
2. To plan the Resettlement and Rehabilitation of Project Affected Families (PAFs), including special needs of Tribals and vulnerable sections;
3. To provide better standard of living to PAFs; and
4. To facilitate harmonious relationship between the Requiring Body and PAFs through mutual cooperation.

Definitions

The Definition of various terms used in this Policy Document are as follows:

1. "Administrator for Resettlement and Rehabilitation" means an Officer not below the rank of District Collector of the State Government appointed by it for the purpose of Resettlement and Rehabilitation of the Project Affected Families of the Project concerned provided that if the appropriate Government in respect of the project is the Central Government, such appointment shall be made in consultation with the Central Government.
2. "Affected zone", in relation to a project, means declaration under this Policy by the appropriate Government area of villages or locality under a project for which the land is being acquired under Land Acquisition Act 1894 or any other Act in force or an area that comes under submergence due to impounding of water in the reservoir of the project;

3. "Agricultural family" means a family whose primary mode of livelihood is agriculture and includes family of owners as well as sub-tenants of agricultural land, agricultural labourers, occupiers of forest lands and of collectors of minor forest produce;
4. "Agricultural labourer" means a person normally resident in the affected zone for a period of not less than three years immediately before the declaration of the affected zone who does not hold any land in the affected zone but who earns his livelihood principally by manual labour on agricultural land therein immediately before such declaration and who has been deprived of his livelihood;
5. "Agricultural land" includes lands used or capable of being used for the purpose of:

- agriculture or horticulture;
- dairy farming, poultry farming, pisciculture, breeding or livestock and nursery growing medical herbs;
- raising of crops, grass or garden produce; and
- land used by an agriculturist for the grazing of cattle, but does not include land used for the cutting of wood only;

6. "Appropriate Government" means

- in relation to acquisition of land for the purposes of the Union, the Central Government;
- in relation to a project which is executed by Central Government agency/Central Government undertaking or by any other agency on the orders/directions of Central Government, the Central Government, otherwise the State Government; and
- in relation to acquisition of land for other purposes, the State Government.

7. The Below Poverty Line Families shall be those as defined by the Planning Commission of India from time to time.

8. "Commissioner for Resettlement and Rehabilitation", in relation to a project, means the Commissioner for Resettlement and Rehabilitation appointed by the State Government not below the rank of Commissioner/ Secretary of that Government.
9. "Displaced Family" means any tenure holder, tenant, Government lessee or owner of other property, who on account of acquisition of his land including plot in the abadi or other property in the affected zone for the purpose of the project, has been displaced from such land or other property;
10. "Family" means Project Affected Family consisting of such persons, his or her spouse, minor sons, unmarried daughters, minor brothers or unmarried sisters, father, mother and other members residing with him and dependent on him for their livelihood.
11. "Holding" means the total land held by a person as an occupant or tenant or as both;
12. "Marginal Farmer" means a cultivator with an unirrigated land holding upto one hectare or irrigated land holding upto half hectare;
13. "Non-Agricultural Labourer" means a person who is not an agricultural labourer but is normally residing in the affected zone for a period of not less than three years immediately before the declaration of the affected zone and who does not hold any land under the affected zone but who earns his livelihood principally by manual labour or as a rural artisan immediately before such declaration and who has been deprived of earning his livelihood principally by manual labour or as an artisan in the affected zone;
14. "Notification" means a notification published in the Official Gazette;
15. "Occupiers" means members of the Scheduled Tribe community in possession of forest land prior to 25 October 1980;
16. "Project" means a project displacing 500 families or more en masse in plain areas and 250 families or more en masse in hilly areas, DDP blocks, areas mentioned

in Schedule V and Schedule VI of the Constitution of India as a result of acquisition of land for any project.

17. "Project Affected Family" means a family/person whose place of residence or other properties or source of livelihood are substantially affected by the process of acquisition of land for the project and who has been residing continuously for a period of not less than three years preceding the date of declaration of the affected zone or practicing any trade, occupation or vocation continuously for a period of not less than three years in the affected zone, preceding the date of declaration of the affected zone.
18. "Resettlement Zone", in relation to a project, means the declaration of any area under this Policy by the appropriate Government acquired or proposed to be acquired for Resettlement and Rehabilitation of Project Affected Families as a resettlement zone;
19. "Requiring Body" shall mean any company, a body corporate, an institution, or any other organization for whom land is to be acquired by the appropriate Government, and includes the appropriate Government if the acquisition of land is for such Government either for its own use or for subsequent allotment of such land in public interest to a body corporate, institution, or any other organization or to any company under lease, license or through any other system of transfer of land to such company, as the case may be;
20. "Small Farmer" means a cultivator with an unirrigated land holding up to two hectares or with an irrigated land holding up to one hectare.

Appointment of Administrator and Commissioner for Resettlement and Rehabilitation and their Powers and Functions

Where the appropriate Government is satisfied that acquisition of land for any project involves displacement of 500 families or more en masse in plain areas and 250 families or more en masse in hilly areas, DDP blocks and areas mentioned in Schedule V and Schedule VI of the Constitution of India as a result of acquisition of land for any project, it shall, by Notification, appoint in respect of that project, an Officer not below the rank of District Collector of the State Government to be the Administrator for R&R in respect of that project.

Provided that if the appropriate Government in respect of the project is the Central Government, such appointment shall be made in consultation with the Central Government.

The Administrator for Resettlement and Rehabilitation shall be assisted by such Officers and employees as the appropriate Government may provide.

Subject to the superintendence, directions and control of the appropriate Government and Commissioner for R&R, the Administrator for Resettlement and Rehabilitation shall take all measures for the Resettlement and Rehabilitation of all Project Affected Families in respect of that project.

The overall control and superintendence of the formulation of Resettlement and Rehabilitation Plan and execution of the same shall vest in the Administrator, Resettlement and Rehabilitation.

Subject to any general or special order of the appropriate Government, the Administrator for Resettlement and Rehabilitation shall perform the following functions/duties:

- Minimize displacement of persons and identify non-displacing or least displacing alternatives in consultation with the Requiring Body;
- Hold consultation with the Project Affected Families while preparing a Resettlement and Rehabilitation scheme/plan;
- Ensure that interest of the adversely Project Affected Families of Scheduled Tribes and weaker sections are protected;
- Prepare a draft plan/scheme of Resettlement and Rehabilitation as required under this Policy;
- Prepare a budget including estimated expenditure of various components of acquisition of land, Resettlement and Rehabilitation activities or

programmes in consultation with representatives of the Project Affected Families and requiring body for whom the land is acquired;

- Acquire adequate land for the project and also for settling the Project Affected Families;
- Allot land and sanction benefits to Project Affected Families;
- Perform such other functions as the appropriate Government may, from time to time, by order in writing, assign.

Administrator for Resettlement and Rehabilitation may, by order in writing, delegate such of the administrative powers conferred and duties imposed on him by or under this Policy to any Officer not below the rank of Tehsildar or equivalent.

All Officers and staff appointed by the appropriate Government under this Policy shall be subordinate to the Administrator for Resettlement and Rehabilitation.

The State Government shall appoint an Officer of the rank of Commissioner/Secretary of that Government for Resettlement and Rehabilitation in respect of such projects to which this Policy applies to be called the Commissioner for Resettlement and Rehabilitation.

For the purposes of this Policy, the Administrator for Resettlement and Rehabilitation and other Officers and employees appointed for the purposes of Resettlement and Rehabilitation of PAFs shall be subordinate to the Commissioner for Resettlement and Rehabilitation.

The Commissioner shall be responsible for supervising the formulation of Resettlement and Rehabilitation plans/schemes, proper implementation of such plans/schemes and redress of grievances as mentioned in this Policy.

Schemes/Plans for Resettlement and Rehabilitation

The procedure mentioned in this Policy shall be followed for declaration of Affected Zone, carrying out survey and census of Project Affected Families, assessment of Government Land available and land to be acquired for the purpose of

Resettlement and Rehabilitation, preparation of draft scheme/ plan for R&R and its final publication.

The appropriate Government may, if it is of the opinion that acquisition of land for a project is likely to displace 500 families or more en masse in plain areas and 250 families or more in hilly areas, DDP blocks and areas mentioned in Schedule V and Schedule VI of the Constitution of India, declare, by notification in the Official Gazette, area of villages or localities as an affected zone of the project and thereupon the contents of this Policy shall apply to the project involved.

Every declaration made under Para 5.1 of this Policy shall be published in at least two daily newspapers (one of them should be in the local vernacular having circulation in villages or areas which are likely to be affected) and also by affixing a copy of the Notification on the Notice Board of the concerned Gram Panchayats and other prominent place or places in the affected zone.

Once the declaration is made under this Policy, the Administrator for Resettlement and Rehabilitation shall undertake a survey for identification of the persons and their families likely to be affected by the project.

Every survey shall contain the following village-wise information of the Project Affected Families:

1. Members of families who are permanently residing, practicing any trade, occupation or vocation in the project affected area;
2. Project Affected Families who are likely to lose their house, agricultural land, employment or are alienated wholly or substantially from the main source of their trade, occupation or vocation;
3. Agricultural labourers and non-agriculture labourers;
4. Project Affected Families who are having possession of forest lands prior to 25 October 1980, that is prior to the commencement of the Forest (Conservation) Act 1980.

Every survey undertaken shall be completed within a period of ninety days from the date of declaration.

On the expiry of the period of ninety days as aforesaid, the Administrator for Resettlement and Rehabilitation shall, by Notification, and also in such other manner so as to reach all persons likely to be affected, publish a draft of the details of the findings of the survey conducted by him for inviting objections and suggestions from all persons likely to be affected thereby.

On the expiry of thirty days from the date of publication of the draft of the details of survey and after considering the objections and suggestions received by him in this behalf, the Administrator for Resettlement and Rehabilitation shall submit the final details of survey with his recommendations to the State Government.

Within forty-five days from the date of receipt of the recommendations of the Administrator for Resettlement and Rehabilitation, the State Government shall publish the final details of survey in the Official Gazette.

The Administrator for Resettlement and Rehabilitation shall ensure that the Project Affected Families may be settled preferably in a group or groups and such sites should form a part of existing Gram Panchayat as far as possible. However, it has to be ensured that the PAFs may be resettled with the host community on the basis of equality and mutual understanding, consistent with the desire of each group to preserve its own identity and culture.

The Administrator for Resettlement and Rehabilitation shall draw up a list of lands which may be available in any existing Gram Panchayat for Resettlement and Rehabilitation of Project Affected Families.

The lands drawn up under shall consist of:

1. Government waste lands and any other land vesting in the Government available for allotment to Project Affected Families.
2. If sufficient Government Land is not available there, then land to be acquired for the purposes of Resettlement and Rehabilitation scheme/plan. However, the Administrator for R&R should ensue that such acquisition of land should not lead to another list of affected families.

The appropriate Government shall, by Notification, declare any area acquired or proposed to be acquired for Resettlement and Rehabilitation of Project Affected Families, as a resettlement zone.

The Administrator for R&R, on behalf of the appropriate Government, may either compulsorily acquire any land under the Land Acquisition Act 1894 or purchase land from any person through consent award and may enter into an agreement for this purpose.

After completion of baseline survey and census of Project Affected Families and assessment of requirement of land for resettlement, the Administrator for R&R shall prepare a draft scheme/plan for the Resettlement and Rehabilitation of the Project Affected Families in consultation with representatives of Project Affected Families, including women and Chairpersons of elected Panchayati Raj Institutions within which the project area is situated.

While preparing a draft scheme/plan, the Administrator for R&R shall ensure that the cost of R&R scheme/plan should be an integral part of the cost of the project for which the land is being acquired and the entire expenditure of R&R benefits and other expenditure for Resettlement and Rehabilitation of PAFs are to be borne by the Requiring Body for which the area is being acquired.

It shall be the responsibility of the Requiring Body to provide sufficient funds to the Administrator for R&R for proper implementation of Resettlement and Rehabilitation scheme/plan of Project Affected Families.

The Administrator for R&R shall keep proper books of accounts and records of the funds placed at his/her disposal and submit periodical returns to the Appropriate Government in this behalf.

Every draft scheme/plan of Resettlement and Rehabilitation prepared shall contain the following particulars, namely:

1. the extent of area to be acquired for the project and the name(s) of the corresponding village(s);

2. a village-wise list of Project Affected Families and likely number of displaced persons, family-wise, and the extent and nature of land and immovable property in their possession indicating the survey numbers thereof held by such persons in the affected zone;
3. a list of agricultural labourers in such area and the names of such persons whose livelihood depend on agricultural activities;
4. a list of persons who have lost or are likely to lose their employment or livelihood or who have been alienated wholly and substantially from their main sources of occupation or vocation consequent to the acquisition of land for the project;
5. a list of occupiers, if any;
6. a list of public utilities and Government Buildings which are likely to be affected;
7. a comprehensive list of benefits and packages which are to be provided to Project Affected Families;
8. details of the extent of land available which may be acquired in settlement area for resettling and allotting of land to the Project Affected Families;
9. details of the basic amenities and infrastructure facilities which are to be provided for resettlement;
10. the time schedule for shifting and resettling the displaced families in resettlement zones;
11. such other particulars as the Administrator for Resettlement and Rehabilitation may think fit to include for the information of the displaced persons.

The Administrator for Resettlement and Rehabilitation shall submit the draft scheme/plan for R&R to the State Government for its approval. It will be the responsibility of the State Government to obtain the consent of Requiring Body before approving the same. The draft scheme/plan may be published in the Official Gazette to give wide publicity to the same in the affected zone. Upon Notification of a scheme/plan, the same shall come into force.

R&R Benefits for Project Affected Families

The Resettlement and Rehabilitation (R&R) benefits shall be extended to all the Project Affected Families (PAFs) whether belonging to Below Poverty Line (BPL) or non-BPL.

Any Project Affected Family (PAF) owning house and whose house has been acquired may be allotted free of cost house site to the extent of actual loss of area of the acquired house but not more than 150 sq.m. of land in rural areas and 75 sq.m. of land in urban areas.

Each PAF of BPL category shall get a one-time financial assistance of Rs. 25,000/- for house construction. Non-BPL families shall not be entitled to receive this assistance.

Each PAF owning agricultural land in the affected zone and whose entire land has been acquired may be allotted agricultural land or cultivable waste land to the extent of actual land loss subject to a maximum of one hectare of irrigated land or two hectares of un-irrigated land/cultivable waste land subject to availability of Government Land in the districts.

Stamp duty and other fees payable for registration shall be borne by the Requiring Body.

The land allotted shall be free from all encumbrances. The land allotted may be in the joint names of wife and husband of PAFs.

In case of allotment of wasteland/degraded land in lieu of acquired land, each PAF shall get financial assistance of Rs. 10,000/- per hectare for land development. In case of allotment of agricultural land, a one-time financial assistance of Rs. 5,000/- per PAF for agricultural production shall be given.

Each PAF having cattle shall get financial assistance of Rs. 3,000/- for construction of cattle shed.

Each PAF shall get financial assistance of Rs. 5,000/- as transportation cost for shifting of building materials, belongings and cattle etc from the affected zone to the resettlement zone.

Each PAF comprising of rural artisan/small trader and self-employed person shall get one-time financial assistance of Rs. 10,000/- for construction of working shed/shop.

Each PAF owning agricultural land in the affected zone and whose entire land has been acquired shall get one-time financial assistance equivalent to 750 days minimum agricultural wages for "loss of livelihood" where neither agricultural land nor regular employment to one member of the PAF has been provided.

Each PAF owning agricultural land in the affected zone and whose entire land has not been acquired and consequently he becomes a marginal farmer shall get one time financial assistance equivalent to 500 days minimum agricultural wages.

Each PAF owning agriculture land in the affected zone and who consequently becomes a small farmer shall get one time financial assistance equivalent to 375 days minimum agricultural wages.

Each PAF belonging to the category of 'agricultural labourer' or 'non-agricultural labourer' shall be provided a one-time financial assistance equivalent to 625 days of the minimum agricultural wages.

Each displaced PAF shall get a monthly subsistence allowance equivalent to 20 days of Minimum Agricultural Wages per month for a period of one year upto 250 days of MAW.

In the case of acquisition of land in emergent situation such as under Section 17 of the Land Acquisition Act 1894 or similar provision of other Act in force, each PAF shall be provided with transit accommodation, pending Resettlement and Rehabilitation scheme. Such families shall also get R&R benefits as mentioned in the above paras under this Policy.

In case of projects relating to Railway Lines, Highways, Transmission Lines and laying pipelines wherein only a narrow stretch of land extending over several kilometers is being acquired, the Project Affected Families will be offered an ex gratia amount of Rs. 10,000/- per family, and no other Resettlement and Rehabilitation benefits shall be available to them.

The Project Affected Families shall be provided necessary training facilities for development of entrepreneurship to take up self-employment projects at the resettlement zone as part of R&R benefits.

The Project Affected Families, who were in possession of forest lands prior to 25th October 1980 shall get all the benefits of R&R as given in the above paras under this Policy.

The PAFs of Scheduled Caste category enjoying reservation benefits in the affected zone shall be entitled to get the reservation benefits at the resettlement zone.

R&R Benefits for Project Affected Families of Scheduled Tribes

Each Project Affected Family of ST category shall be given preference in allotment of land.

Each tribal PAF shall be entitled to get R&R benefits mentioned in the above Paras under this Policy.

Each Tribal PAF shall get additional financial assistance equivalent to 500 days minimum agriculture wages for loss of customary rights/use of forest produce.

Tribal PAFs will be resettled close to their natural habitat in a compact block so that they can retain their ethnic, linguistic and cultural identity.

Tribal PAFs shall get land free of cost for community and religious gatherings.

Tribal PAFs resettled out of the district/taluka will get 25 per cent higher R&R benefits in monetary terms.

The Tribal Land alienated in violation of the laws and regulations in force on the subject would be treated as null and void and the R&R benefits would be available only to the original tribal land owner.

The Tribal Families residing in the Project Affected Areas having fishing rights in the river/pond/dam shall be given fishing rights in the reservoir area.

Tribal PAFs enjoying reservation benefits in the affected zone shall be entitled to get the reservation benefits at the resettlement zone.

Basic Amenities to be Provided at Resettlement Zone

While shifting the population of the affected zone to the Resettlement Zone, the Administrator for R&R may as far as possible, ensure that:

1. In case the entire population of the village/area to be shifted belongs to a particular community, such population/families may be resettled en masse in a compact area so that socio-cultural relations (social harmony) amongst shifted families are not disturbed; and
2. In case of resettlement of Scheduled Castes PAFs, it may be ensured that they are resettled in sites close to the villages.

The Project Affected Families shall be provided the basic amenities and infrastructural facilities at the resettlement site as per norms specified by the Appropriate Government. It is desirable that provision of drinking water, electricity, schools, dispensaries and access to the resettlement sites amongst others be included in the Resettlement Plan formulated by the Administrator for R&R.

Dispute Redress Mechanism

R&R Committee at Project Level

In respect of every project to which this Policy applies, the State Government shall constitute a Committee under the Chairmanship of the Administrator of that Project to be called the Resettlement and Rehabilitation Committee to monitor and review the progress of implementation of scheme/plan of Resettlement and Rehabilitation of the Project Affected Families.

The Resettlement and Rehabilitation Committee constituted as above shall inter alia include as one of its members:

1. a representative of women residing in the affected zone;
2. a representative each of the Scheduled Castes and Scheduled Tribes residing in the affected zone;
3. a representative of a voluntary organization;
4. a representative of the lead bank;

5. Chairman or his nominee of the PRIs located in the affected zone; and
6. MPs/MLAs of the area included in the affected zone.

Procedure regulating the business of the Resettlement and Rehabilitation Committee, its meeting and other matters connected thereto shall be prescribed by the Appropriate Government.

Grievance Redress Cell

In respect of every project to which this Policy applies, the State Government shall constitute a Grievance Redress Cell under the Chairmanship of the Commissioner for Resettlement and Rehabilitation for redress of grievances of the PAFs.

The composition, powers, functions and other matters relating to the functioning of the Grievance Redress Cell shall be such as may be prescribed by the Appropriate Government.

Any Project Affected Family, if aggrieved, for not being offered the admissible R&R benefits as provided under this Policy, may move an appropriate petition for redress of its grievances to the Grievance Redress Cell.

The form and manner in which and the time within which complaints may be made to the Grievance Redress Cell and disposed of shall be such as may be prescribed by the Appropriate Government.

The Grievance Redress Cell shall have the power to consider and dispose of all complaints relating to Resettlement and Rehabilitation against the decision of the Administrator/ R&R Committee at project level for Resettlement and Rehabilitation and issue such directions to the Administrator for Resettlement and Rehabilitation as it may deem proper for the redress of such grievances.

Inter-State Projects

In case a project covers an area in more than one State or States or a Union territory where the Project Affected Families are or had been residing, or proposed to be resettled, the

Central Government in the Ministry of Rural Development (Department of Land Resources) shall in consultation with concerned States or Union territory, as the case may be, appoint the Administrator for Resettlement and Rehabilitation and the Commissioner for Resettlement and Rehabilitation for the purposes of this Policy.

The method of implementation of plans/schemes for Resettlement and Rehabilitation shall be mutually discussed by the State Governments and the Union Territory administration and the common plan/scheme shall be notified by the Administrator for Resettlement and Rehabilitation in the State or Union territory administration, as agreed to, in accordance with the procedure laid down in this Policy.

If any difficulty arises in the implementation of the schemes/plans, the matter shall be referred to the Central Government in the Ministry of Rural Development (Department of Land Resources) for its decision and the decision of the Central Government shall be binding on the concerned States and Union Territory.

Monitoring Mechanism

National Monitoring Committee

The Central Government, Ministry of Rural Development, Department of Land Resources shall constitute a National Monitoring Committee, to be chaired by the Secretary, Department of Land Resources, for reviewing and monitoring the progress of implementation of Resettlement and Rehabilitation scheme/plan relating to all projects to which this Policy applies. The Committee will have the following or his/her nominee not below the rank of Joint Secretary as its members:

Secretary, Planning Commission
Secretary, M/o Social Justice and Empowerment
Secretary, M/o Water Resources
Secretary, M/o Tribal Affairs
Secretary, M/o Railways

Secretary, M/o Power
Secretary, M/o Coal

Besides, the Secretary of the administrative Ministry/ Department of the project for which the land is to be acquired shall be invited as one of the Members. The functions and duties of this Committee shall be prescribed by this Ministry.

The National Monitoring Committee shall be serviced by the National Monitoring Cell to be constituted by the Department of Land Resources for reviewing and monitoring the progress of implementation of Resettlement and Rehabilitation scheme/plan relating to all projects to which this Policy applies.

The National Monitoring Cell constituted under this Policy shall be headed by an Officer not below the rank of Joint Secretary to the Government of India.

Applicability

The National Policy on the Resettlement and Rehabilitation of Project Affected Families (NPRR 2003) shall come into effect from the date of its publication in the Gazette of India (Extraordinary).

3

Ethics of Governance

Key Words

Communist Party of India (Marxist), Communist Party of India (Marxist-Leninist), Democratic Decentralization, Dialectical Materialism, Ideology, Information Technology, Infrastructure Development, Land Reforms, Land Rights, Left Front Government, Operation Barga, People's Democratic Revolution, Security of Tenure.

Executive Summary

This chapter makes an attempt to examine the lessons learnt and best practices of development ethics identified in the earlier chapters in the context of the Left Front Government regime in West Bengal that commenced since 1977.[1] The different dynamics and ethos of development as practised by the ruling communists in the state are analyzed in this connection in order to understand the critical process of reconciling the ideology of communism with the market demands of the parliamentary democratic system.

Introduction

The case of West Bengal is a classical study that indicates how copybook communists conforming to different shades of ideologies ranging from pink socialism to hardcore Marxism-Leninism have grappled with the realities of Statecraft in order to continue in office for close to three decades since 1977 when they first came to power following the conclusion of the infamous Emergency (1975-77).

Photograph 1: Jyoti Basu being sworn in as Chief Minister of West Bengal on 21 June 1977[2]

Prologue

The Communist Party of India (Marxist) has always led the successive Left Front Governments that have ruled West Bengal since 1977 when the first Left Front Government came to power riding the wave of the historic socialist movement led by veteran leader Jayaprakash (JP) Narayan. Prominent Left Front allies have been the Communist Party of India (that joined later), the Forward Bloc and the Revolutionary Socialist Party. Other smaller parties are also part of this ruling coalition.

We would concentrate exclusively on the evolution of the CPI (M) as the leading party in power that has effectively tackled the demerits of incumbency to institutionalize a series of stints in government that has redefined the meaning of regime in order to identify it with the more value-loaded term of hegemony. The party has effectively reconciled the apparently divergent trends of movement and government so as to evolve as a unique practical political outfit that depends on organization, entrenchment, networks, patron-client relationships and a pragmatic pro-people/pro-poor image that can radically declass itself as and when required.

Map 1: Political Map of West Bengal[3]

The first ever Left Front Government adopted certain important policy decisions. These were relevant in the volatile political context of the mid-1970s when the single party dominant rule of the monolithic Indian National Congress led by Indira Gandhi was effectively challenged by the upsurge of an alternative politics that was supposed to have emerged from the grassroots and supported by local as well as regional long-term aims and aspirations.[4]

Such new political ambitions were not entirely unexpected. A long and sustained period of Congress rule had led to a profound sense of relative deprivation on the part of the local political actors that were eager to play in the multicultural and pluralist political arena of the Indian liberal democratic system. Another critical factor that was operational in this regard in West Bengal was the misgovernance factor.

Misrule 1967-77

West Bengal was not properly governed during the decade of 1967-77 that has been described by various political scientists and social historians as the critical and disturbed period of *interregnum* that was provoked by successive Union Front Governments led by Ajoy Mukerjee of Bangla Congress (that was a breakway splinter from the ruling Congress Party led by Prafulla Chandra Sen). Profound cabinet instability marked both the Union Front Governments that were formed in 1967 and 1969.

Jyoti Basu of the CPI (M) happened to be the Deputy Chief Minister in Ajoy Mukherjee's Cabinet. This was an ideological dichotomy of the Union Front Governments that experimented with strange bedfellows like the communists (who were more radical in their political outlook at this point of time) and the mainstream Bangla Congress leadership that was more comfortable with the centrist mode of politics informed by the norms and conventions of the parliamentary democratic system.

Radical firebrand leaders such as Harekrishna Konar and Subodh Banerjee led the land grab and gherao movements to ensure social justice in the state. But the fact that they themselves were part of the Establishment during this period confused their political agenda further and subsequently led to a period of total anarchy and misrule against a most volatile political background that ultimately facilitated growth of the well-known Naxalite Movement during the late 1960s till the early 1970s.

Naxalite Radicalism

This agrarian movement was ideologically located well within the tradition of the Tebhaga and Telengana Movements that emerged due to agrarian injustice and oppression exercised on the part of the unduly privileged classes who were a product of the Permanent Settlement introduced by Lord Cornwallis way back in 1793 in Undivided Bengal. The landless agricultural labourers, the share-croppers and the tenant farmers were the worst-affected classes under this land revenue system that created a category of absentee landlords who stayed in their estates in Kolkata (erstwhile Calcutta) and elsewhere and depended upon their managerial staff to collect revenue.[5] The Zamindari Abolition Act and the Land Ceiling Act were passed in the 1950s to secure agrarian justice but land reforms in the objective sense of the term were not carried out till 1977 in West Bengal.

Student intellectuals of Kolkata were inspired by the revolutionary teachings of Mao Ze Dong (Chairman of the Chinese Communist Party). These student activists mainly joined the Naxalite Movement from the famous Presidency College of Kolkata that was established as the Hindu College way back in 1817 even before Calcutta University was founded in 1857.

Naxalite leaders believed in radical doctrines such as the source of power lies in the barrel of the gun and that the Parliament is a pigsty where revisionists and reactionaries conspire with the bourgeoisie to relentlessly oppress the proletarian classes by institutionalizing a mode of production whose productive forces adversely condition the uneven relations of production by hoarding any surplus value created by the labourers.

But the essential problem with the Naxalite Movement was that it was organized by city-bred young intellectuals who cherished a noble dream without being equipped with the resources that were require to transform their vision of egalitarian social change into reality. Student leaders had no organic intellectual or even psychological connection whatsoever with the grassroots represented by the tea garden workers for whom they first took up arms against the police and state authorities at Naxalbari Village in North Bengal.

It is worthwhile to note at this point that more prominent Naxalite leaders like Charu Mazumdar, Kanu Sanyal and Jangal Santal had formed a new political outfit called the Communist Party of India (Marxist-Leninist) by breaking away from the CPI(M) that had itself broken away from the Communist Party of India in 1964 due to differences in perception about the bourgeois democratic revolution and the people's democratic revolution among other related ideological concerns.[6]

Naxalite leaders subsequently championed the politics of assassination that soon degenerated into the politics of vendetta led by the lumpen proletariat. The high point of this period of misgovernance was reached during the infamous Baranagar Cossipore Killings in North Kolkata when allegedly CPI(M) and Congress activists rounded up and massacred several Naxal supporters (supported by the police authorities) during one single night.

Failures of the Naxalite Movement point to certain political lessons. This was an early attempt to conjoin the issue of economic development with the ethics of governance but the movement still was destined not to succeed because it was not supported by a mass base, perspective planning, organizational strength, visionary leadership and essential resources. The type of urban guerilla warfare that the Naxalite activists had started practising ultimately backfired when stiff resistance was offered by their political opponents and the police forces (who were reported to have engaged in a series of fake encounters to liquidate Naxal leaders and their followers).

Historic Context

This aborted movement signified virtually the end of a revolutionary dream and the end of the so-called project of emancipation. One must remember that this period also witnessed the Liberation War in East Pakistan that culminated in the creation of Bangladesh just across the international border. Refugee influx into West Bengal was a critical problem during this period. This problem in fact continued right from the Partition of India and Independence at 1947. The communists promptly utilized the refugees as a political weapon to agitate against the ruling Congress Party during the 1950s and 1960s.

The 1950s and 1960s constituted the disturbed period when several communist-led agitations took place, including the food movements that were organized to protest against the public distribution system policies of the Congress Government. The infamous War for a Pice also occurred at this juncture to protest against the fair hike in public trams.

The communists did not allow the refugees to resettle in the Andaman and Nicobar Islands and Dandakaranya. But it was an irony of history that the first Left Front Government unleashed police repression against the refugees at Marichjhanpi in 1978.

Maoist Insurgency

The incidents of armed insurgency led by the Maoist outfits (that maintain liaison with their counterparts in Nepal and Sri Lanka) in West Bengal during the present decade point to the fact that the basic tenets of organized protest are still very much present in the state. Poverty, inadequate development, unemployment etc continue to haunt the communists in office.

Even starvation deaths have been reported widely in the popular media. Security forces have cracked down upon the militants while the rebels themselves have inflicted heavy casualties on the police personnel deployed in the arid and generally backward districts such as Purulia, Bankura and West Midnapore.

The Maoist rebels who frequent the forest areas of these districts are heavily armed and use remote-controlled explosives and anti-personnel landmines to challenge the police forces. Their communication networks are well-maintained and the local villagers act as their conduits of information either for fear or favour.

These rebels are also located in states like Andhra Pradesh and Bihar where they fight bloody wars with the security forces and illegal private armies of feudal landlords. Maoist rebels are gradually trying to establish a regional alliance in South Asia. They have already influenced the course of history in neighbouring Nepal where the King has been forced to usher in an era of parliamentary constitutional reforms led by the democratic parties.

Indian communist leaders have even taken part in deliberations with the Maoist leaders of Nepal to initiate this process of a historic transfer of power. This indicates a steady understanding between the CPM and the Maoists in the international context while the picture is entirely different in the case of West Bengal.[7]

Left Front Regime

The first Left Front Government started on a cautious note and spelt out its policies in certain areas at the very outset of its rule. The state government came out with its own official stand *vis-à-vis* India's federal political system, and added that no unsolicited political intervention whatsoever from the Government of India would at all be tolerated, especially in the most sensitive area of administrative autonomy exercised by the Government of West Bengal. This fear psychosis was actually provoked by Prime Minister Indira Gandhi's peremptory dismissal of non-Congress state governments that had incurred her party's displeasure.

The state government also abolished English language teaching from the primary level and even wanted (at least party mandarin Pramod Dasgupta promoted this idea) to introduce a new class of barefoot doctors (quacks) to take care of the public health situation of rural West Bengal. The state government also declared its resistance to the entry of computers in order to continue the labour-intensive mode of production.

Historic agrarian land reforms in the form of Operation Barga followed soon. Landless agricultural labourers were given land rights or *patta* by the state government to ensure and institutionalize redistributive justice. This was a landmark achievement of this young government that attracted global attention and scholarly acclaim. Academic researchers worldwide focused their attention on West Bengal's dynamic experiments in the rural sector. This focus intensified when successive Left Front Governments returned to power in 1982, 1987, 1991, 1996, 2001 and 2006.[8]

But the initial wonder that accompanied the first generation of land reforms in the state has subsided somewhat as realization has dawned that excessive fragmentation of land holdings has negatively affected the productivity of land and the economic scale of operations. Agriculture has ceased to continue as a profitable venture, at least for small and marginal farmers as well as share-croppers. The state government is now poised to amend the existing Land Ceiling Act in order to facilitate transfer of large plots of land to investors who are interested to set up knowledge cities, health cities, Special Economic Zones, townships and automobile factories in the districts of North and South 24 Parganas, Howrah and Hooghly that are adjacent to Kolkata.

Policy Shift

Chief Minister Buddhadeb Bhattacharjee and Industries Minister Nirupam Sen have reiterated that potential investors should be given land wherever they demand, and not in remote areas of the state where there is abundant land. The problem is that the land adjacent to Kolkata is fertile where multiple cropping is carried out each year. But the arid zones in Bankura, Birbhum and Purulia are not attractive enough due to inadequate infrastructure and poor rail and road and air and water connectivity.

Nirupam Sen has even categorically spelt out that the state government would not compel potential investors to engage local-level labour in their various projects. He has pointed out that such a demand essentially violates the basic norms of market capitalism. Cheap and skilled labour force will be brought from outside West Bengal to implement the projects currently in the pipeline in a cost-effective manner.

The state government is at least expected to request private investors to provide adequate compensation to the Project Affected Families who would lose land or immovable assets or both due to implementation of these projects. The Left Front Governments in the past had at least on paper announced that adequate compensation would be paid to affected persons during implementation of infrastructure development projects. But the case of Rajarhat New Town adjacent to Salt Lake City suggests otherwise.

This paradigm shift in ideology and political priorities in terms of the development agenda and moral values was perhaps a historic compulsion that was necessitated by the increasing flight of capital from West Bengal and the closing down of industrial units, especially in the famous Jute Belt area along the River Hooghly. A similar incident happened way back in 1991 when India's first generation of belated economic reforms was catalyzed by an acute crisis in the country's foreign exchange reserves.

So now the communist leadership of West Bengal has realized that Deng Ziao Ping of the People's Republic of China was at his pragmatic best when he had declared that it was glorious to be rich and that it was not important what the cat brought back home, a white or a black mouse, as long as it was still a mouse![9] This cryptic statement actually meant that it was of no value splitting ideological straws regarding the political nature of economic investments so long as the cash flow continued to enrich and energize the economy.

The CPM admits that the Chinese Communist Party is its ideological inspiration. So it has opted for the path of its much-flaunted path of an alternative development championed by Finance Minster Ashim Dasgupta. The market socialist policy of China happens to somewhat inform the ideological baggage of the CPM-led Left Front Government at this present juncture. Nirupam Sen has even advanced one strategic step forward when he recently declared that the state government is following an open market liberal approach to attract capitalists to the state. He has also pointed out that it cannot always be expected that industry would play a socially committed role in its pursuit of profits.

Policy Critique

Several criticisms against the present Left Front Government's industrial policy have been put forward by social scientists, especially economists, who have questioned the moral justification of infrastructure development, commercial activities and profit-making ventures by acquiring fertile agricultural land that happens to be the only source of (subsistence) livelihood on the part of most peasants who either own the land or else cultivate the same on a share-cropping basis. The issue of tenant farmers and marginalized landless agriculture labourers has also assumed especial significance in this context, as only the legal owners of land are entitled to monetary compensation.

Detailed entitlement matrices have to be drafted to ensure that all categories of stakeholders dependent on agricultural land for their principal sources of livelihood are adequately compensated. Social security measures have to be also introduced by the state government in due consultation with the project promoters in order to establish an entrenched network of support mechanisms. The basic purpose of development would be defeated in terms of good governance driven by a set of ethical standards.

But several economists and political commentators have of late raised the issue of ethical choice in the context of acquiring prime agricultural land around Kolkata in order to subserviently cater to the demands raised by prospective investors. The new investor-friendly Industrial Policy framed by the Government of West Bengal in the recent past under the leadership of Chief Minister Jyoti Basu was itself a much delayed proposition that materialized when the state was on a rapid downhill slide in terms of industries and investments.

Such an alarming state of affairs prompted the Destination West Bengal slogan and the rhetoric of an improved Left Front (after the exit of Jyoti Basu and entry of Buddhadeb Bhattacharjee as the new Chief Minister of the state). It has been proclaimed that the only viable substitute for the Left Front Government is an improved version of the Left Front

Government itself that is much more pro-technology (the capital intensive and not the labour intensive version) and industry-friendly.

Economists have repeatedly pointed out in the media that the compensation fixed for land should be calculated not on the basis of the present market value in the concerned areas but on the projected value of land that would be enhanced due to infrastructure development and addition to capital assets in the locality in the near future. Proximity to highway, port, airport, township, chemical hub, knowledge city, food park, health city etc would automatically increase the market value of land. So when it is imperative to freeze land transactions in the proposed areas to prevent unethical speculation, it is also important to scientifically arrive at a realistic value of land based on projected figures.

Next arises the question of entitlements, benefits and project support. There are several categories of stakeholders dependent upon agricultural land who are not formally the owners of land, and hence not entitled for any sort of monetary compensation. How to safeguard their livelihood in order to ensure sustainable development? The state government has announced that the issue of employment for one member of affected families whose land would be acquired for the project would be sympathetically considered. But what kind of employment has the government considered for this labour force that is only skilled in agricultural activities?

The state government launched a campaign before the Legislative Assembly Election of 2006, namely Agriculture is Our Base, Industry is Our Future. This actually follows the classical Base-Superstructure Theory of Marxism that conforms to the notions of Dialectical Materialism. So are we in fact witnessing a historical shift from thesis to antithesis in West Bengal today? There are ample examples of the unity and struggle of opposites and the emergence of qualitative policy stances from quantitative electoral gains in the context of strategic negation of tactical negations.

But the Left Front Government is not ideologically strait-jacketed while posed to launch a series of development projects in the state unprecedented since the rule of Congress Chief Minister Dr Bidhan Chandra Roy. But while Dr Roy focused more on infrastructure augmentation in the public sector, the communists have opted for technology-intensive industrialization in the private sector, perhaps compelled by the new world order of liberalization, privatization and globalization.

Operation Barga

The famous land reforms movement launched by the first Left Front Government in West Bengal was code named Operation Barga.[10] This was the first ever concerted initiative to guarantee security of tenure for the sharecroppers who earned their livelihood by tilling the land owned by an affluent and exploitative class of the feudal rich (*jotedar*). Agrarian reforms were in fact even attempted by earlier Congress Government, but the real impact in terms of widespread social change was achieved during the Left Front regime. Land rights were given to the marginalized and landless cultivators in an effort to empower them against social and economic injustice.

"As a multitude of studies have discussed, well-conceived legislation coupled with political will brought West Bengal's land reform efforts substantial success over the last 25 years. While land reform has made little headway in most of India, West Bengal has been an exception. Progress has occurred in three areas:

1. regulating sharecropping relationships (Operation Barga);
2. redistributing ceiling-surplus lands in ownership; and
3. distributing homestead plots.

"In all, approximately half of rural households in West Bengal have received land reform benefits. Through serious and sustained land reform implementation, West Bengal has made remarkable progress in agricultural growth and in some aspects of poverty alleviation. In the 20-year period after setting land reforms in place, agricultural growth skyrocketed. More important, rural poverty declined sharply and both food intake and wages in the countryside increased significantly.

"West Bengal's land reform success was not achieved in a single legislative step, but in a series of major steps and minor corrective revisions over several decades. The state government has not just rested on past land reform laurels, but instead has taken numerous, incremental steps to further improve the land reform legislation and implementation over time. Many such steps were pragmatic responses to changes in the economic, social, and/or political environment in the countryside. The state government currently (and appropriately) recognises that some additional improvements may now be needed to further benefit the rural poor and marginalised and to facilitate rural economic growth."[11]

Critics have repeatedly pointed out that in several cases the *parcha* (land record) has been kept under the CPI (M)'s control in order to ensure mass loyalty to the party. Excessive fragmentation of landholdings has also led to reduced productivity of land. Collective farming by using mechanized equipment cannot also be carried out in fragmented agricultural plots. The issue of agricultural inputs such as pesticides, fertilizer, seeds and water for irrigation purpose is also a critical factor, as rural indebtedness may easily occur when the cultivators have to approach local moneylenders to buy such items.

Total implementation of Operation Barga in West Bengal is a mammoth exercise that requires significant time and administrative involvement. Suicides on the part of farmers in different parts of India (provoked by rural indebtedness) have not been generally observed in the case of West Bengal. But rural poverty has led to starvation deaths in pockets such as Amlashole. Naxalite disturbances are also on the rise due to rural backwardness in places like Beliatore and Shalboni.[12]

Panchayati Raj

Local self-government and democratic decentralization/ devolution of political power and accountability have been important landmarks for the protracted Left Front Government rule in West Bengal. The most significant political rhetoric in this regard was the well-known Power to the People slogan. This ensured that the rural population in the backward agrarian pockets would now have a voice and choice in their overall arrangement of political participation.

The three-tier *panchayati raj* system of local governance has prepared the ground for an effective alternative politics that would be guided by pro-people as well as pro-people political institutions at the level of the grassroots and the material conditions of everyday life. Scholars have employed the neo institutional analytical framework to critically address the dialectical relationship between actors and their institutions in the context of the politics from below system.

Political commentators have pointed out that decentralization of corruption has taken place in rural West Bengal along with decentralization of political power. They have also repeatedly alleged that the panchayats have steadily emerged as localized pockets of vested agrarian interests in the countryside. Panchayats controlled by the communists and their coalition allies now happen to dictate the political destiny of the rural population, it has been added.

"Elected local governments (panchayats) have played an important role in the implementation of various poverty alleviation programs in West Bengal since 1978. These programs include land reform, delivery of credit, farm inputs and local infrastructure projects designed to generate employment for the poor. It is widely believed that these programs were effectively targeted in favour of the poor, due in part to the involvement of the panchayats in their implementation. The West Bengal experience thus suggests that decentralization of delivery of anti-poverty programs can result in reduction of targeting failures which have plagued traditional delivery mechanisms entrusted to centralized bureaucracies.

"The literature on decentralization of service delivery however stresses some potential pitfalls. The most important of these is the possibility that local democracy may not function well in some contexts *e.g.* where the distribution of assets, literacy and social status is highly unequal, a tradition of widespread political participation does not exist, and political competition is lacking. Under such conditions, political parties may be prone to capture by special interest groups, participation in elections may not be widespread, and voters may be swayed more by campaign rhetoric or political handouts rather than genuine policy issues.

"Political competition for panchayat seats is undoubtedly jointly determined along with anti-poverty policies of the panchayat ... the electoral successes of the Left Front in gram panchayat elections were driven primarily by wider shifts in voter loyalties (as gauged by vote shares at the district level in elections to the state legislature occurring around the same time) and pro-incumbency bias among voters, rather than local patterns of land distribution, literacy or caste.

"One could continue to examine whether the evidence fits any other hypothesis of endogeneity bias. Instead we conclude our discussion by noting that the hypothesis of lower political accountability of local governments to the poor when they are more vulnerable provides a parsimonious explanation of the observed targeting patterns in a wide variety of programs."[13]

Jyoti Basu had often boasted about the successful experiment with the panchayats and coalition politics in West Bengal. But the fact of the matter remains that the CPI (M) has extended and entrenched its rule based on the philosophy of the iron law of oligarchy[14] in the state by penetrating both the private as well as the public spheres of everyday politics.

Epilogue

So the hiatus between the priorities of development and the exercise of ethical choices of such priorities remains a pertinent question in present day West Bengal ruled by the Left Front Government that at least ideologically tries to maintain (equal) distance from bourgeois and reactionary and communal parties such as the Indian National Congress and the Bharatiya Janata Party. But the policy imperatives of even such a party with an ideological difference do not offer much new thought for an alternative politics or even alternative development. In the ultimate analysis the compulsions of continuing in power supersede any possibility of deviating from the mundane but familiar path of the so-called mainstream model of development that cannot afford to bother itself about the larger question of values and the moral order of development.

Conclusion

Our analysis of the Left Front regime in West Bengal comes to an inconclusive end while we are still trying to grapple with value-loaded terms like ethics and development. But it is still worthwhile to raise a few questions The answers may not always be forthcoming but that should not deter us from framing the questions at least that keep on emerging at most critical and uncomfortable junctures. We cannot deny the fact that the communists have been able to achieve much in terms of social change. But we are also more or less convinced that their experiments have not yet ended and should continue in tandem with their journey towards exploring political alternatives and sustainable answers to some of the most baffling questions of ethical development. We cannot be sure that rulers in parliamentary democracies all over the world always exercise ethical choices. But we should continue with our initiatives at the level of the civil society to ensure that conscientious efforts on the part of the political elite are oriented towards development underpinned by humane considerations. The agenda of intellectual emancipation and economic independence loses much of its significance if it is not supported by a political order that is moral in its conviction and developmentalist in its worldview.

REFERENCES

Appu, P.S. (1996), *Land Reforms in India*, Vikas Publishing House, New Delhi.

Banerjee, A. (2004), "Who is Getting the Public Goods in India: Some Evidence and Some Speculation," in K. Basu (edited), *India's Emerging Economy: Performance and Prospects in the 1990s and Beyond*, MIT Press, Cambridge MA.

Bardhan, P. (1996), "Decentralized Development", *Indian Economic Review*, vol. 31, no. 2.

——— (2002), "Decentralization of Governance and Development," *Journal of Economic Perspectives*, Fall 2002, 16(4), 185-206.

——— and D. Mookherjee (2000), "Capture and Governance at Local and National Levels," *American Economic Review*, May 2000, 135-139.

——— (2002), "Decentralizing Anti-Poverty Program Delivery in Developing Countries," mimeo, Boston University.

——— (2003a), "Decentralization and Accountability in Infrastructure Delivery in Developing Countries," Working Paper, Institute for Economic Development, Boston University.

——— (2003b), "Political Economy of Land Reforms in West Bengal 1978-98," mimeo, Boston University. http://econ.bu.edu/dilipm/wkpap.htm/wkpaphmpg.html

——— (2003c), "Pro-Poor Targeting and Accountability of Local Governments in West Bengal," mimeo, Boston University. http://econ.bu.edu/dilipm/wkpap.htm/wkpaphmpg.html

Bird, R. (1995), "Decentralizing Infrastructure: For Good or Ill?" in A. Estache (ed.), *Decentralizing Infrastructure: Advantages and Limitations*, World Bank Discussion Papers 290, Washington D.C., 1995.

Crook, R. and J. Manor (1998), *Democracy and Decentralisation in South Asia and West Africa*, Cambridge: Cambridge University Press, 1998.

Dreze, J. and A, Sen (1989), *Hunger and Public Action*, Oxford University Press, New Delhi.

Faguet, J.P. (2003), "Decentralization and Local Government in Bolivia," paper prepared for a conference on The Rise of Local Governments in Developing Countries, London School of Economics, May 2003.

Galasso, E. and M. Ravallion (2000), "Distributional Outcomes of a Decentralized Welfare Program," Working Paper no. 2316, World Bank Research Department.

Kohli, A. (1997), "From Breakdown to Order: West Bengal," in P. Chatterjee (ed), *State and Politics in India*, Oxford India Paperbacks, Oxford University Press, New Delhi.

Lieten, G.K. (1992), *Continuity and Change in Rural West Bengal*, Sage Publications, New Delhi.

——— (1996), "Panchayats in Western Uttar Pradesh," *Economic and Political Weekly*, 28 September 1996, 2700-2705.

Manor, J. (1999), *The Political Economy of Democratic Decentralization.* Washington DC: The World Bank, 1999.

Mathew, G. and R. Nayak, "Panchayats at Work: What It Means for the Oppressed?" *Economic and Political Weekly*, July 6, 1996, 1765-1771.

Mookherjee, D. (2004), *The Crisis in Government Accountability: Essays on Governance Reforms and India's Economic Performance*, Oxford University Press, New Delhi.

Prud'homme, P. (1995), "The Dangers of Decentralization," *World Bank Research Observer*, 10, 1995, 201-20.

Ravallion, M. and D. van de Walle (2002), "Land Allocation in Vietnam's Agrarian Transition," Working Paper, World Bank Research Department.

Sengupta, S. and H. Gazdar (1996), "Agrarian Politics and Rural Development in West Bengal," in Drèze, J. and A. Sen, Editors, *Indian Development: Selected Regional Perspectives*, Oxford India Paperbacks, Oxford University Press, New Delhi.

Swaminathan, M. (1990), "Village Level Implementation of IRDP: A Comparison of West Bengal and Tamil Nadu," *Economic and Political Weekly*, XXV, 13:A17-A27.

Tanzi, V. (1996), "Fiscal Federalism and Efficiency: A Review of Some Efficiency and Macroeconomic Aspects," in M. Bruno and B. Pleskovic (Edited), *Annual World Bank Conference on Development Economics 1996*. Washington DC: The World Bank.

Webster, N. (1992), *Panchayati Raj and the Decentralization of Development Planning in West Bengal*, KP Bagchi and Co., Calcutta.

Wittenberg, M. (2003), "Decentralisation in South Africa," Working Paper, University of Witwatersrand, Johannesburg, presented at a conference on The Rise of Local Governments in Developing Countries, London School of Economics, May 2003,

World Development Report 2004, *Making Services Work for Poor People*, The World Bank, Washington DC., Oxford University Press.

Suggested Readings[15]

Afshar, Haleh (1991). *Women, Development and Survival in the Third World.*Longman Press, NY.

Ahmed, Iftikhar (1994). "Technology and Feminisation of Work." *Economic and Political Weekly*, April 30: pp. WS-34.

Batliwala, S. (1993). *Empowerment of Women in South Asia: Concepts and Practices.*

Basu, Amrita (1992). *Two Faces of Protest: Contrasting Modes of Women 's Activism in India.* Zed Books, London.

Calman, Leslie (1992). *Toward Empowerment: Women and Movement Politics in India.* Westview Press, Boulder.

Chen, Martha (1991). *A Quiet Revolution. Women in Transition in Rural Bangladesh.* BRAC Prokashana, Dhaka.

Clark, Alice ed. (1993). *Explorations of South Asian Systems. Gender and Political Economy.* Oxford University Press, Delhi.

Duza, Asfia (1993). *Emerging New Accents: A Perspective of Gender and Development in Bangladesh.* Women for Women, Dhaka.

Feldman, Shelley (1987). "Overpopulation as Crisis: Redirecting Health Care Services in Rural Bangladesh."*International Journal of Health Services.* 17(1):113.

Feldman, Shelley (1992). "Crisis, Islam and Gender in Bangladesh: The Social Construction of the Labour Force." in Feldman, Shelley and Beneria, Lourdes. *Unequal Burden.* Westview Press, Boulder.

Franke, Richard; Barbara Chasin (1996). "Female Supported Households. A Continuing Agenda for Kerala Model?" *Economic and Political Weekly*, March 9:625.

Ganguly Thukral, Enakshi (1996). "Development, Displacement and Rehabilitation. Locating Gender." *Economic and Political Weekly*, June 15:1500.

Ghosh, Jayati (1994). "Gender Concerns in Macro-Economic Policy." *Economic and Political Weekly*, 2 April 30:WS-12.

Huq-Hussain, Shahnaz (1995). "Fighting poverty: the economic adjustment of female migrants in Dhaka." *Environment and Urbanization*, 7(2): October.

Jeffrey, Patricia; Roger Jeffrey and Andrew Lyon (1989). *Labour Pains and Labour Power.* Zed Books, London.

Kabeer, Naila (1994). *Reversed Realities. Gender Hierarchies in Development Thought.* Verso, London.

Moser, Caroline (1993). *Gender Planning and Development.* Theory, Practice and Training. Routledge, NY.

Raju, Saraswati; Bagchi, Deipica (1993). *Women and Work in South Asia: Regional Patterns and Perspectives.* Routledge, London.

Ranadive, Joy (1994). "Gender Implications of Adjustment Policy Programme in India. Significance of the Household." *Economic and Political Weekly*, April 30:WS-12.

Redclift, Nanneke and M. Thea Sinclair ed. (1991). *Working Women. International Perspectives on Labour and Gender Ideology.* Routledge Press, NY.

Rose, Kalima (1992). *Where Women are Leaders. The SEWA Movement in India.* Zed Books Ltd, London.

Shah, Nandita et al (1994). "Structural Adjustment, Feminisation of Labour Force and Organisational Strategies." *Economic and Political Weekly*, April 30: WS-39.

Sharma, Kumud (1994). "Gender,Environment and Structural Adjustment." *Economic and Political Weekly*, April 30:WS-5.

Shiva Kumar, AK (1996). "UNDP Gender Related Development Index. A Computation for Indian States." *Economic and Political Weekly*, April 6:887.

Spodek, Howard (1994). The Self-Employed Women's Association (SEWA) in India: Feminist, Gandhian Power in Development. *Economic Development and Cultural Change*.

Venkateswaran, Sandhya (1995). *Environment, Development and the Gender Gap*. Sage Publications, New Delhi.

Viswanath, V. (1991). *NGOs and Women's Development in Rural South India: A Comparative Analysis*. Westview Press, Boulder.

Vlassoff, C. (1994). "From rags to riches: the impact of rural development on women's status in an Indian village." *World Development*, 22(5): 707-719.

White, Sarah (1992). *Arguing With the Crocodile: Gender and Class in Bangladesh*. Zed Books, London.

Wieringa, Saskia ed. (1995). *Subversive Women. Women, Movements in Africa, Asia, Latin America and the Caribbean*. Zed Books, London.

APPENDIX-I

West Bengal State Elections: Left Front Lurches Further Right

By Arun Kumar and Keith Jones (8 May 2006)[16]

The Left Front's campaign to win re-election in West Bengal, India's third most populous state, has exemplified its role as a political prop and servant of the Indian bourgeoisie.

Led by the Stalinist Communist Party of India (Marxist) [CPM], the Left Front is seeking to win a seventh-consecutive term as West Bengal's state government by exploiting residual popular illusions in its claims to be pro-toiler and socialist, even while pledging to the Indian bourgeoisie that it will press forward with economic restructuring.

The Left Front has made the pivot of its election campaign the call for industrialization—a euphemism for making West Bengal a cheap-labour cog in the manufacturing, research and business-processing operations of Indian and international capital.

"The industrialists have realized that the Left Front government is an investment-friendly government," boasted West Bengal Chief Minister and CPM Politburo member Bhuddhadeb Bhattacharjee in a press interview last month. "Several industrial houses have come to Bengal, and more are coming. ... We are engaged in the task of development within a capitalist structure."

In pursuit of investment, West Bengal's Left Front government has relaxed labour standards and effectively banned strikes in the state's information technology and business-processing sectors, given the green light to the expropriation of small farmers so that their lands can be used for private industrial development, and sought to win the confidence of international-lending agencies by contracting out public sector jobs and curbing social spending.

In the first four decades following independence, the CPM and its main Left Front partner, the Communist Party of India, justified their support for India's state-led national development strategy on the grounds that the "anti-imperialist" sections of the national bourgeoisie had to be supported against the pro-imperialist wing and feudal reaction. Now, in an even cruder perversion of Marxism, the Stalinists claim, citing China as their model, that the path to socialism lies through West Bengal's transformation into a cheap labour magnet for international capital.

"I am trying," said Bhattacharjee, "to work accepting the present reality...since we are practical, we know it is wise to be capitalist at the moment when the whole world is wooing capitalism".

The Left Front government is particularly concerned at dispelling the notion of West Bengal as a center of worker militancy. Bhattacharjee made a point of reporting for work last September 29, when the unions and Left Front staged a one-day strike to protest the economic policies of the central government, and he angrily denounced workers whose protests crippled the operations of Kolkata's IT sector that day, vowing his government will ensure no like disruption ever occurs again.

The Left Front's "development model" stresses the need for "harmonious relations" between management and labour, Bhattacharjee told a meeting at the Calcutta Press Club, April 13. "It is not the management's responsibility alone to run industry, but labourers should also co-operate so that disputes are settled through discussions. I can't encourage militant trade unionism and shut down factories."

Among the Left Front government's main arguments in wooing investors is that it can better ensure "labour peace" than other state governments, because of its close ties to the trade union apparatus. But when the labour bureaucracy has proven unable to quell worker militancy, the West Bengal Left Front regime has not shied away from using police repression, a point Bhattacharjee himself made when speaking to a business audience in Mumbai last August. After denouncing those who know only how "to formulate a charter of demands, raise slogans and disturb production," Bhattacharjee declared, "We have acted firmly by calling in police when the unions turned militant at Bata and a Pepsi factory."

According to the corporate media, there is strong support for the Left Front government's re-election in business circles. An April 26 Reuters report gave the example of a real estate developer, Pradip Chopra, whose business has grown tenfold in the last five years. "I am comfortable with this government and will support it," said Chopra. "They have changed Kolkata's image of a dying city to one that is vibrant and a happening place to invest." Another businessman, Rajat Kandoi, a partner in a company that does overseas business-processing, told Reuters, "I never dreamed I would vote for the Communists. But this time, I would like this government to return to power."

A poll conducted by the Indian Chamber of Commerce (ICC), the results of which were released last month, rated West Bengal the third most attractive state in which to invest, after Gujarat and Maharashtra. More than half of the ICC's respondents termed the Left Front government's performance in respect to "industrialization and the creation of a congenial business environment" good, while 78 per cent lauded the measures that Chief Minister Bhattacharjee has taken to boost business confidence.

The CPM and Left Front leaders themselves admit that they are courting business support. Jyoti Basu, who served as the West Bengal's chief minister from 1977 to 2001, told a rally, "So far, we have won election on the strength of the poor's vote. Now, we want votes from every stratum of the society."

"Left turns right in Bengal's biz belt," exclaimed on April 25, CNN-IBN report. It pointed to Narayan Jain, the Left Front's candidate for the Chowringee constituency, as symbolic "of the Left's growing clout among business leaders and professionals." His "core group of supporters are all businessmen."

Jain, adds the report, "pushes an unabashed pro-reform, pro-business line. His main concern is to make West Bengal safe for business. 'The laws which are not relevant today, should be scrapped. And after the new government comes, we will take that initiative,' he says."

Led by the CPM, the Left Front is also playing a critical role at the all-India level in supporting the Indian bourgeoisie in imposing its neo-liberal program of privatization, deregulation, and the gutting of worker rights and farmer-price supports. The Left Front's 60-plus MPs are providing the minority, Congress Party-led United Progressive Alliance (UPA) coalition with the votes needed to sustain it in office, while working to contain the mass opposition to the growth of economic insecurity and social inequality within the confines of trade union and parliamentary protests. In the West Bengal elections, which have been held in five phases ending today, the Left Front has been opposed by two, rival multi-party alliances.

The split in the opposition virtually guarantees the Left Front will be re-elected to an unprecedented seventh-term and is indicative of the general satisfaction of big business and the ruling elite with the current government.

The first alliance is led by the Trinamool Congress, a split-off from the Congress Party of Sonia Gandhi and Prime Minister Manmohan Singh, and includes the Hindu supremacist Bharatiya Janata Party (BJP). Although the BJP is the second largest party in India's national parliament, it is only a marginal player in West Bengal politics.

The Trinamool or "grassroots" Congress (TMC) is led by Mamata Bannerjee, a populist demagogue who makes Bengali-chauvinist and strident anti-communist appeals, while trying to exploit popular anger over some of the anti-worker and anti-poor actions of the Left Front government. In the late 1990s, Bannerjee's TMC became the focus of an attempt on the part of sections of big business to oust the Left Front government, which was perceived as insufficiently supportive of economic restructuring. But her stock has fallen as the Left Front has moved right and as sections of West Bengal's urban middle class have benefited from the growth in India's economy.

The Congress, which heads an eight-party [West Bengal] United Democratic Alliance, spurned Bannerjee's pleas for a *mahajot* or grand anti-Left alliance. Sections of the West Bengal Congress party apparatus were inclined to accept Bannerjee's offer, but the all-India party leadership would not hear of it.

Publicly the Congress justified its refusal to ally with the TMC on the grounds that Bannerjee would not break her ties with the BJP and its National Democratic Alliance. Clearly this was a factor, since any alliance with the BJP would undermine the Congress' posture as a progressive, secular party.

But even more importantly, an electoral alliance with the TMC would have constituted a threat to the continued existence of West Bengal's Left Front government, which provides the Stalinists with much of their leverage in official politics. By allowing the return to power of West Bengal's Left Front government with only token opposition, the Congress leadership has smoothed the way for retaining the Left's pivotal support for the UPA government at the Center.

APPENDIX-II

Who are the Naxalites?[17]

The Naxalites, also sometimes called the Naxals, is a loose term used to define groups waging a violent struggle on behalf of landless labourers and tribal people against landlords and others. The Naxalites say they are fighting oppression and exploitation to create a classless society. Their opponents say the Naxalites are terrorists oppressing people in the name of a class war.

How many Naxalite groups are there?

Many groups operate under different names. The Communist Party of India (Marxist-Leninist) is the political outfit that propagates the Naxalite ideology. There are front organisations and special outfits for specific groups such as the Indian People's Front.

The two main groups involved in violent activities, besides many factions and smaller outfits, are the People's War Group, the group many believe is responsible for the attempt on Naidu, and the Maoist Communist Centre.

Where do they operate?

The most prominent area of operation is a broad swathe across the very heartland of India, often considered the least developed area of this country. The Naxalites operate mostly in the rural and Adivasi areas, often out of the continuous jungles in these regions. Their operations are most prominent in (from North to South) Jharkhand, Chhattisgarh, Madhya Pradesh, eastern Maharashtra, the Telengana (north-western) region of Andhra Pradesh and western Orissa. It will be seen that these areas are all inland, from the coastline.

The People's War Group is active mainly in Andhra Pradesh, western Orissa and eastern Maharashtra while the

Maoist Communist Centre is active in Bihar, Jharkhand and northern Chhattisgarh.

Who do they represent?

The Naxalites claim to represent the most oppressed people in India, those who are often left untouched by India's development and bypassed by the electoral process. Invariably, they are the Adivasis, Dalits and the poorest of the poor, who work as landless labourers for a pittance, often below India's mandated minimum wages.

The criticism against the Naxalites is that despite their ideology, they have over the years become just another terrorist outfit, extorting money from middle-level landowners (since rich landowners invariably buy protection), and, worse, even extorting and dominating the lives of the Adivasis and villagers who they claim to represent in the name of providing justice.

Who do the Naxalites target?

Ideologically, the Naxalites claim they are against India as she exists currently. They believe that Indians are still to acquire freedom from hunger and deprivation and that the rich classes—landlords, industrialists, traders etc—control the means of production. Their final aim is the overthrow of the present system, hence the targeting of politicians, police officers and men, forest contractors etc.

At a more local level, the Naxalites have invariably targeted landlords in the villages, often claiming protection money from them. Naxalites have also been known to claim 'tax' from the Adivasis and landless farmers in areas where their writ runs more than that of the government.

When did this movement start? How did it get its name?

The earliest manifestation of the movement was the Telengana Struggle in July 1948 (100 years after the Paris Communes were first set up, coining the word Communist). This struggle was based on the ideology of China's Mao Zedong, with the aim of creating an Indian revolution. Not surprisingly, the ideology remains strong in this region of Andhra Pradesh.

But the Naxalite movement took shape after some members of the Communist Party of India (Marxist) split to form the Communist Party of India (Marxist-Leninist), after the former agreed to participate in elections and form a coalition government in West Bengal. Charu Mazumdar led the split.

On May 25 1967, in Naxalbari village in Darjeeling district, northern West Bengal, local goons attacked a tribal who had been given land by the courts under the tenancy laws. In retaliation, the tribals attacked landlords and claimed the land. From this 'Naxalbari Uprising' came the word Naxalite.

Was it ever popular?

In the late 1960s and early 1970s, the Naxalite movement was popular. There were reports of brilliant students, including from the famed IITs, dropping out of college to join the struggle for the rights of the tribals and landless labourers. But as has been the case with many movements set up with high principles, over the years the Naxalite movement is seen as having lost its vision and having compromised its principles. Nevertheless, the fact that it has an endless supply of men and women joining its ranks shows that many still believe in its cause.

Do the Naxalites face much opposition?

Yes they do, almost from the entire Indian political spectrum. Noticeably, when the Naxalite movement first started in the late sixties in West Bengal, it was the CPI-M that cracked down hardest on the Maoist rebels, with ample support from the Congress at the Centre. At village levels, the Naxalites' terror tactics have spawned local armies to provide protection to the landlords and others. The most infamous of these is the Ranvir Sena in Bihar and Jharkhand, formed by Bhumihar caste landlords, which kill tribals, Dalits and landless labourers either in retaliation or to enforce their domination.

NOTES

1. The Left Front government in West Bengal enters its 30 year of existence on June 21, 2006. This is a historic day which comes in the background of an equally historic election victory which has led to the formation of the seventh Left Front government. The three decades of the Left Front government is of enormous significance in the annals of the communist movement in the country. It has also acquired international significance. It is necessary to recall the past history in order to understand the long and arduous political struggle that has gone into the creation of a stable Left political formation and a stable Left Front government in West Bengal.
http://pd.cpim.org/2006/0625/06252006_prakash.htm
2. http://pd.cpim.org/2006/0625/06252006_prakash.htm
3. http://www.worldproutassembly.org/archives/2006/05/west_bengal_sta.html
4. Regional parties first began influencing India's federal politics during and after the country's Fourth General Election in 1967—an event that is widely thought to be the major watershed of Indian politics. The Congress Party's exclusive control was severely challenged, and the party's "deinstitutionalization" began soon after its unprecedented electoral setback. In that election, the Congress Party's majority was reduced from 361 to 284 seats in the House of the People, the lower house of parliament. The Congress even lost its majority in the lower house in 1969. However, the minority government of Indira Gandhi (daughter of India's first Prime Minister, Jawaharlal Nehru, of the Congress) managed to continue in power with the support of the Communists and regional parties such as the Akali Dal from Punjab and the Dravida Munnetra Kazagham from Tamil Nadu. Before 1967, the Congress managed to win 70 per cent or more of the seats in the House of the People while polling less than 50 per cent of the popular vote. This was due to India's first-past-the-post electoral system. The next largest party in Parliament was the Communist Party of India with a presence that ranged from 16 to 29 seats. The Jana Sangh (forerunner of the BJP) was even weaker, with 3 to 14 seats. Even then, however, the Congress could not dominate the state legislative assemblies. This was repeatedly the case in the Patiala and East Punjab States Union (merged with Punjab in 1956), in North India and Madras (present-day Tamil Nadu), and in Andhra Pradesh in South India. The Communists had already formed the first ever non-Congress government in Kerala as early as 1957. And the Congress increasingly had to rely on coalitions

with regional political parties such as the Jharkhand Party or Ganatantra Parishad in Orissa. In the early 1960s the Congress lost heavily in the state assemblies of West Bengal, Bihar, Orissa, Kerala, Madras (South India) and Punjab. Some regional opposition parties had started entering into federal electoral alliances with one another against the Congress. This had the effect of consolidating the anti-Congress vote. This further encouraged splits within the Congress and defections in the country's legislatures. However, the various coalitional state governments that came to power in 1967 were mostly unstable power arrangements. They suffered from what was described in the press as a convenient, short-term "ideological promiscuity" that was exclusively aimed at unseating the Congress rather than designing any coherent political alternative. Such a shift in the arrangements of the party system in India has informed the country's present-day politics, characterized by Goliaths like the Congress or BJP aligning with Davids at both the central and regional levels to win elections and successfully run coalition governments. http://www.forumfed.org/publications/pdfs/vol1_no5_summer_2001.pdf

5. The aim of any bourgeois-democratic land reform is to abolish the ownership right of non-cultivating landowners over the land. This is what a bourgeois politician like Devraj Urs did in Karnataka. The land was transferred to the tenants by paying compensation to the non-cultivating landowners which was recovered from the tenants over a period of 18 years. But Operation Barga was far inferior to even Urs' land reforms since it had no provision to transfer the land from the absentee landowners to the tenants and provided them no option to purchase the land even with similar state assistance. As is evident from the field study, absentee landlordism appears to be quite strong in Bengal. Among the lessors, those whose primary occupation is also cultivation accounted for 43.92% and those in primarily non-agricultural occupations like service or trade accounted for 54.12% in the advanced region and the figures for backward region is 38.22% and 58.60%. Transfer of land from these categories to the tenants, even by giving compensation where necessary, should have been the logical next step after OB. Even after nearly two decades after its introduction such a step is nowhere is in sight. http://www.cpiml.org/liberation/year_1996/october/article.htm
6. The Communist Party of India (Marxist), or CPI(M), is a political party in India. It is strongest in the states of Kerala, West Bengal and Tripura. In West Bengal and Tripura states, as of 2004, it currently holds the government. It split from the Communist Party of India in 1964 because of what it describes as the latter's

revisionism and sectarianism. It claims to have 814,408 members as of 2002.

http://en.wikipedia.org/wiki/Communist_Party_of_India_(Marxist)

7. This week Kolkata had to share the trauma of terrorist attacks against Mumbai, India's commercial capital. A red alert was declared throughout the state of West Bengal, and this included the city of Kolkata, India's cultural capital. Railway stations and airports and major industrial centers along with public offices were put under strict surveillance. The authorities even carried out large-scale evictions of illegal encroachers along the Eastern Metropolitan Bypass on the fringes of Kolkata in order to carry out the road widening works of this important thoroughfare. Security was cited as a sensitive issue to dismantle the illegal structures along a sizable section of this road. Widespread speculation and rumor was fanned by the incident of an explosion inside a parked car at Jadavpur in South Kolkata. Apparently the reason for this explosion was the presence of a carbon dioxide gas cylinder that was inside the vehicle. But the police arrested the owner of the car and have started investigations in this regard. It is a well-documented fact that insurgents from Pakistan and Bangladesh have been using Kolkata as a safe haven for quite sometime now. We keep on reading about incidents where police forces from outside West Bengal have nabbed wanted criminals from Kolkata without soliciting any intelligence backup or logistic support from the local authorities, anticipating information leaks at strategic levels. Even shootouts and encounters have taken place in the heart of Kolkata without the local police authorities having any advance information on the same. The long and insecure international border that West Bengal shares with Bangladesh is porous, to say the least. Smuggling of cows, rice, narcotics and gold and trafficking in women and children are among the several illegal activities that take place in the border area. Coupled with this is the constant terror of crossfire between the Border Security Force and Bangladesh Rifle. While BSF tries to pushback illegal immigrants, the BDR ensures that the Indian security forces' actions and attempts are thwarted, according to Press and Media sources. Some years back there was this infamous terrorist attack against security personnel stationed before American Center at Kolkata. The gang responsible for this daredevil attack in broad daylight was later identified as an inter-state criminal organization that also specializes in kidnapping of celebrities against hefty ransom demands. Terror is a mind game that is targeted to numb the citizens' morale and emasculate the State's repressive apparatuses. It is an intellectual resource whose physical deployment is a constant reminder of forces that operate

within and without or boundaries for ulterior purposes of evil. Security preparedness of the local police authorities needs to be upgraded at all levels. This is also true for combating the radical left activists in the state. Even the Chief Minister's residence is apparently not quite safe. It is true that inadequate development and growth of militant radical left politics are complementary forces, but it is also relevant to explore the ways and means to strengthen the State's vigil so that the lives and properties of peace-loving and innocent civilians are safeguarded. Gory incidents like the Mumbai explosions prove how insecure we all are in this age when terror has been globalized in its philosophy, impacts and application. Kolkata should be always alert to avert such incidents in the future. But the cosmopolitan character of Kolkata is a hindrance to locate strangers. The assassin of Phulan Devi (Bandit Queen turned Member of Parliament) was recently arrested from Kolkata by the police force of another state. This indicates the lack of confidence in Kolkata Police on the part of other police forces. West Bengal is under constant threat from insurgent of terrorist organizations located in Pakistan, Bangladesh and even Nepal, where the Maoist rebels have recently succeeded to topple the last Hindu King from his throne and have entered the constitutional arena of parliamentary politics. India's muddle and meddle foreign policy is largely responsible for this sorry state of affairs. We have failed to exhibit the iron hand in the velvet glove whenever and wherever required. Kicks and kisses were required to maintain a viable balance of power in South Asia, but we have constantly toyed with the morale of our military forces and have chosen the wrong allies at historically wrong junctures. India should have consolidated her military gains during the series of wars it had fought since Independence. But she had squandered the military advantages in the name of *Panchasheel* policy that propagates non-aggression, non-interference, mutually peaceful existence and regional cooperation etc. But critical issues like Kashmir and Siachen cannot be simply solved on the basis of goodwill. Confidence-building measures also fail in the face of trans-border terrorism. So tough measures short of actual warfare appear to be the only solution. Riding piggyback on Big Brother United States will not actually help India, as the US of A will never ever allow India to emerge as a regional superpower in South Asia. So strategic alliance with China and Russia would appear to be the short-term tactical policy that India should adopt in order to fight terrorism in Kashmir and elsewhere in the country. The lessons for Kolkata in this context are to tighten community vigil and citizen watch in all public and private places that have sensitive value or strategic importance. Terrorists are cowards in the final estimation, so community policing is an essential requirement at this hour of crisis when the security of the state is in grave question (16 July 2006). http://www.boloji.com/diary/kolkata/010.htm

8. The communists have again returned to power in West Bengal. This time around the allegation of electoral malpractice was not raised so much by the Opposition as the Election Commission of India had ensured free and fair polls in the state. Kolkata as such did not witness the mindless electoral tempo as restrictions on campaigning were observed in a stringent manner in the City. This should be the hallmark of a mature liberal democratic political system. People know who perform and who do not, and they accordingly cast their vote. There is no need for any additional fanfare before the election to make people aware of policies and performance. The Election Commission of India must be congratulated for the commendable measures taken before, during and after the polls in West Bengal. Even an ordinarily volatile metropolitan city like Kolkata did not have the faintest opportunity to erupt in pre-poll or post-poll violence despite the explosive and provocative comments made by some leftist political leaders. The Rule of Law has been established firmly in the state and one hope that this newly entrenched tradition of stable political ethos continues in the City in the future as well. The presence of Opposition politics in Kolkata in particular and West Bengal in general is limited to fanfare and more often than not ineffective slogan campaigns and long drawn out processions and demonstrations and sit-ins. One must admit that the Opposition parties have been found wanting in terms of their political resources and wisdom while the Left Front Government has been able to successfully formulate its own political rhetoric couched in the appropriate ideological idiom.
http://www.boloji.com/diary/kolkata/003.htm
9. Refer to the excerpts from the West Bengal CPI (M)'s review report on the peasant front as adopted by the party's 20th State Conference held in Kolkata from 22 to 25 February, 2002 in this connection. On the Land Question: It is true that the key slogan of the peasant movement is radical land reforms. But the slogan of radical land reforms can only be a propaganda slogan in the present structural framework. The effective slogan in this context is: land reforms within ceiling limits. ... Of the 1.3 million acres of land vested with the state, more than 1.05 million acres have been redistributed among more than 2.3 million landless beneficiaries. ... The land tribunal has initiated the process of disentangling some more land for redistribution, but unless this land is fast redistributed there is every danger of the land being locked again in litigation at High Court level division benches. Comrades are lacking in alertness

and initiative on this score. Thanks to the land reforms movement and increasing fragmentation of erstwhile joint and big families, there is little concentration of land ownership left in the state. The land-ownership pattern in the state yields the following picture: 11,00,701 small holdings (16.81% of total holdings), 50,03,845 marginal holdings (76.42%), 4,41,936 medium holdings (6.75%) and 1,152 large holdings of over 10 acres (0.2%). This also includes 11,05,957 acres of land being cultivated by 14,97,418 bargadars or sharecroppers. Generally speaking, landlords thus no longer dominate the agrarian scene of the state. The land seizure and redistribution movement has therefore lost its old fervour and momentum. In the changed context of land and production relations shaped through land reforms, the peasant movement has come to acquire a multifarious and multidimensional character. But this realisation is yet to dawn on our comrades working on the peasant front. We therefore hear from some quarters demands to lower the ceiling limits so as to give an impetus to the peasant movement. At the same time we also hear a few comrades question the very relevance of the peasant front in the state.

On Sharecroppers: Operation Barga has secured the cultivation rights of 14,97,418 sharecroppers over 11,05,957 acres of land. This security of tenancy has generated enthusiasm among the sharecroppers and led to a rise in production. But some sharecroppers tend to confuse their cultivation rights with ownership rights and thus they refuse to hand over the due share of crops to the owners. This is an opportunist tendency, which is harmful for the peasant movement and detrimental to the cause of broad peasant unity. Fighting out this opportunism is a key task of the peasant movement. This tendency is witnessed particularly in those areas where the landowners do not reside in the concerned villages and activists of the peasant movement remain oblivious of their responsibilities in this regard. We must wage a sustained struggle against this trend. We are noticing a new twist to the Barga question in recent times. This is not a question of eviction of bargadars nor has the peasant front taken any initiative to stop or overcome the barga practice. Many new occupations are now available in rural areas or in neighbouring urban areas. In some cases, bargadars feel compelled by real life conditions to switch over to other occupations. There are also instances of landowners seeking a settlement with bargadars so they can sell off the land or use it for other purposes. With growing penetration of capital into agriculture, barga practice is bound to become a thing of the past. Time and again we have discussed the subject among peasant front comrades. This is becoming a common feature in rural areas and in many cases our comrades are intervening and mediating in settlements where the bargadars are being paid very little compensation. We have decided that in such situations if land owners and bargadars both agree then our principled position would be to ensure that bargadars get half the land or half the value of the land. On Wage Struggles: The number of landless agricultural labourers is not insignificant. Redistribution of 1.05 million acres of land among the landless may have temporarily checked the number of the landless in the state, but against the backdrop of intense countrywide crisis and the relentless process of immiseration, the number of landless labourers is bound to go up. A section of small peasants too has to resort to wage labour. Wage increase is the natural and primary demand of this growing section of the rural population. The growth of democratic forces in the countryside can only proceed on the solid and organised foundation of agricultural labourers. In spite of our consistent emphasis on this aspect, most of our district leaders are yet to realise the importance of this front. Instead of building up planned movements for wage increase, temporary market-induced increases in wages are often sought to be projected as fruits of wage struggles. ... As a result of the policies of economic liberalisation, the prices of foodgrains and other crops are showing a downward trend. Consequently we now see inhibition to wage struggles even in places accustomed to such struggles. We however believe that even under the present conditions it is possible to assess the per capita surplus value generated by agricultural labourers by deducting the average input cost from the sale price of crops, and consequently it is also possible to decide on the fraction of that surplus value for which we can conduct wage struggles of agricultural labourers. ... http://www.cpiml.org/liberation/year_2002/june/specialfeature.htm

10. Though the Zamindari system was abolished by an enactment in the state Assembly way back in 1957, the land holding pattern had undergone little change. A vast majority of the cultivators had little or no land in their possession. In an effort to penetrate and widen its support base in the rural areas, the CPM, after coming to power, initiated steps to correct the existing imbalance in land relations. For this CPM, a dopted a two-prong strategy. On the one hand, it stressed the empowerment of the landless and marginal farmers—'Operation Barga'. Additionally, it tried to complete the unfinished task of distributing surplus land vested from the landlords. On the other, the Left Front government introduced a three-tier panchayat system and in 1978 held its first election. The panchayat system was important for it was expected to give the people a participatory role in the process of rural development. We shall

see later that the effort was not extended to its logical next step; rather it was abandoned halfway.

http://www.india-seminar.com/2001/497/497%20rajat%20ray.htm

11. http://www.rdiland.org/PDF/PDF_Publications/EPW-Bargadars&Landownership.pdf
12. The impact is already visible. Since January 1, 2006, eight persons —six CPI-M and two Jharkhand Party activists—have been killed and the police apprehend more violence. 'Somen', the CPI-Maoist 'state secretary', declared on April 5, 2006, "It hardly matters which party gains out of this—CPM or Jharkhand Party. This is part of our campaign strategy and we will enforce this call in our base areas in West Midnapore, Bankura and Purulia." Responding to a query on who are the targets, he unambiguously stated: "The political leaders, who have been hand-in-glove with the administration to unleash repression."Significantly, electoral campaigning has been on a low key in many villages in Purulia as a result of the Maoist threat, as candidates for the April 17 polls in the District drew up their campaign itinerary carefully avoiding the CPI-Maoist strongholds. Some leaders of the ruling CPI-M in the two other 'base' districts—Bankura and Midnapore—have reportedly refused police escort, apprehending that the Maoists could target them more easily if they took police assistance. The fear also extends to the police, and senior police officials in the three Districts have received over 250 applications for transfer to 'safer' areas, fearing Maoist attacks. There are also reports of Maoists from Andhra Pradesh and Jharkhand infiltrating into West Bengal to disrupt the elections. The role of cadres from Andhra Pradesh was underlined by Chief Minister Buddhadeb Bhattacharjee, who has been insisting on de-linking the old and new Maoist movement in the State, describing the present genre of Maoists as "exports from Andhra and Jharkhand." According to the state's Inspector General of Police (Law and Order) Raj Kanojia, the Police have identified 13 'sensitive' police stations in the three Districts. Special security arrangements were ordered for Belpahari, Salboni and Bagmundi Police Stations in West Midnapore; Bandwan, Jhalda, Jajpur and Manbazar Police Stations in Purulia; and Salimpur, Sarenga and Simlipal Police Stations in Bankura. About 90 per cent of the booths in the three Maoist-affected districts were said to be 'sensitive'. While some 300 companies of paramilitary forces were deployed in the whole of West Bengal during the 2001 Assembly elections, this time around nearly 600 companies of paramilitary forces would be deployed in 7,479 polling stations across these three Districts alone. Maoists have been making inroads into the tribal hinterland of south Bengal

since the late 1990s. According to the Maoist blueprint, these arid and backward tracts, covered with hills and forests, are to be targeted vigorously to eventually become 'liberated zones', a strategy that the outfit is following in similar terrain in other Maoist-affected States. To this end, the CPI-Maoist has consistently sought to highlight the plight of tribals, a majority of whom are below the poverty line and without access to basic amenities. The Census 2001 indicated that basic amenities such as safe drinking water, sanitation and electricity are yet to reach most tribal homes in West Bengal. Scheduled Tribes constitute 6.37 per cent of the State's total population and the tribal concentration in the Southern Districts is the largest in Purulia—18.98 per cent, followed by Bankura, 10.43 per cent, and Midnapore, 8.4 per cent. Similarly, electricity has reached only 19.03 per cent of tribal homes as against 37.45 per cent of the total State population. In all three districts, 93-96 per cent of tribal families are dependent on kerosene for light. These districts are relatively backward with 4.47 per cent of the people in Purulia still fetching drinking water from rivers and canals. Many villages in the forests are still inaccessible, with health centres located far off. That these districts are crucial for the Maoists is also visible in the fact that they are using the corridor of Bandwan, Ranibandh in Bankura district and Belpahari in the Midnapore district to facilitate operations between Jharkhand and West Bengal. Further, Nepalese Maoists use the Bihar-Nepal border to enter West Bengal to secure a safe haven. The Maoists have also augmented their weaponry to further their goal of reclaiming their lost stronghold in the State. A 2006-study carried out by A.K. Maliwal, Chief Security Officer to the Chief Minister, indicates that the Maoists, who earlier used lower-end command wire-based explosive devices, are of late using sophisticated bombs, including vehicle-borne and remote-controlled improvised explosive devices, to substantially increase their impact. The study also notes a shift from home-made to factory-produced explosives and the use of target-activated bombs, as well as a resort to triggering parallel and simultaneous explosions. Meanwhile, the Subsidiary Intelligence Bureau has cautioned the government about changes in the Maoists' modus operandi, with a shift from conventional ambushes and landmines, and an increasing potential of tactics such as hijacking, which could prove more useful at a time of heightened security. The report also noted that the Maoists may also attempt to blow up radio and telephone towers. West Bengal has been ruled by the mainstream Left Front since 1977, and has been largely successful in combating Left Wing extremism through a judicious mixture of political and security measures. But with the dangerous expansion of Maoist influence and activities in the

neighbouring states, the future for West Bengal is becoming increasingly uncertain as well.
http://naxalwatch.blogspot.com/2006/04/polls-under-maoist-shadow-in-west.html

13. http://globetrotter.berkeley.edu/macarthur/inequality/papers/BardhMookhPanchayats.pdf
14. In his classic research paper into parties, Robert Michels provided evidence for the "iron law of oligarchy" (rule of the few). Michels assumes that every organization unavoidably produces a ruling class, but is unable to control it effectively over the long-term. Certainly, the necessity for executive officials, the superior knowledge of the party leadership and the rampant specialization of politics bring about a certain degree of independence for the party apparatus. Nevertheless, whether or not an internal party process for forming a political will, which is instigated from the top and works its way down, actually exists and, if so, to what extent, remains to be established. Clusters of people with political office and (associated with this) a concentration of power represents a serious problem for all large parties (...) An improvement in the way in which opinion is exchanged within parties for the purpose of reducing hardened party structures is just as necessary as increased mobilization of party members. Oligarchic tendencies in large democratic parties are, to a certain degree, also caused by a lack of participation on the part of many citizens. Only a small minority of those voting and sympathizing with a party are prepared to become members. (...). This being said, it would be wrong to presume that political parties were not using this increasing criticism and a general level of disaffection among the population, which is reflected in a loss of loyal voters, falling memberships and a clear lack of enthusiasm among younger voters, as a motive to carry out reforms to the way in which parties are organized. The large "people's parties" have, indeed, been taking actions in this area (...). Reforms are being discussed such as the introduction of rules to regulate the amount of time individuals can spend in office and to prevent accumulations of office; the expansion of schemes to encourage party sympathizers to participate without them having to become formal members; and more consideration for women and young people at party conferences and in committees.
http://www.dadalos.org/int/parteien/Grundkurs5/oligarchie. htm
15. South Asia Development Studies and Political Economy Bibliography compiled by Jody Ranck (December 1996).
16. http://www.worldproutassembly.org/archives/2006/05/west_bengal_sta.html
17. http://ushome.rediff.com/news/2003/oct/02spec.htm

4

Ethics of Globalization[1]

Key Words

Capacity-Building, Civil Society, Development, Ecology, Environment, Foreign Direct Investment, Freedom, Globalization, Grassroots, Progress, State, Structural Adjustment Programs, Third World.

Executive Summary

The idea of human freedom is essentially rooted in the concept of human development, according to Noble Laureate Professor Amartya Sen's "Development as Freedom" thesis [that outlines an entitlement to capacity-building process]. And the idea of human progress is a construct that is designed around the axis of freedom. What is freedom? Is it only lack of societal constraint, withdrawal of discipline and punishment willing suspension of the panoptic Super Ego that they address as the "mainstream"? Or is freedom a concept much more fundamental, to be read into the texts of Rabindranath Tagore, Romain Rolland or even *Walden*?

Introduction

Globalization has been described (Kegley Jr. and Wittkopf, 1997: 249) as the "intensification of economic, political and cultural relations across borders" that is noticed in the following pieces of evidence: the average daily turnover in foreign exchange increased from $200 billion in the mid-1980s to approximately $1.2 trillion in 1996; net capital flows to developing countries grew from an annual average of $44 billion for the period 1983-88 to $197 billion in 1996; and Foreign Direct Investment increased from $10 billion to $91 billion (Echeverri-Gent, 1997). However, it has also been noticed (Lee, 1996: 382) that "the worldwide gap between the rich and the poor has become a vast chasm. Both within and between countries, the rich grow richer at the expense of the poor." Lee adds that the share of income of the poorest 20 per cent of the global population has fallen from 2.3 to 1.4 per cent in the last 30 years while the share of the richest 20 per cent of the global population has increased from 70 to 85 per cent. More than 1 billion people live in countries where average per capita income fell between 1980 and 1993. Lee has even quoted the United Nations Development Program administrator, Gustave Speth, who maintains that if the world continues down its current path, "economic disparities between industrial and developing nations will move from inequitable to inhuman."

The Janus Face of Globalization

The contemporary states system informed by globalization is like a double-faced Janus: it has, generally speaking, a robust face in the developed North but an almost impotent face in the developing or underdeveloped South. So globalization necessitates a dialogue between the rich and the poor outside its essentialist assumptions of an uneven power discourse as conditions of Good Governance and Structural Adjustment Programs (Gary and Mayo, 1995) that benchmark most Third World postcolonial democracies (Ray, 1989, 1996) today.

While there are contentions (Rapley, 1996) that aggressive market forces make it difficult for welfarist governments to protect their citizens from transnational actors that are as elusive as their hot money, there are also counter-arguments (Keohane, 1998) that institutions like the International Monetary Fund or the World Trade Organization actually safeguard citizens from the administrative limitations of their respective national governments. There appears to be a consensus, however, that powerful markets tend to undermine political élites at home (Barber, 1996; Cox, 1993; McGrew, 1992; and Slater, 1996). But does this also suggest that national governments have been so thoroughly undermined today that the Global Village can eventually replace the state?

John Echeverri-Gent (1997) has pointed out that if globalization, on the one hand, facilitates decentralization then, on the other, it also helps develop pockets of dynamic Free Trade Areas in large developing countries like China and India by reorganizing their economic geography, Foreign Direct Investment and global commodity chains. This process, however, creates large hinterlands of economic backwardness and entrenches economic inequality within the developing South. Globalization, therefore, intensifies regional disparities in the Third World. John Rapley (1996) has found that Structural Adjustment Programs have varied widely in the results they have yielded. While Latin America has partially benefited from structural adjustment, Africa has not. Rapley has also argued that rolling back the state *i.e.* less government (as an imperative of contemporary globalization) does not always lead to enhanced economic growth.

Globalization, therefore, would appear to be an open-ended journey toward a globalized world order whose weightless economy (Huws, 1999: 32) may be described as one that defies both national and international borders so far as economic transactions are concerned. This is a situation where freight charges are nil and trade/tariff barriers would disappear. Such a pilgrim's progress, however, is nothing new. Technological innovations during the past five centuries have steadily helped integrate the global community into an emergent global civil society. Transatlantic communications have developed from sailing boats to steamships, to the telegraph, the telephone, the commercial aircraft and now the Internet where even nationalism as a conventional political ideology has been reduced to 'banal nationalism' (Billig, 1995).

Progress and Development

Sociologists claim that civilization is what we are and culture is merely an arrangement of artifacts that we happen to use during the course of our politics of everyday life. But then civilization is also a system of values that is handed down generations as a movement of socialization that laymen identify as "progress".

But how can progress be distinguished from "development", if at all? A most prominent item on today's humanitarian global agenda, apart from mantras like good governance, social capital, neo-liberal communitarianism, grassroots empowerment, civil societal capacity-building and gender sensitization, is certainly the notion of sustainable development.[1] This has become almost a catchword of sorts in the Third World, decolonized state nations that are more or less grappling to muster a political system around pluralistic identities of nationhood enmeshed in ethnicity, language, religion, region and mutual distrust. It is almost as if "soft/ fragile states" are hanging loose and can only be brought back on to the fast track of development by way of external intervention and advocacy on the part of the Eurocentric West.

Development, it may be appreciated at this point, is not anything extrinsic like politics imposed from the above without any regard whatsoever to the end-users of limited political resources. Actors who are supposed to interface with their very own institutions are nearly always better comfortable if left alone with the material conditions of daily life that breed organic ethos of community existence. This is where the colonial masters went wrong in Asia, Africa and South America when they bled the colonies white and left behind a legacy of comprador bourgeois and crony capitalism that, in turn, fostered a repressive state apparatus and a perverted anti-people bureaucratic managerial state system that was not only anti-people but was also occasionally anti-progress.

What Richard Cobden implies by "Cabinets or Foreign Offices" is actually this mechanistic attitude of the political élite [in capitalist systems] and party leadership [in socialist societies] that are smug in the cocoon of their mistaken convictions that people at the top echelons of power, authority and influence have necessarily a working knowledge of "the greatest good of the greatest number". This is not a utilitarian or even a welfarist state approach—it is actually self-defeating as amply evidenced in the erstwhile USSR where an insane arms and space race with the United States [incidentally the only country in the entire world to have actually materially gained from the First and Second World Wars with minimum military casualties] led the once powerful communist country to a more or less incredible situation of mind-boggling bankruptcy.

Military hardware and nukes were being manufactured at the cost of basic consumer requirements like bread, potatoes and vodka, following Stalin's rhetoric of an entire generation making sacrifices [read being purged if found to be politically incorrect] for the cause of a better Russia of the future. Moscow's huge and sprawling department store GUM was always nearly empty while the party's top brass were running around in their imported limousines, shopping in dollar shops selling Swiss chocolates and watches, Scotch whisky, French champagne and perfumes. Add rampant corruption and repression to accept a second-hand political ideology not originating from the ground realities of people and you have ideal recipes for killing fields like the infamous Prague Spring.

Whither States System?

But states, meanwhile, have not ostensibly lost their importance and, on the contrary, even Third World governments' capacities to tax and redistribute incomes, control their domestic economies and hegemonize civil societal activities have expanded in a significant manner (Aziz and Arnold, 1996). This is notwithstanding the fact that "In any corrupt regime people enjoy the benefits of bypassing the government regulation. Under-reporting of income leads to tax savings which helps both the taxpayer and the assigning official who receives a bribe. But, this is not an unmixed blessing. In a society where corrupt officials can wield power of coercion and harassment, people are forced to pay bribe to avoid problems. Thus corruption entails benefits as well as cost" (Marjit *et al*, 1999: 23).

However, the present-day transition of state efficacy—from welfare to Good Governance—has to be explained in terms of a paradigm shift that can even lead to deinstitutionalization of state apparatuses in postcolonial democracies as the conventional manner of looking at the welfarist state as a sponsor of nation building (Kothari, 1976) is subverted in the process. James Manor (1996: 8-9) would confirm that "In recent years, many Western aid and development agencies have increasingly emphasised the need to promote 'good government' in their programmes ... Many scholars ... regard 'good government' agendas and the conditionality that goes with them as an example of latter day imperialism. Many also worry that some of these agendas entail considerable hypocrisy on the part of Western funders ... The contents of some 'good government' agendas are rather curious. Some place enormous stress on the need for market forces to predominate, which is not everyone's idea of 'good government'. Some mix that emphasis and pressure to enact structural adjustment programs with pressure for democratization, decentralization, respect for human rights, legal reform, poverty alleviation, transparency and accountability. There is a degree of dissonance between some of these varied elements ... Capitalism requires the existence of state institutions, no matter how many free marketeers loosely claim that what it most needs is the disappearance of government. As economic liberalization proceeds, there is a greater need for contract law and for judicial and executive institutions to ensure that it actually makes an impact."

Globalization entails another paradox—it requires Good Governance underpinned by Structural Adjustment Programs that can, however, erode the popular bases of democratic governance (March and Olsen, 1995), and lead to collapse of entire régimes. Malcolm Waters (1995: 99-101) has pointed out that "In the third quarter of the twentieth century the corporate welfare state hit a multiple and widely recognized crisis ... The response to this multiple crisis was a process of disétatization or state-weakening ... state intervention by command was reduced but at the same time states sought to increase the scope and scale of the market. Many government services were opened to competitive tendering between the public and private sectors and, as is well known, many state-owned industries were returned to the private sector. Many states stopped providing welfare in certain areas ... The crisis of the state contributes to the reflexivity of globalization."

Globalization, therefore, would increasingly come across as the transition of world capitalism from one stage to another, safeguarding investments of global capital in this process. Globalization also increasingly requires disinvestment, prompting Anthony Giddens (1995: 140-1) to argue that "The relation between the decline of the welfare state and the changing character of the global order of states was to some extent masked by the very political successes of the New Right. The neoliberals led the attack on the 'overloaded' welfare state in the name of freedom of competitive enterprise from bureaucratic burdens and from enfeebled labour markets. Simultaneously, however, they not only defended the state and nation but called for a 'strong state' in the international arena. The paradoxical character of this position was soon noted by critics, and corresponded to the wider paradoxes of New Right political theory ..."

Available evidence, as mentioned earlier, suggests that average incomes have increased while the income gap between rich and poor countries has also widened (Albo, 1997; Altvater, 1997; Echeverri-Gent, 1997; Epstein *et al*, 1996; Lee, 1996; and Wallis, 1996). Both trends have been evident for more than 200 years—it is only now, however, that improved global communications have resulted in a growing awareness among citizens of poor countries of income inequalities, and compelled them to increasingly immigrate to rich countries. Rich countries, consequently, have been provoked to pass laws that discourage mass immigration (Kalpagam, 1994). It has even been mentioned that (Fix *et al*, 1994) "Although there is no evidence to date of broad job displacement and the evidence regarding major wage effects is inconclusive, concerns have been raised about the impact of high levels of immigration on the growing wage inequality in the U.S."

Public Action Enterprises

Operation Flood in Anand (Gujarat, India) and the Lijjat and Kissan enterprises are other such brilliant instances of people working toward their common good [based on innovative techniques like outsourcing of manpower and material resources, subcontracting or leasing of plant and machinery, breaking down the production process to delimit financial risk liability ventures somewhat akin to Adam Smith's exposition of the division of labour dynamics] without any outside intervention whatsoever. One must remember that neither India nor Bangladesh tends to practise authoritarian régime maintenance. What was possible once in Beijing's Tiananmen Square when the People's Liberation Army crushed pro-reform students under tanks and armored carriers is unimaginable in either India or Bangladesh (that secured its liberation in 1971 by way of Indian military cooperation). So democracy is an essential requirement if "the progress of freedom" is to continue unabated.

Voice of the People

By democracy we ordinarily mean popular authority or rule. As made popular by Jean Jacques Rousseau, one of the ideologues of the French Revolution (that effectively altered the course of European history by beginning the disintegration process of the medieval and feudalistic Age of Empires), the voice of God is heard in the voice of the People. This was a far cry from the autocratic self-styled pronouncement of French Emperor Louis XIV—"I am the State". It was no wonder that Louis XVI's wife Marie Antoinette [later sentenced to die to rather unceremoniously at the guillotine] had once expressed her wonder in such a naive fashion on hearing about the simmering discontent among the Parisian mob standing in endless queues or bread lines and more often than not starting violent riots among themselves—"If they cannot eat bread why don't they eat cake!"

This vulgar ignorance of the ruled on the part of their rulers is rather inimical to democracy. But we must remember that democracy as dynamic capacity-building agency in the post 9/11 world has all of a sudden underscored its long-ignored extrinsic quality. Democracy is not really insular, stretching from the East Coast to the West Coast of the US. If the notion of external sovereignty has suffered quite extensively since the height of the Cold War when the world was almost vertically divided into the NATO and Warsaw Pact countries (save the NAM states being led by Nehru, Nasser and Tito), the idea of external democracy has gained much popular and diplomatic acceptance.

Simply put, powerful nations can no longer ignore internal human rights or civil rights agendas *vis-à-vis* world public opinion. But this is what the US is consistently trying to follow as its most shortsighted foreign policy since the Malta Summit Conference when President George Bush Senior and CPSU General Secretary Mikhail Gorbachev officially declared the end of the Cold War, a historic event that even prompted Francis Fukuyama to write a banal work on the end of history and the last man.

Since the days of its Nineteenth Century isolationist Munroe Doctrine the US has put up apparently impregnable walls around itself that couldn't even be dismantled during the Marshall Plan for the Reconstruction of Europe after the Second World War or establishment of first the League of Nations (as an initiative of President Woodrow Wilson's historic Atlantic Charter) and then the UNO, the International Monetary Fund, World Bank and now the omnipotent World Trade Organization that apparently dictates the movements of a new specter of the new millennium, namely Globalization. US foreign policy has always been designed on lines of "muddle and meddle"—Vietnam, Korea, Bay of Pigs, Iran Contra scandal, Afghanistan and now Iraq. The country boasts of democracy and swears by it, boiling with righteous motivation to export Yankee democracy around the under-developed world, but has, however, classified the JFK assassination archives for no apparent reason whatsoever. Clandestine covert operations, the strategic defense initiative [Star Wars], research in biological and chemical weapons—you name it and you would find the dirty trick invariably up America's [read the CIA and FBI's] sleeves. In fact, it is the only nation to date that has used atomic weapons during a war, destroying Hiroshima and Nagasaki in the process to avenge the Pearl Harbor attack and crippling generations of Japanese children long after the holocaust as a result of toxic radioactive radiation carried forward genetically by succeeding generations.

Since the Gulf War fought by Senior Bush as the much-hyped Operation Desert Storm so graphically shown by CNN across millions of idiot boxes around the world, nobody knows exactly how many innocent Iraqi children have died from malnutrition, disease and hunger due to the US-imposed and UNO-condoned sanctions against Iraq. The US condemns Osama bin Laden but should actively engage in soul-searching regarding its own virulent international terrorist status in our contemporary unipolar world where might is right in a Hobbesian state of affairs where human life, property and security are all indeed "solitary, poor, nasty, brutish, short". The US, in brief, should radically reorient its foreign policy to address the dignity of human life and internal sovereignty of nation states around the world.

'The US is Us'

This, however, tends to reduce the global economy to an exclusivist power arrangement that also draws on McDonaldization/Coca-Colonization—or cultural homogenization—indicated largely by the one-way-traffic (*ie* infiltration and withdrawal of global capital into the Third World at will but not likewise when infiltration of Third World labour into the North is concerned). According to Eric Helleiner (1994: 173), "the globalization of finance has ... aided the U.S. in preserving its policy autonomy in the face of growing external and internal deficits ... the U.S. in fact actively cultivated the globalization phenomenon partly for this reason, beginning with its support of the Eurodollar market, carrying through opposition to capital controls in the early 1970s, and culminating in its enthusiasm for financial liberalization during the Reagan years.

Globalization benefited the U.S. because of its hegemonic position in the new open global financial system, a position derived primarily from the unique attractiveness of U.S. and Eurodollar financial markets to foreign investors."

Rich countries steadfastly maintain their immigration barriers and discourage agricultural imports while most poor countries have not been quite successful to attract much Foreign Direct Investment due to misgovernance on the part of their national governments. Rich countries, however, may as well concede that politics is a fundamental informant of economic inequality since they are not likely to lower their agricultural and immigration barriers in the near future in order to facilitate protectionism at home. Rich countries may also review the performance of the Washington Consensus[2], which assumes that free markets necessarily promote economic convergence and underscores important issues (like the rule of law, property rights and transparent banking systems) to sustain dialogs between the North and the South.

Nicola Bullard, in 'The Beginning of the End of the Washington Consensus' (1998a), had observed that "In spite of the economic malestrom threatening to engulf the world, this year's IMF and World Bank meetings were notably subdued. It was clear to everyone that the global economy was in trauma: Long Term Capital Management, one of the world's biggest hedge funds, had just been bailed out by what the *New York Times* described as 'Wall Street cronyism' (with some arguing that not to (do) so would have threatened world financial markets). Asia's economies are showing little sign of recovery in spite of massive IMF intervention. Russia, suddenly and catastrophically, has been reduced to a cashless pariah (not that anyone dared speak about Russia—obviously its spectacular collapse is not a topic for polite company!). Brazil, meanwhile, is desperately trying to keep the speculators from the door, and Japan is seemingly unable to muster the political will to restructure its failing banks. Things were looking bad, and no one knew what to do".

Rich countries may also on occasion encourage poor countries to Think Globally, Act Locally *i.e.* design glocal—rather than global—development strategies that would be locally grounded within the larger context of globalization. According to Bullard (1998b), "Redistribution of wealth and purchasing power to the four-fifths of the world who are not being given a chance to pull us out of this recession would give the (US) economy a kick start, would ease the problem of overproduction, and provide all sorts of useful ways to recycle profits. It would also cool down global capital markets.

"However, creating this demand requires significant social reform in terms of asset and income distribution. It means land reform and wage and labour reform. Industrialisation via cheap labour and natural resource exploitation is no longer viable. We have reached the point where further economic growth can only be achieved by expanding domestic markets and by expanding our definition of what is productive to include public goods, culture, the environment, and human security. We are at a moment in history where economic necessity coincides with social justice."

Globalization and Human Rights

Globalization has occasionally been regarded as a solution to problems like underdevelopment, malnutrition and violation of human rights, and important human rights institutions have been set up and incorporated into the global human rights régime. Governments are finding it increasingly difficult to violate their citizens' human rights without attracting the attention of the media and international organizations as a result of developed telecommunications and global interdependence. Indeed, overall human rights practices have improved worldwide during the last decade or so. However, this improvement has neither been universal nor linear.

Globalization, *i.e.* the growing interpenetration of states, markets, (tele)communications and ideas across borders is one of the major informants of the contemporary world order. International agencies for the protection of human rights are now more developed while an emergent global civil society facilitates avenues of appeal for citizens repressed by their own states. But assaults on fundamental human dignity continue, and the very obliteration of borders and promotion of transnational actors that had originally sponsored the global human rights régime may also generate *newer* sources of human rights abuse. Even as they are more widely propagated and accepted, the rights of individuals have come to depend increasingly on an entire range of actors and forces—from the multinationals to the missionaries! What are the patterns of the human rights impact of globalization? Are new problems replacing, intensifying or mitigating state-sponsored repression? How effective are new forms of human rights accountability? Can new global human rights problems be addressed by the global human rights institutions developed to combat state abuses? Are certain dynamics of globalization generating both problems and prospects? How can new opportunities be used to offset new problems?

State and Civil Society

Liberal democratic régimes like India or even the US can only be politically successful, deliver the common good and thereby continue in power in a more stable [read pro-people] manner if they are able to correctly read the obtainable ground realities and problems thereof. These problems are more or less popular in nature, and have a propensity to develop into discontent of the ruled actors against their ruling institutions. So the actors in power have to continuously shuffle and delicately balance priorities of human development, well-being and accessible freedoms like the ever-important agenda of human rights and civil liberties, a responsive and responsible administrative machinery, transparency at all levels of public expenditures and domestic and international peacekeeping projects rather than playing mutually harmful "spy versus spy" games.

Eminent political scientist Subrata K. Mitra (1997: 23) has quite rightly cautioned that "If the wielders of power concede the point to those who challenge established values and norms, they risk losing their legitimacy. On the other hand, the failure to give satisfaction to the discontented might deepen their sense of outrage and alienation which can further reduce their legitimacy."

Powers-that-be ["Cabinets or Foreign Offices"] will do well to continually redress grievances of political actors at the grassroots in a political manner by establishing and ably handling pro-people institutions. Only then organic identification would bind actors with institutions—only then the incipient involvement noticed at the level of "actors and institutions" would, arguably enough, transcend itself to the level of "actors in institutions", consolidating both the level and the quality of progress of freedom in the process.

Narmada Bachao Andolan

The Government of India claims that the multi-purpose Sardar Sarovar Project (SSP) would irrigate more than 1.8 million hectares (mostly in Gujarat and some in Rajasthan) and solve drinking water problems in drought-prone areas like Kutch and Saurashtra in Gujarat. The Sardar Sarovar Dam is the largest among the 30 'big dams' planned to be constructed on the Narmada River[1] in central and western India. This dam, with a proposed height of 136.5 meters (455 feet), has emerged in the not-so-recent past as the focal point of the Narmada Bachao Andolan's concerted opposition and resistance.

The NBA has steadfastly maintained that 'tall' claims on the part of the government are exaggerated and untenable. The SSP would instead displace more than 320,000 persons and adversely affect the livelihood of innumerable others. NBA activists have even estimated that a population of at least 1 million would be dislocated if the SSP were to be completed (as a result of displacements caused by the canal system and other allied projects). Although Varma's conclusions on the basis of the actual performance (karma) of large dams in India can be questioned he eloquently describes the growing need for water and power in India and concludes that it is the duty (or dharma) of dams to meet these growing needs.

The NBA has been opposing this project for a decade now, and its activists sought to highlight demerits of the SSP during 1990-91 by employing statements of protest like *dharnas*, or sit-ins, and *satyagraha*, or non-violent non-cooperation. The World

Bank (that was about to finance the dam for $450 million) was subsequently compelled to set up an independent review committee, the Morse Commission, the first of its kind. The Morse Report indicted the World Bank on many counts, and (tacitly) supported the major human ecological concerns raised by the NBA. Adverse international reaction that had followed the Morse Report finally decided the World Bank against financing the SSP.

The Supreme Court of India, the country's highest court, had suspended further construction of the dam in 1995, at a height of 80.3 meters, following a writ petition by the NBA demanding a comprehensive review of the SSP. However, the Supreme Court, in an interim order (February 1999), had given go-ahead for the dam's height to be raised to a height of 88 meters (85m + 3m of 'humps'). But this can lead to floods during the monsoon season displacing 2,000 tribal households in about 50 villages.

The Supreme Court finally delivered judgement on the SSP on 18 October 2000; it permitted immediate construction of the dam up to a height of 90 meters (in a 2 to 1 majority judgement). The judgement further authorized construction up to the originally planned height of 138 meters in 5 meter increments, subject to approval by the Relief and Rehabilitation Sub-group of the Narmada Control Authority.

The Supreme Court's judgement has not fundamentally altered the Narmada Water Disputes Tribunal Award (NWDTA) that had earlier decided that land should be made available to the dispossessed at least a year in advance before sub-mergence [Clause IX, Sub-clauses IV(2)(iv) and IV(6)(i))]. The Supreme Court's clearance of the SSP, moreover, has not been able to resolve critical issues involved, like cost-benefit analyses of development and displacement (especially in a post-colonial democracy like India's) (Ray, 1989, 127-149; Ray, 1996, 101-112; Ray, 1991, 97-98), rehabilitation and social justice, grassroots (dis)empowerment, and environmental and human ecological problems (Iyer, 1991, 97-98).

This chapter, therefore, would make an attempt to study the NBA as an important social movement in present-day India.

We would argue that big river dams are informed by a certain definition of development that is intellectually hegemonized by the compulsions of globalization. Such a definition would not only reorient one's notion(s) of sustainable development but would also reorient one's worldview. This is, therefore, a politics of subversion of knowledge that ought to be first challenged and next resisted by alternative vision(s) of public action and development underpinned by civil societal initiative in the context of unequal exchange and an as-yet-unjust North-South dialogue.

According to the World Commission on Dams (22 March 2000), India is second only to China in terms of population (1 billion) and dam building, with 4,291 dams. Irrigation is the primary or only function of 96% of the dams; only 4.2% were built for hydropower generation. Estimates of the number of people displaced by large dams in India range from 21 to 40 million

Ensuring food security is one of the main objectives of India's development policy. Its irrigation potential increased from 22.6 million hectares in 1951 to 89.6 million hectares by 1997 and food production grew fourfold to 200 million tonnes, two thirds of the increase coming from irrigated land. Analysis of the costs and benefits of dams in India is hampered by a lack of post-construction assessment.

The global debate about large dams is at once overwhelmingly complex and fundamentally simple. It is complex because the issues are not confined to the design, construction, and operation of dams themselves but embrace the range of social, environmental, and political choices on which the human aspiration to development and improved well-being depend. Dams fundamentally alter rivers and the use of a natural resource, frequently entailing a reallocation of benefits from local riparian users to new groups of beneficiaries at a regional or national level. At the heart of the dams debate are issues of equity, governance, justice, and power-issues that underlie the many intractable problems faced by humanity.

We also argue in this paper that the very logic of globalization cannot be always reconciled with the institutions and imperatives of democratic politics. However, globalization can, and actually does, facilitate a certain kind of development that is more often than not biased in favour of the North rather than the South. Globalization, therefore, entails a paradox of sorts: its dynamics require an enabling exercise of good governance characterized by democratic freedom, rule of law, civil liberties, and human rights.

Construction of large dams on the River Narmada in Central and Western India, and its disastrous impact on millions of people inhabiting this river valley have emerged as one of the most controversial socio-ecological issues in contemporary India.

NGOs and other activist groups like Friends of River Narmada, an international coalition of volunteer individuals and organizations (primarily of Indian descent) provide a support and solidarity network for the Narmada Bachao Andolan. They communicate grassroots viewpoints to the global community through dedicated websites in order to generate debates on whether the SSP (and such similar projects) should be allowed to continue or not in the larger interests of human ecology and sustainable development.

The Indian State, however, has never really been able to reciprocate any similar grassroots-level dialogue, and has even treated the SSP as an exercise in pragmatrix that would focus on cost-benefit analyses in terms of an authoritative definition of development.[5] The State's intransigent attitude is yet to be entirely overhauled despite the President of India's (implicit) criticism of his own government on December 6, 2000 during presentation of the Ambedkar International Award for Social Change to environmental activist Baba Amte.

While we are not convinced with the treatment of present-day narratives as a collection of so-called grand narratives, we are also not always in consonance with the politics-from-below point of view that tends to examine contemporary social activism and public action as an absolute discourse in terms of black and white.

We cannot, therefore, afford to discuss our categories of analysis in straitjacketed terms like either the subaltern or the élite. We are not quite comfortable with such categories and would rather interrogate these in order to explore other in-between areas of our research.

This is why we do not want to examine the marginalized subaltern as someone who is bereft of any further paraphernalia of identity. There are intra-subaltern strife and tension, problems of sustaining a workable stock of *social capital* (Coleman, 1994, p. 304) within the subaltern ranks and file. Moreover, can we at all afford to look at the subaltern as a class or should we rather focus on a neoinstitutional (actor-oriented) argument that has to be located within the framework of post-colonial India's politics of State repression and displacement?

It is thus clear by now that the judgement on Sardar Sarovar Project by the high court permits further construction of the dam, which will lead to forcible eviction and destitution through flooding of houses and lands, without rehabilitation of a few thousand families. The judgement thus has paved the way for violation of right to life and livelihood of innocent toiling masses and integrated natural resource-based communities. Will it not be a violation of the Constitution itself?

The judgement on the dam is then symbolic of both; the court's supporting violation of the Constitution against the common people from disadvantaged sections of society and judgements (such as the ones in Bhopal Gas tragedy, Enron and Niyogi murder, etc.) based on misinformation due to outdated, inadequate process and procedures to appraise the complex reality. While the judiciary is one of the four pillars of democracy, the time has come to recognize that peoples' movements and civil society groups make an additional fifth one taking the role of changing the judiciary, its value framework, its anti-people biases, and bringing in not just judicial reform, but revolution (Tandon, 1997, p. 39).

Battles of everyday life are sometimes best resolved with the help of organic resources. But subaltern actors are often without the *permission to* narrate (Spivak, 1995, pp. 24-28) and are, as a result, almost inevitably relegated to the margins of an élitist grand narrative that is empowered by superior (?) knowledge of the material conditions of existence (Smart, 1985).

NBA activist Shripad Dharmadhikary has itemized the movement's *alternative* agenda so that civil societal engagements can effectively resist implementation of the State's *developmentalist* agenda:

- The NBA would try to involve all aspects of the civil society;
- The NBA envisions the issue (in hand) as much larger than fight(s) over a specific project ... the NBA is a coalition that challenges development philosophy, supports 'right to life', and challenges power/energy policy;
- The coalition works to mobilize locally affected people;
- The coalition demands local rights to fisheries;
- The NBA would take steps toward decommissioning/ removal of dams;
- The coalition advocates re-operation/partial decommissioning to free land for people who have not been resettled;
- Dam decommissioning is the next logical step as part of a spectrum from re-operation to decommissioning;
- Experiences with decommissioning would help change mindsets;
- It is important to share information and debate issues.[7]

The Narmada struggle has been non-violent, but certainly assertive. It has sought to innovate, sharpen and widen the means of non-violent *satyagraha,* which otherwise had become a routine affair, often ineffective. Like every movement, the Andolan has developed its own means, idioms, and work culture for spreading and sharpening the issues at stake.

So when do people at the grassroots finally begin to identify themselves with their *own* institutions? This can only happen when they are compelled to de-identify themselves with the state's agencies (of coercion) that have been *mai baap* (*i.e.* as parents) (Chatterjee, 1982, pp. 9-38) to them, as in India, since time immemorial. Popular institutions serve as indices to assess the quality of grassroots activism. Such institutions, moreover, have a proclivity to become somewhat indispensable as their networks expand and become increasingly detailed in terms of organization; their levels of encompassment and embeddedness in the everyday politics at the grassroots rise accordingly.

The role of social trust and networks of cooperation in the context of such 'decentralized' governance is rather vital. As Confucius had once remarked that trust is *the* single most important factor in the political lives of men.[8] Trust leads to social bonds and intra- as well as inter-institutional connectedness, and this actually coheres institutions, so to say.

Trust indicates a system of values; a system of values implies social mores; and social mores are themselves an important institution. So trust can, and often does, lead to the sustenance of institutions. Neoinstitutionalism as a dominant frame of reference in present-day political sociology serves to explain the reality of governance or even the lack of it; it introduces a fresh way of looking at and handling institutions.

But this is not encouraged so far as environmentalist values of the establishment in India are concerned. We have to also remind ourselves that democratic political systems are required to grapple with adaptation, goal attainment, integration, and latent pattern maintenance. Mitra has cautioned that "if the wielders of power concede the point to those who challenge established values and norms, they risk losing their legitimacy. On the other hand, the failure to give satisfaction to the discontented might deepen their sense of outrage and alienation which can further reduce their legitimacy" (Mitra, 1997, p. 23).

Our neoinstitutional argument is also supported by rational choice analysis that suggests that any democratic régime (Kohli, 1987, p. 29; Kohli, 1991; Kohli and Basu, 1998) would legitimately prefer entrenchment(s) of its own power and authority rather than problems of governance; this, however, prompts an essential cost-benefit analysis, namely what amount of political investment to establish pro-people, responsive institutions at the grassroots would yield good governance?

Conclusion

However, the political élites of rich countries may even find it occasionally convenient to overlook their own immigration and tariff barriers since such barriers are considered absolutely vital to their own domestic political stability. The amount of clout rich countries command at multilateral platforms like the International Monetary Fund or the WTO more often than not makes it difficult for developing countries to successfully negotiate such barriers.

Jan Aart Scholte (1996: 55) has analyzed in this connection that "Globalization has to date mostly been an extension of modernization. At the same time, the rapid rise and wide-ranging reach of this transformation of social space has brought great instability to capitalism, made traditional conceptions of sovereignty unviable, heightened worries about ecological sustainability, injected much confusion into the construction of identity and encouraged reactions against reason. To this extent, globalization has opened space for critical theory and a fundamental rethink of production, governance, ecology and community, as well as the nature and purpose of knowledge itself."

We would conclude by maintaining that the contemporary states system may well be compared to Janus—it has a strong face in the developed North where immigration and tariff barriers have been erected to discourage further redistribution in terms of income transfer entitlements among Third World immigrants; the United States has even imposed embargo on import of Indian carpets ostensibly because their production involve child labour *i.e.* human rights violation! But the post colonial state almost necessarily assumes a rather weak face in the developing South where governments have repeatedly failed to come up with Good Governance despite their modernizing, albeit non-Westernizing, civil societies (Huntington, 1968, 1996). However, the state located within the contemporary post-capitalist/post-industrial globalization discourse is yet to wither away—we may regard it (among its different *avatars*) as an important facilitator in the uneven, if not multi-cultural, North-South dialogue. We may even also regard it as an actor that would continue to engage its civil societies and public sphere (Habermas, 1992a, 1992b) *vis-à-vis* critical issues like Good Governance, Structural Adjustment Programs and social capital formation (Loury, 1987; Putnam *et al*, 1993; and Coleman, 1994) or otherwise.

So the question we are left with while winding up is: do we prefer freedom backed up by minimum government or would we be merely satisfied with sobriety that is imposed on our lives and liberty by the dictates of high politics from the above. It is amply clear by the beginning of a new millennium already imperiled by the grim possibility of a nuclear war that civilized human beings organized as systems of politics across porous international borders can no longer afford to unquestioningly follow the policy prescriptions of their domestic governments, foreign offices and state departments. More intense people-to-people contacts should be sustained on a long-term basis as such transnational networks can better work toward the so-called Track Two diplomacy between intellectuals and academics, social activists, policy analysts, development consultants and the common people (Maiti, 2001).

NOTES

1. Earlier versions of this paper appeared in *Globalization* [Volume I: Issue 1 (Fall 2001) and Volume 3: Issue 1 (Spring 2003)] and *Electronic Green Journal* [Issue 14 (Spring 2001)]. The usual disclaimer applies
2. Economist John Williamson's prescriptions that had informed the Washington Consensus were (1) Fiscal discipline, (2) Redirection of public expenditure, (3) Tax reforms, (4) Financial liberalization, (5) Adoption of a single, competitive exchange rate, (6) Trade liberalization, (7) Elimination of barriers to Foreign Direct Investment, (8) Privatization of state-owned enterprises, (9) Deregulation of market entry and competition, and (10) Ensuring secure property rights.

REFERENCES

Albo, Gregory (1997). 'A World Market of Opportunities? Capitalist Obstacles and Left Economic Policy'. *Socialist Register.*

Altvater, Elmar (1997). 'Financial Crisis on the Threshold of the 21st Century'. *Socialist Register.*

Aziz, Abdul and D.D. Arnold (eds) (1996). *Decentralised Governance in Asian Countries* (New Delhi: Sage).

Barber, Benjamin R. (1996). *Jihad versus McWorld*. New York: Ballantine.

Billig, Michael (1995). *Banal Nationalism*. London: Sage.

Bullard, Nicola (1998a). 'The Beginning of the End of the Washington Consensus'.

Bullard, Nicola. (September 1998b) 'Regulation or Barbarism'. http://www.focusweb.org/publications/1998/Regulation%20or%20Barbarism.htm

Chatterjee, Partha. (1982). Agrarian relations and communalism in Bengal, 1926-1935. In Ranajit Guha (Ed.), *Subaltern studies: Writings on South Asian history and society.* Delhi, India: Oxford University Press.

Coleman, James S. (1994). *Foundations of Social Theory.* Cambridge, MA: Harvard University Press.

Coleman, James S. (1994). *Foundations of Social Theory*. Cambridge, Massachusetts/London: Harvard University Press.

Cox, Robert (1993). "Gramsci, Hegemony and International Relations: An Essay in Method". S. Gill (ed), *Gramsci, Historical Materialism and International Relations.* Cambridge: Cambridge University Press.

Echeverri-Gent, John (July 1997). "Governance in a Globalizing World: Deconstructing Decentralization in India, China and the United States." Charlottesville: Department of Government and Foreign Affairs, University of Virginia (mimeo).

Epstein, Gerald et al (November 1996). 'Winners and Losers in the Global Economic Game'. *Current History.*

Fix, Michael et al (May 1994). 'Immigration and Immigrants: Setting the Record Straight'.

Gary, Craig and Marjorie Mayo (Eds.). (1995). *Community Empowerment: A Reader in Participation and Development*. London: Zed Books.

Gary, Craig and Marjorie Mayo (eds) (1995). *Community Empowerment: A Reader in Participation and Development*. London/New Jersey: Zed Books.

Gary, Craig and Marjorie Mayo (eds) (1995). *Community Empowerment: A Reader in Participation and Development*. London/New Jersey: Zed Books.

Giddens, Anthony (1995). *Beyond Left and Right: The Future of Radical Politics.* Cambridge: Polity Press.

Habermas, Hans-Jürgen (1992a). *The Structural Transformation of the Public Sphere: An Inquiry into the Category of Bourgeois Society*. Cambridge: Polity Press.

Habermas, Hans-Jürgen (1992b). 'Further Reflections on the Public Sphere'. Craig Calhoun (ed), *Habermas and the Public Sphere*. Columbia: Columbia University Press.

Helleiner, Eric (1994). 'From Bretton Woods to Global Finance: A World Turned Upside Down'. Richard Stubbs and G.R. Underhill (eds), *Political Economy and the Changing Global Order*. London: Macmillan. http://immigration.about.com/newsissues/immigration/gi/dynamic/offsite.htm?site=http%3A%2F%2Fwww.urban.org%2Fpubs%2Fimmig%2Fimmig.htm

http://www.focusweb.org/publications/1998/The%20Washington%20consensus.htm

Huntington, Samuel P. (1968). *Political Order in Changing Societies*. New Haven/London: Yale University Press.

Huntington, Samuel P. (November-December 1996). 'The West Unique, Not Universal'. *Foreign Affairs*.

Huws, Ursula (1999). "Material World: The Myth of the Weightless Economy". Leo Pantich and Colin Leys (eds), *Socialist Register*. London: Merlin.

Iyer, Ramaswamy R. (2000 October 27). *A judgment of grave import*. Retrieved from the World Wide Web: http://www.narmada.org/sardar-sarovar/sc.ruling/iyer.article.html

Kalpagam, U. (1994). *Labour and Gender: Survival in Urban India*. New Delhi/London: Sage.

Keohane, Robert O. (Spring 1998). "International Institutions: Can Interdependence Work?" *Foreign Policy*.

Kohli, Atul, and Amrita Basu (Eds.). (1998). *Community Conflicts and the State in India*. Delhi, India: Oxford University Press.

Kohli, Atul. (1987). *The State and Poverty in India: The politics of reform*. Cambridge, England: Cambridge University Press.

Kohli, Atul. (1991). *Democracy and Discontent: India's growing crisis of governability*. Cambridge, England: Cambridge University Press.

Kothari, Rajni (ed) (1976). *State and Nation Building: A Third World Perspective*. New Delhi: Allied.

Lahiri-Dutt, Kuntala. (2000 July 1-7). Imagining Rivers. *Economic and Political Weekly*, 35 no. 27.

Loury, Glenn (1987). 'Why Should We Care about Group Inequality?' *Social Philosophy and Policy* (5).

Maiti, Prasenjit (2001). "Toward Alternatives of Conflict Resolution in South Asia". *Journal of Social Sciences*.

Manor, James (1996). 'Recent Trends in the Study of State-Society Relations'. Mette Halskov Hansen and Arild Engelsen Ruud (eds),

Weak? Strong? Civil? Embedded? New Perspectives on State-Society Relations in the Non-Western World. Oslo: Centre for Development and the Environment, University of Oslo.

March, James G. and Johan P. Olsen. (1995). *Democratic Governance*. New York: Free Press.

March, James G. and Johan P. Olsen (1995). *Democratic Governance*. New York/London: The Free Press.

Marjit, Sugata *et al* (May 1999). 'Harassment, Corruption and Economic Policy'. Munich: CESifo Working Paper No. 189.

Mazrui, Ali A. (1996). The Frankenstein state and uneven sovereignty. In D.L. Sheth and Ashis Nandy (Eds.), *The Multiverse of Democracy: Essays in Honour of Rajni Kothari*, . New Delhi, India: Sage.

McGrew, A. (1992). "Globalization". Stuart Hall et al (eds). *Modernity and Its Futures*. Cambridge: Cambridge University Press.

Mitra, Subrata K. (1997). "Legitimacy, Governance and Political Institutions in India after Independence." In Subrata Mitra and Dietmar Rothermund (Eds.), *Legitimacy and Conflict in South Asia*. New Delhi, India: Manohar.

Mitra, Subrata Kumar (1997). "Legitimacy, Governance and Political Institutions in India after Independence". Mitra and Dietmar Rothermund (eds), *Legitimacy and Conflict in South Asia*. Manohar, New Delhi.

North, Douglass C. (1990). *Institutions, institutional change and economic performance*. Cambridge, England: Cambridge University Press.

Putnam, Robert D., Robert Leonardi, and Raffaella Nanetti. (1993). *Making Democracy Work: Civic traditions in Modern Italy*. Princeton, NJ: Princeton University Press.

Putnam, Robert, D. *et al* (1993). *Making Democracy Work: Civic Traditions in Modern Italy*. Princeton, New Jersey: Princeton University Press.

Rapley, John (1996). *Understanding Development: Theory and Practice in the Third World*. Boulder, Colorado: Lynne Rienner.

Ray, Aswini K. (1989). "Towards the Concept of a Post-Colonial Democracy: A Schematic View". Zoya Hasan *et al* (eds), *The State, Political Processes and Identity: Reflections on Modern India*. New Delhi: Sage.

Ray, Aswini K. (1989). Towards the Concept of a Post-Colonial Democracy: A Schematic View. In Zoya Hasan, S.N. Jha, and Rasheeduddin Khan (Eds.),*The state, political processes and identity: Reflections on modern India*. New Delhi, India: Sage, 1989.

Ray, Aswini K. (1996). "Democratic Rights in a Post-Colonial Democracy". Agora Project Working Papers (Uppsala: The University of Uppsala).

Ray, Aswini K. (1996). Democratic Rights in a Post-Colonial Democracy. *Agora Project Working Papers*. Uppsala, Sweden: University of Uppsala.

Ray, Prasanta. (1991). *Conflict and State: Exploration in the Behaviour of the Post-Colonial State in India.* Calcutta, India: Sarat Book House.

Sangvai, Sanjay. (2000). *The River and Life: Story of the Narmada Bachao Andolan.* Mumbai, India: Earthcare Books.

Scholte, Jan Aart (1996). 'Beyond the Buzzword: Towards a Critical Theory of Globalization'. Elenore Kofman and Gillian Youngs (eds). *Globalization: Theory and Practice.* London: Pinter.

Singh, Shekhar. (2000 October 25). The Karma of Dams. *Indian Express.*

Slater, David (1996). "Other Contexts of the Global: A Critical Geopolitics of North South Relations". Elenore Kofman and Gillian Youngs (eds). *Globalization: Theory and Practice.* London: Pinter.

Smart, Barry. (1985). *Michel Foucault.* Chichester, England: Ellis Horwood.

Spivak, Gayatri Chakravorty. (1995). Can the subaltern Speak?" In Bill Ashcroft, Gareth Griffiths, and Helen Tiffin (Eds.), *The Post-Colonial Studies Reader.* London: Routledge.

Tandon, Rajesh. (March, 1997). Grassroots Democracy. *Seminar.*

Varma, C.V.J. (October 23, 200-). Reservoirs for the Future: The Dharma of Dams. *Indian Express.*

Wallis, Victor (January 1996). 'Socialism under Siege'. *Monthly Review.*

Waters, Malcolm (1995). *Globalization.* London/New York: Routledge.

Williamson, John (ed) (1990). *Latin American Adjustment: How much has Happened.* Washington DC: Institute for International Economics.

5

Quantifying Development[1]

Key Words

Infrastructure, Operation and Maintenance, Stakeholders, Development Agencies, Infrastructure Impact Assessment, Community, User Groups, Indicators.

Executive Summary

Infrastructure Impact Assessment refers to the exercises by which beneficial impacts of urban development projects may be assessed. To ensure that project facilities are managed efficaciously and that benefits accrue to target groups, IIA programs are mandated by urban development projects. Such programs monitor the delivery of services as planned under development projects and measure benefits as they accrue.

Introduction

Sustainable urban development happens to be one of the major concerns of the new millennium at the policy choice level as this underpins an array of growth, risk and assumption factors predicated by a mode of production that is in a state of perpetual flux itself due to fluid forces and relations of production. Such a state of affairs entails that global bodies such the UN-Habitat[2] and UNDP[3] start exploring viable alternatives to sustain cities and their hinterlands, as these are the growth centers and conurbations that largely determine the direction of the world economy. Urban development, therefore, emerges as a serious business that needs to be addressed in terms of workable strategies. One such methodological tool that is readily available is the Infrastructure Impact Assessment strategy that periodically takes stock of urban development projects.

M&E

IIA generally comprises (i) the preparation of indicators and analyses of benchmarks and (ii) monitoring and evaluation studies to assess the benefits of development projects. This is done by carrying out periodic sample surveys in order to determine the changes in key social and technical indicators over time. Monitoring is the systematic collection of data to provide management, donors and other stakeholders with an indication of project progress. Evaluation is the systematic and objective assessment of an ongoing or completed project, including its design, implementation and results. Evaluation leads to more informed decisions, allowing those involved in the project to learn from experience and to be accountable to donors and stakeholders. Both Monitoring and Evaluation should be used to demonstrate accountability and to understand the dynamics of the program. The differences in the objectives, methodology and purposes of Monitoring and Evaluation are shown in the table below. It is important to keep in mind that Monitoring does not replace Evaluation.[4]

SCP

Stakeholders' Consultative Process involves different issues and concerns of IIA. In order to scientifically implement project-related activities it is imperative to develop a time-frame of proposed activities to be carried out during project cycles. Any development agency's social action plan will elaborate and schedule the activities to be undertaken in accordance with the aims and objectives of SCP as mandated by the scope of physical works of different urban development projects.

SCP is in fact an interactive dialogue process that handles issues such as resource mapping, benefit mapping, needs assessment, priority ranking and participatory development so that physical interventions may become all the more effective and sustainable at the community-level.

WTP

Willingness to Pay underscores the projected revenue earnings of municipal authorities in terms of user charges/fees so far as Operation and Maintenance of civic assets (and affordable access to the same on the part of primary stakeholders/project beneficiaries) are concerned. Better supervision of existing urban infrastructure indicates optimum utilization of manpower presently available *i.e.,* streamlining human resources and avoiding "free rider costs"/non-merit expenditures incurred on non-performing assets (that leads to underemployment) in the process. Both these benchmarks examine the "value for money" concern of urban good governance as a central issue of sustainable development underpinned by the stakeholders' consultation process.

IIA

Impact assessment of development projects in terms of new civic infrastructure created is also an exercise related to physical progress measurement of engineering interventions and designs at the level of implementation. It is important to understand that impact assessment studies also include in their purview the issues and concerns of participatory development. Non-Government Organizations and other voluntary organizations/development agencies that engage social entrepreneurs focused on capacity-building rather than mere service delivery in terms of philanthropic humanitarianism (especially during disaster and (tactical) crises management) may interact with the primary stakeholders at the grassroots who are perceived by the secondary stakeholders as potential and/or prospective project beneficiaries.

Such interactions may include a basket of participatory rapid appraisal tools and strategies such as focus group discussions, personal interviews, community meetings, transacts, priority ranking and matrix scoring. Needs assessment exercises of physical resources as perceived by the primary stakeholders will be based on such participatory observation methods. These exercises will also be predicated by resource mapping of the proposed project area by consultants. Micro planning will be developed next in association/consultation with the primary stakeholders. Resource Persons, Key Informants and/or Community (-Level) Representatives will take part in such grassroots planning in order to make such exercises as broadbased as feasible.

Table 5.1: Differences between Outcome Monitoring and Outcome Evaluation 5

	Outcome Monitoring	*Outcome Evaluation*
Objective	To track changes from baseline conditions to desired outcomes	To validate what results were achieved and how and why they were or were not achieved.
Focus	Focuses on the outputs of projects.	Compares planned with intended outcomes achievement. Focuses on how and why outputs and strategies contributed to achievement of outcomes. Focuses on questions of relevance, effectiveness, sustainability and change.
Methodology	Tracks and assesses performance (progress towards outcomes) through analysis and comparison of indicators over time.	Evaluates achievement of outcomes by comparing indicators before and after the intervention. Relies on monitoring data to information from external sources.
Conduct	Continuous and systematic by Task Managers, Project Managers and key partners.	Time-bound, periodic, in-depth. External evaluators and partners.
Use	Alerts managers to problems in performance, provides options for corrective actions and helps demonstrate accountability.	Provides managers with strategy and policy options, provides basis for learning and demonstrates accountability.

Development agencies cannot aspire to capture the aspirations of the community without getting involved in such empathetic interactions. It should always be kept in mind that development is intrinsic to local-level realities. It is imperative to be attuned to the local for development to succeed at the macro-level of society. Engineers will attend all such community-level interactions in order to sensitize themselves with the priorities and perceptions of the community. Such choices may also be informed by gender orientations to development.

IIA indicators may be both quantitative and qualitative in nature in order to include process indicators, progress indicators and qualitative indicators. These will provide primary (field-level) data to monitor the project, evaluate progress of physical work and guide the implementing agencies as well as consultants so far as effective utilization of resources is concerned. IIA indicators may also evaluate the impact of the project on the quality of life of primary stakeholders before and after the project and examine the increased level of community participation and awareness-generation *vis-à-vis* project interventions:[6]

> Indicators are new professional tools for management of housing and urban programmes. The Arabic equivalent of the word indicators is pointers, indicating the outcomes or path to choose, "what approach is more effective" from amongst a possible range of policy solutions. The indicators are in the nature of a diagnostic tool that facilitates the assessment of the current health of the activity that is being assessed, such as the housing conditions, reach out and quality of basic services, income distribution pattern, economic environment or efficacy of governance. The utility of these "pointers" depends upon the quality of the data and the capacity of the users to analyse and interpret them and link them to the specific task in hand. Some of the indicators which have been in use for a considerable time are well-understood. Classic examples are GDP growth rate, unemployment rate, poverty ratio. Such well-recognised indicators in the

> housing and urban sector have not yet been developed and the indicators programme is an attempt towards this goal. Indicators at present are highly aggregated and have to be disaggregated as per the requirements to contribute significantly to the policy and project formulation process. The decision to disaggregate, the extent of disaggregation and the methodology to do it will, again, depend on the capacity of the users as well as producers of the indicators.[7]

Under different baseline assessments the infrastructure and socio-economic conditions across different sections of potential beneficiaries may be studied in order to gain meaningful insights into the deep text of the problems to be addressed. Such problems may occasionally assume gender-specific orientations (as already mentioned earlier). Local women inhabitants belonging to low-income categories may perceive issues of community-level infrastructural development in a different manner from the men.

WatSan

Critical areas related to water supply and sanitation services, safe drinking water, bathing spaces and abru walls (for women), toilet units with proper security and water arrangements, provisions for security lighting, solid waste disposal litterbins/vats/containers, efficient sewerage and drainage systems, wide enough pathways, plantation of trees, a community hall (for women to meet and undergo vocational training if feasible), safe electricity connections, access to telephone booths and post offices and police stations and transport networks may be highlighted during discussions with women focused on infrastructural improvements in their locality.

Gender

Women (as well as women-headed households) happen to primarily nurture the infrastructure-related impacts of development. So it is imperative to involve them as much as possible during the course of developmental dialogues in order to mainstream gender and factor in specifics of gender-driven discourse *vis-à-vis* project designs, goals, objectives and deliverables.

Thrust Areas

The major heads of study that may be covered under IIA programs may include critical areas of sustainable urban development such as solid waste management, sewerage and drainage, water supply and sanitation and slum improvement. Social action plans of development agencies that provide time frames to IIA plans may also lay down strategies for collection of data and assessment of the infrastructure under each head (mentioned above). SAP may also take into account and investigate socio-economic conditions of the principal stakeholders and analyze their perceptions with regard to the available urban infrastructure. Data under these heads may be collected using both qualitative and quantitative methods in order to freeze the ground realities and design physical interventions under urban development projects. IIA programs are generally participatory underpinned by the stakeholders' consultation process. SCP is central to the methodology of IIA whose central objective is to move away from conventional top-down approaches (to monitoring and evaluation) that involve measurement of project performance against pre-set indicators by using standardized procedures and tools.[8] The strategy to facilitate community mobilization and participation campaigns under IIA programs may be divided phase-wise as follows:

1. Devising an institutional structure for participation that entails community networks of mutual trust and cooperation in order to cohere a sustainable stock of social capital.
2. Establishing and putting into operation mechanisms for the effective functioning of such an institutional

structure so that a communitarian approach to development may be adopted.

3. Defining roles and responsibilities for planning, implementation and monitoring *vis-à-vis* primary and secondary stakeholders.

IIA programs underpinned by the rationale of participatory development may (i) define statements of measurable objectives in terms of physical interventions, (ii) design a structured set of indicators covering outputs of goods and services and their possible impact on project beneficiaries and (iii) include provisions for data collection/analyses and reporting to the client and project consultants:

1. Participation of the stakeholders creates conditions for consensus and potential conflict resolution.
2. People's participation not only makes programs and policies more acceptable but also makes them cost-effective and enhances ownership.
3. The stakeholders once brought into a participatory mode undertake significant follow-up activities on their own accord and enhance social mobilization. These are key contributions to sustainable development.[9]

MIS

The client's/executing agency's Management of Information System may serve to streamline the project's database to coordinate inflow and outflow of information *vis-à-vis* the Project Management Unit, development agencies and consultants in terms of IIA findings.[10] The executing agency's expanding database will necessitate exploration of information storage and sharing techniques facilitated by local area networking and made secure by firewalls built into the system. The project's performance at a certain stage may critically depend on the rate and precision of information flow available between PMU, development agencies and consultants.

MIS may reorient "good practices" of Information Technology by broadbasing IT applications to the development sector and may be divided into (1) data collection, (2) data examination, (3) data processing, (4) data organizing, (5) data analysis and (6) data utilization in terms of heuristic strategies and (tactical) projections. PMU may install an internal messaging system that will be cost-effective and provide an instant interface between PMU, development agencies and consultants. This may also be utilized to hold e-meetings with donors and funding agencies. Dedicated project websites may be constantly updated and uploaded in order to learn from comparable case studies around the world. This will facilitate information exchange and drawing of lessons on a global scale and promote transparency of all project-related activities. Vital information exchange relates to a worldview of interaction between stakeholders. This also underscores the need for e-governance where citizen-government interface and public-private participation may be suitably facilitated to sustain urban development projects.

Any information management exercise happens to be a sharing of data between peer groups in order to revise strategies and reorient good practices of development. Learning from one another in the light of lessons derived from ongoing project interventions may constitute a key component of management information systems. MIS may be designed in a realistic manner so that the work packages, milestones, parameters, goals, objectives, philosophy and aspirations of projects are suitably captured within its ambit.

Change Management

Change management constitutes an important component of MIS. Any social change that is to be brought about by project interventions may be incorporated in MIS so as to gauge the amount of effective community-level progress realized under specific projects. Adequate indicators need to be developed in order to monitor and evaluate this process.

Process indicators are benchmarks that are concerned with the dynamics of change *i.e.*, how change is to be effected at the grassroots, how the process of change is to managed with the help of external interventions and internal facilitation, how best change can be reconciled with conventions *vis-à-vis* the primary stakeholders?

For instance: Operation and Maintenance is a difficult area to be implemented under projects that are funded by global donor agencies. There may not be any moral compulsion to explore the Willingness to Pay factor on the part of the primary stakeholders as there are no financial obligations involved on the part of the executing agency to pay back the amount of project assistance along with interest (staggered across a given number of years).

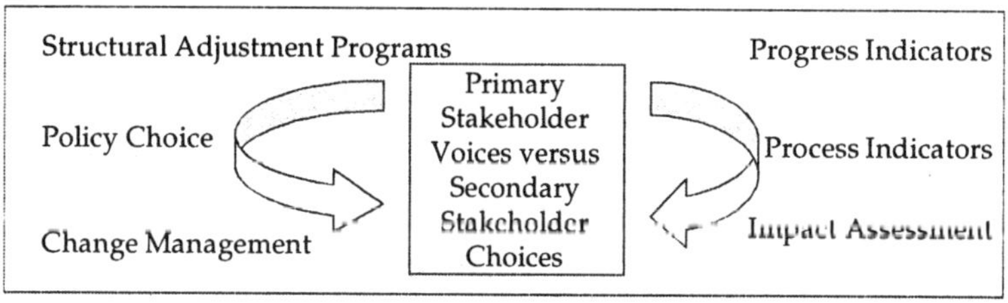

Voices-Choices Model

IIA survey reports submitted by development agencies may serve to update PMU, consultants and implementing agencies *vis-à-vis* physical progress of the project. Reassessment and reorientation exercises may be carried out to adjust project priorities in accordance with new demands and perceptions on the part of primary stakeholders.

Urban development projects cannot always follow predetermined approaches. Development more often than not emerges from chaos but subsequently leads to cohesion by resolving the tension between priorities and utilities. MIS may guide PMU, development agencies and consultants to better coordinate project-related activities and avoid overlapping of jurisdictions.

MIS may primarily focus on IIA programs in order to serve as the consultant-stakeholder interface impacting on crisis management (short-term) and sustainable urban development (long-term). MIS may also stress on transparency, coordination, accountability and cooperation in order to lend a socially relevant face to information technology.

IIA indicators may be designed keeping in view the fact that development agencies aim to facilitate need-based awareness-generation programs and the stakeholder's consultation process. Benchmarks may be utilized as indices against which baseline, mid-term and post project surveys may be carried out:

> Henry Taylor and Sam Cole discuss the turning point approach to neighbourhood change as it relates to the barrier and enabler theory. The turning point theory of neighbourhood change challenges existing concepts of urban development, such as the neighbourhood life-cycle theory. Taylor and Cole argue that for substantive community revitalization to occur, a city must make a large-scale commitment to removing impediments to societal development by improving housing and education. Then it must create enablers, such as introduction of local commerce and beautification of neighbourhoods, to generate community competence. Community competence, in turn, promotes healthy communities.[11]

IIA sample surveys may be undertaken on a continuous basis throughout the duration of the project in tandem with mid-term and post-project reviews. Consultations with primary beneficiaries as well as project surveys may be scheduled to supply information that may be utilized to plan future project-related activities and reorient ongoing physical interventions. IIA is a continuous process in terms of project-related interventions.

Another critical debate that may be outlined in this context relates to the primary stakeholder versus project beneficiary controversy *i.e.*, whether project affected persons as the defining axes of urban development projects may be described as primary stakeholders who define a multiplicity of stakes *vis-à-vis* physical interventions as against the contending role definition of beneficiaries at the center of development predicated by state welfarism and subsidies. One of the main thrusts of IIA-related initiatives may be the creation of Model Slums on completion of basic infrastructure development works. A slum with a relatively higher level of community cohesiveness and the initiative to assume greater responsibilities may be targeted in this regard.[12]

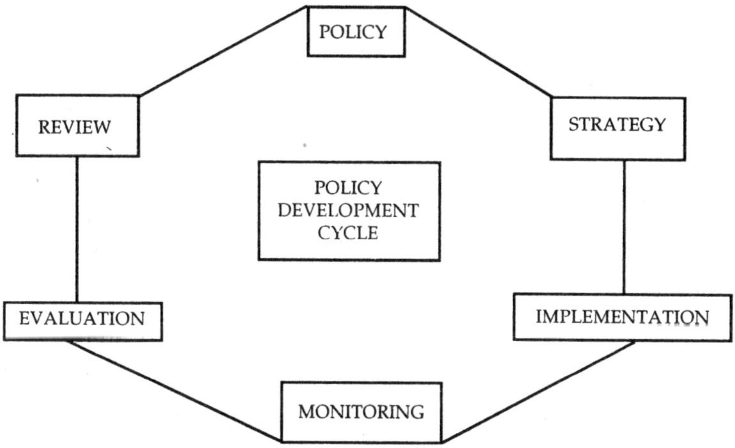

Policy Development Cycle[13]

Intensive community mobilization and participation activities as well as awareness-generation campaigns may be undertaken in such designated slums to ensure maximum role of the community *vis-à-vis* delivery of civic services during implementation of physical works. Formation/facilitation of efficacious community-based institutional arrangements for managing and sustaining project interventions will be the main feature of developmental activities in Model Slums.[14] Water user groups among local women may be formed/facilitated by development agencies in order to ensure O&M of water supply and sanitation services as well as create employment opportunities at the micro-level of the community. These are imperative measures that may be undertaken to highlight as well as entrench project sustainability measures.

Participation may be defined as an interactive process during the passage of which primary stakeholders gain access to the decision-making process either directly or via institutionalized representation. SCP underscores that community participation is imperative as

1. It helps identify the needs and perceptions of primary stakeholders.
2. It sustains civic amenities after withdrawal of implementing agencies.
3. It monitors progress of physical works.
4. It streamlines community-level institutional mechanisms.
5. It develops ownership among community members *vis-à-vis* collective assets.

Participatory monitoring and evaluation exercises as a backup to IIA sample surveys are important in order to:

1. Assess the progress of physical works and ensure that maximum benefits accrue to the community in terms of repair/new construction of civic assets and physical infrastructure; and
2. Mobilize the community so that primary stakeholders may undertake Operation and Maintenance of collective assets.[15]

While the first task may be carried out by examining the progress of physical works and interacting with the community in terms of structured as well as unstructured logistics, the second task may be performed by organizing focus group discussions (with community members) related to primary health and hygiene, water supply and sanitation services, safe community practices and poverty alleviation programs:

CMP

Community mobilization and participation activities also seek to build and sustain a stock of social capital at the local-level that may well facilitate monitoring, supervision and evaluation of physical works undertaken during the project cycle. Social capital may also ensure that the community continues to maintain its collective assets after completion of the project and phased withdrawal of interventions.

Community participation strategies operate at two levels: (1) the communitarian level where the community is brought back into developmental focus in order to build and sustain a proprietary sense among primary stakeholders[16] and (2) the neoinstitutional level where "actors and institutions" are transformed into "actors in institutions" *i.e.*, end-users of institutionalized civic services are mobilized suitably to identify their personal agenda with community interests. These are in effect utilitarian tools to motivate the community to become proactive and safeguard collective concerns at the level of collectives.

Awareness-generation programs constitute one of the principal tools utilizing which the community may be made aware of the need for basic services like water supply and sanitation. AGPs may form an integral part of SCP. Based on physical interventions designed by urban planners and policy-makers, development agencies may design awareness-generation campaigns to inform and educate primary stakeholders (intended project beneficiaries) with regard to proposed project interventions, probable outputs of the project (as well as related environmental impacts) and the roles and responsibilities of various project stakeholders as follows:

1. Community mobilization and participation campaigns in order to provide an efficacious/conducive civil societal backdrop against which the progress of physical works and participatory monitoring and evaluation of such works may be ascertained. CMP exercises may also facilitate formation/institutionalization of formal user groups and representative committees from among the community in order to streamline issues and concerns of a commercially viable Operation and Maintenance system of physical infrastructure (collective civic resources) in the discernible future when "free rider costs/non-merit expenditures" (subsidies) may be discontinued by the concerned municipal authorities.

2. Awareness-generation programs with regard to primary health and hygiene, sustainable urban development (and best practices associated with such user-friendly type of participatory development), literacy, gender empowerment, community development, civic responsibility and a general sense of urban wealth and well-being sustained by neighbourhood groups/civil societal organizations/ community-based organizations.

Such exercises may primarily focus on areas that have comparatively low educational and literacy levels such as city slums.[17] Community mobilization and participation activities and awareness-generation programs may be initiated during the inception phase of urban development projects so that such interventions on the part of development agencies continue throughout the project cycle in order to effectively promote sustainable urban development[18] and best practices of good urban governance that is characterized by the principles of sustainability, subsidiarity, equity, efficiency, transparency and accountability, civic engagement and citizenship and security, and that these principles are interdependent and mutually reinforcing. [19]

Participation is an interactive process whereby primary stakeholders take part in the decision-making process either in a direct manner or via CBOs/NGOs. Community development events and awareness-generation campaigns are generally strategized to streamline project-related interventions and facilitate dialogues between primary and secondary stakeholders. Such programs serve to build empathy at the community-level and facilitate dialougic rather than pedagogic terms of discourse at the project implementation, monitoring and evaluation levels. Community mobilization and participation activities are not an end but a means to secure rapport-building that may ensure acceptance of development interventions on the part of project affected persons.[20]

Primary stakeholders may be suitably empowered to sustain developmental impacts of the project *i.e.*, their entitlements should be converted into capacities (following Amartya Sen). This will ensure that project interventions and their benefits sustain over a considerable period of time and motivate future development and further popular initiatives at the grassroots level where communities have been made capable to make critical decisions affecting the quality of their everyday life.[21] Axes of civic participation and/or preparedness should be identified in order to plan NGO/CBO/Civil Society Organization interventions in consultation with local-level resource persons and/or key informants. Interventions should be scientifically implemented and underpinned by a definitive plan of action. This is despite the fact that development generally emerges out of flux and can seldom be planned in a rigid manner. Field-level lessons (and insights)—therefore—should be utilized to coordinate between theory and praxes.[22]

Conventional urban development approaches more often than not fail to build the capacities of primary stakeholders to reflect, analyze and act on their own initiative. By contrast, participatory approaches consider primary stakeholders as the agency, rather than the object, of project monitoring and evaluation. Key differences between conventional and participatory M&E are as follows:

Conventional versus Participatory M&E[23]

Issues and Concerns	*Conventional M&E*	*Participatory M&E*
Who plans and manages interventions	senior managers or outside experts	local people, project staff, managers and other stakeholders, often helped by a facilitator
Role of Primary Stakeholders (intended beneficiaries)	provide information only	design and adapt the methodology, collect and analyze data, share findings and link them to action
How success is measured	externally defined, mainly quantitative indicators	internally defined indicators, including more qualitative instruments
Approach	predetermined	adaptive

There are different forms of PM&E that are predicated by the type of participants, at what stages such actors are involved and the exact targets of urban development projects. The following principles are generally at the core of PM&E:

1. Participation *i.e.,* making the project design flexible to include primary and secondary stakeholders in data analyses and planning and implementation of physical interventions.
2. PM&E inclusiveness requires negotiations to agree on what will be monitored and evaluated and how, what are the implications of data analyses and how survey findings will be shared and action taken to streamline project-related activities.
3. This facilitates learning of lessons that constitute the basis for subsequent project interventions.
4. Flexibility is essential since the number, role and skills of stakeholders, the external environment and related factors change over time.[24]

The advantages of using a participatory approach to IIA (according to United Nations Development Program guidelines) are as follows:

However, following a participatory approach to IIA can be constrained by low literacy levels in the community, insufficient time, intensity of analytical work to be undertaken during the monitoring/evaluation process and the fact that several issues covered during M&E may not be directly relevant to primary stakeholders. SCP may underpin a participatory approach to IIA. The first step of a participatory IIA program is to identify key stakeholders whose participation will be sought from a large array of institutions and individuals that could potentially affect—or be affected—by proposed project interventions. The borrowers, donor/funding agencies, beneficiaries, affected groups and other interested groups may be studied in this connection. Participatory evaluations are useful when there are questions about implementation difficulties or program effects on different stakeholders or when information is wanted on stakeholders' knowledge of program goals or their view of progress.[25]

Identification of stakes is critical to project designs and will involve assessment of the following items of inquiry:

1. What are the stakeholders' expectations from the project?
2. What benefits are there likely to be for the stakeholders?
3. What resources are the stakeholders able and willing to mobilize?
4. Which interests of the stakeholders are in conflict with project goals?

Once the key stakeholder groups have been identified, their possible interests in the project or economic and sector work may be considered. Certain stakeholder interests are less obvious than others and may be difficult to define, especially if these happen to be covert, multiple or in contradiction with the stated aims/objectives of the organization/individual.

The above questions and answers may guide further inquiries into the interests of each key stakeholder or group. In the case of certain stakeholder institutions/organizations these questions may be answered by reviewing secondary information. For more informal groups, assessment of their interests will probably require consultations either directly with these stakeholders or with persons who are familiar with these groups (resource persons/key informants). With this background, consideration can be given to how the project might affect these interests: positively or negatively. The process for establishing stakes in a participatory manner is discussed below. Community mobilization and participation strategies may be divided into the following phases:

1. Formation/facilitation of institutional structure(s) for participation.
2. Establishing and operationalizing mechanisms for the effective functioning of these structure(s).
3. Defining roles and responsibilities for planning as well as implementation and M&E.

This is a comprehensive strategy and may be followed in a flexible manner as per the situation available on the ground. This strategy may be developed keeping slums in mind. The first stage involved in mobilizing the community to participate in project-related activities is to set up an institutional structure whereby participation of primary stakeholders may be solicited in a formal manner. This structure would be the community-project interface, utilizing which secondary stakeholders can hold intervention-related consultations, receive feedback and make decisions with regard to planning, implementation, monitoring and evaluation of project-related activities. This is imperative as it is not always practicable to involve everyone at the community-level during all the stages of project-related interventions. Community-level feedback may inform decision-making in a structured manner on the part of secondary stakeholders to generate tangible outputs.

CMP is not an end but a means to secure rapport-building that—in its turn—may ensure acceptance of consultants at the community level. This acceptance would finally serve the following purposes: (1) needs assessment with regard to civic services/assets and physical works, vocational training programs and income-generation activities (for poverty reduction purposes), (2) awareness-generation with regard to health and hygiene and safe (*i.e.* eco-friendly) community practices and (3) monitoring and evaluation of physical works carried out for the community by the community itself.

Several formal and informal groups exist within the community. Factors binding the members to a group could be social, economic, cultural or political. Other organizations and institutions, such as NGOs, CBOs and CSOs are also important members of the community exerting influence over group dynamics and community-level interactions.

The first step would be to build rapport with these groups, organizations and institutions. A common way to gain acceptance is to organize creative communication events at the community-level so that primary stakeholders may unite and relate to proposed project interventions. Such events serve as a community-level access while depending all the same on the level of community preparedness in order to assess needs and plan project interventions.

There may already be representative group(s) at the community-level representing different sections of primary stakeholders. Development agencies—in such cases—will have to ensure that all groups (especially the weaker/vulnerable sections or those most impacted by lack of water supply and sanitation facilities) have been adequately represented. The structure created to institutionalize participation should be as representative of the community as possible. The tasks that will be undertaken for this specific objective are as follows:

An initial listing of Resource Persons/Key Informants within slums may be undertaken. This will be achieved through regular interactions with community members, though on a random basis. Assistance of community-based institutions may also be sought in this regard. RPs are community-level spokespersons and opinion-makers who may represent a particular socio-cultural/economic group. They may also have specific political affiliations. RPs may be identified and their profiles prepared for further consultation purposes. Efforts may be made to identify RPs from various geographical locations within slums so that all major settlements are suitably represented. The domain of influence of each RP may also be mapped. Final selection of RPs may be made on the basis of RP profiles and maps.

In order to facilitate participation of women, it may be ideal to identify at least one woman RP per slum. In communities where participation from women would generate overall disapproval, development agencies may ensure that women's views find a place in core committee (user group) consultations. RPs may prepare a list of formal and informal groups within the community and prioritize these from the perspective of planning and implementing project-related activities. RPs may also select representatives from the prioritized groups (formal or informal). Criteria for selection may be determined by RPs. The objective would be to form a core committee of community-level representatives. The representative group may comprise individuals as identified and selected by RPs. This representative group will be formed during a joint meeting of RPs and group representatives. Agenda of this meeting may vary. This may depend on the level of preparedness of group representatives to discuss project-related issues, beginning with needs assessment exercises. Advice of RPs may be sought in this connection.

This will involve delegating roles and responsibilities among core committee members and depend on how members want to orient themselves *vis-à-vis* roles and responsibilities. It is important to note that the representative group may decide to function in an informal manner without creating a formal structure. If representative groups already exist (equipped with established procedures and mechanisms) then these will be assessed and developed to ensure community mobilization and participation. Operational details of functioning, such as frequency of core committee meetings, may also be decided. Similarly, election/nomination of representative group members to responsible positions, criteria for decision-making etc. may also be decided. To what extent these processes/functions can be formalized may be left to core committee members to decide.

Roles and responsibilities of core committee members may define the areas where their capacities need to be enhanced in order to enable them to carry out designated functions. The areas in which capacities of core committee members need to be enhanced will be identified by development agencies in consultation with RPs. Needs assessment is the first stage of facilitating community mobilization and participation in the project. It will involve undertaking the following set of tasks at the core committee-level. At any stage of these consultations (especially those requiring decisions to be taken), RPs or representatives of formal/informal groups may interact with respective group members for further consultations to facilitate feedback at the core committee-level.

Baseline assessment findings may be discussed with representative groups. A list of identified needs will be accordingly prepared and discussed. The core committee will be requested to comment on identified needs in terms of the severity of problems and urgency of redress. This exercise will generate a list of problems/prioritized needs on the basis of certain criteria that will be suggested by core committee members (who will also rank problems in order of priority). It is important that problems thus identified and prioritized should be existing and not probable or future ones:

> At the heart of the DISCUS research is the exploration and understanding of the interaction between institutional and social capital. There is naturally a link between these—for example we can assume that existing and well performing local government institutions within the field of sustainable development in the local community can, in fact, create a natural and balanced as well as a supportive environment for different sectors of civil society to further develop those skills necessary to improve their "performance". Putnam (2000) distinguishes between "bonding" and "bridging" forms of social capital. In brief, bonding social capital refers to the networks, links and relationships, which tend to reinforce identities and homogenous groups. In contrast, bridging social capital is more outward looking, often encompassing people from diverse social and geographical backgrounds.[26]

Community-level problems may be identified and cause-effect relationships determined in this process. This may also help to identify benchmarks of solution impacts (facilities proposed to be provided under urban development projects). The problems identified may be converted into need-based statements. This exercise will require discussions and listing prioritized need statements. Development agencies may next determine areas within slums that need to be upgraded.

A detailed stakeholders analysis may be carried out subsequently, needs and area-wise. Stakes will be established for various settlements in the areas (of slums) that have been identified for upgradation. These settlements may be those that are likely to benefit directly if that need is addressed in that area. This process will be beneficial to determine mechanisms for cooperation from these groups and avoid possible conflicts in the future. Development agencies may share engineering designs (based on community-level feedback) with representative groups. Community meetings may be organized for this purpose.

Representative Groups (or Group Representatives)/ Resource Persons/Key Informants may suggest proposals that will increase income and accordingly increase the effective demand for basic services being provided/strengthened in slums. Skill development needs may be identified accordingly:

> Supporting the development and maintenance of 'bridging social capital' could be through the mechanism of Community Leadership. This term has been applied both to leaders within the community, and to the role that local government plays in encouraging social capital to develop. The literature in this area emphasises the importance of community leaders within civil society organisations (such as social and environmental NGOs). However, emphasis is also placed on local government providing leadership in terms of 'enabling' communities to develop capacity, but also in the context of municipal entrepreneurship—the role of officers and politicians in promoting and developing a municipality's profile and effectiveness. We need to have some understanding of leadership in order to be able to disentangle charismatic individuals from the processes that might permit both individual and institutional leadership to emerge.[27]

There are different ways to ensure that the community's perspective is taken into account. Early indications of impact may be obtained by surveying beneficiaries' perceptions *vis-à-vis* project progress/services. Such a leading indicator has the twin benefits of consultation with stakeholders and advance warning of problems that may arise.

The achievement of project objectives generally depends on how project beneficiaries respond to the goods or services delivered by the project. Evidence of their response and the benefits they derive requires consultation and data collection that are outside the scope of regular management activities. It is important to identify how beneficiaries are expected to respond to project services because the client and funding/ donor agencies may require evidence of that response if they need to modify activities/strategies. SCP for IIA is relevant in this connection.

Implementing agencies involved need to be responsive to the recommendations that emerge from IIA programs. Flexibility, a quick response system and beneficiary-orientations are essential characteristics of an implementing agency that will use participatory M&E approaches in an efficacious manner. Consultations with beneficiaries and/or surveys will be scheduled to provide information for use in planning further project activities/rectifying ongoing interventions.

Dissemination of IIA assessment results should include feedback to the stakeholders involved at all the levels of the project, including presentations at the field-level for community representatives, an informal review meeting with project staff and a final workshop with senior project officials:

> Good monitoring is the foundation for good evaluation because it creates a repository of data and other information aimed at assisting evaluators in their work.[28]

PM&E

For participatory approaches to M&E to be effective, these need to be incorporated into the overall project and undertaken on a continuous basis. The results of an initial self-evaluation exercise, for instance, can provide certain preliminary findings that may constitute the groundwork for follow-up assessments. These results, in turn, can be used to refine the key issues and generate new questions during subsequent M&E. IIA programs for urban development projects may simultaneously develop new activities and encounter new problems, which may affect the stakeholders' perceptions of project-related activities.

Communities may also experience changes from other sources that may have an impact on the progress of the project. All these factors may be built into IIA programs.[29]

IIA studies in fact act as indices against which project progress in terms of physical work and developmental interventions may be quantified. Such periodic surveys provide insights on the part of both primary as well as secondary stakeholders in the sense that strategies may be revised, goals redefined and praxes reformulated in the light of field-level lessons learnt during implementation of project targets. Such a critical and heuristic manner of learning from past mistakes and making necessary amendments during the project cycle to aim at moving targets more often than not underpin IIA exercises and place such surveys in their proper context from which a panoptic ombudsman role may be played by development agencies *vis-à-vis* project-related interventions.

IIA strategies focus on a central concern of development *i.e.* development for the people, of the people and by the people. IIA strategies lay due importance on the fact that development cannot be like a politics of knowledge discourse that is more often than not imposed from the above without any consideration of ground realities *i.e.*, what does the community located at the receiver's end of such development prefer.

Such a superior politics is generally the result of scientific knowledge and an assumption that developmentalist best practices are bound to lead to human wealth and well-being. These are equated with the idea of progress at a material level of the politics of everyday life. But this is just another version of the white man's burden. Although orientalism as a counter philosophy of identity politics was made to suffer considerably by its critics, this much may be asserted that Edward Said's basic challenges and contentions with regard to the claims of superior culture root paradigms and knowledge discourses among civilizations (or constructs and artifacts that we prefer to address as civilizations) still remain largely valid.

IIA studies basically reorient the best practices of community development by bringing back the primary stakeholders into the central focus of interventions. This entails a critical debate between progress versus development and strategy versus interventions:

1. Stage of Exploring: identifying lessons that are of value for redesigning the project or that can be used by others working in the same field.
2. Stage of Explaining: codifying knowledge in such a way that it can easily be identified and used by others.
3. Stage of Exporting: disseminating among other team members, management, or other organizations in the form of lessons learned, the knowledge obtained from the monitoring and evaluation work.[30]

Progress is much more ideational and value-specific *i.e.*, community progress indicates changes at the level of value systems, broadbased worldviews, evolution of new managing agencies at the level of the mode of production and dynamic interfaces cohered among the representative collectives who happen to manage community affairs and the agenda of institutionalized civic participation mechanisms. Development—on the other hand—indicates a compromise between alternative choices, a resolution of policy-level conflicts and exercises in manufactured consent (following Noam Chomsky[31]). Such discourses may be represented as follows:

Development Discourses Model

Progress	Culture	Values	Institutions	Policies
Trusteeship	Identity	Planning	Participation	Choices
O&M	Benefits	Sustainability	Interventions	Decisions
Social Capital	Community	Beneficiaries	Stakeholders	Information

The above matrix may be read from any point in a logical sequence that will happen to correlate development with perceived benefits, institutions with social capital that facilitates participation, O&M with trusteeship and identity, culture with values, planning by the community for sustain-ability, decisions with regard to interventions, choices informed by policies and stakeholders finally emerging as beneficiaries:

"Sustainable community development is the ability to make development choices which respect the relationship between the three Es—economy, ecology and equity:

1. Economy—Economic activity should serve the common good, be self-renewing, and build local assets and self-reliance.
2. Ecology—Human beings are part of nature, nature has limits, and communities are responsible for protecting and building natural assets.
3. Equity—The opportunity for full participation in all activities, benefits, and decision-making of a society."[32]

Conclusion

IIA—therefore—emerges as an analytical exercise that may be able to reconcile contending role definitions between stakeholders and beneficiaries[33] as well as resolve the tension of dynamics between the subtle idea of progress and the much more down-to-earth utilitarian notion of sustainable urban participatory development.[34]

NOTES

1. Originally published in *Southern Initiatives Journal of Sustainable Development*, Vol. 2, Issue 1, pp. 63-93.
2. The Global Urban Observatory (GUO) addresses the urgent need to improve the world-wide base of urban knowledge by helping Governments, local authorities and organizations of the civil society develop and apply policy-oriented urban indicators, statistics and other urban information. The GUO was established by UN-HABITAT (United Nations Human Settlements Program) in response to a decision of the United Nations Commission on Human Settlements, which called for a mechanism to monitor global progress in implementing the Habitat Agenda and to monitor and evaluate global urban conditions and trends. http://www.unhabitat.org/programmes/guo/
3. See United Nations Development Program's Millennium Development Goals in this connection. http://www.undp.org/mdg/
4. Adapted from the UNDP Handbook on Monitoring and Evaluating for Results.

5. *Ibid.*
6. Participation of the stakeholders create conditions for consensus and potential conflict resolution; people's participation not only makes programmes and policies more acceptable, they make them cost-effective and enhance ownership; and the stakeholders, once brought into a participatory mode, undertake significant follow-up activities on their own accord and enhance social mobilization. These are key contributions to sustainable development. http://www.ecouncil.ac.cr/rio/national/reports/asia/bangladesh/ban4.htm
7. Stuti Lall (ed), *Economic and Social Indicators for Managing the Growing Economics* (New Delhi: Society for Development Studies, 1996), Chapter III.
8. Participatory Monitoring and Evaluation: Learning from Change. IDS Policy Briefing, Issue 12, 1998. http://www.ids.ac.uk/ids/bookshop/briefs/brief12.html
9. http://www.ecouncil.ac.cr/rio/national/reports/asia/bangladesh/ban4.htm
10. http://solutionportals.com/Components/Overview.htm
11. http://www.utexas.edu/lbj/rhodesprp/01_02/divide/needs.htm
12. Networks of community cohesion are sustained by an obtainable level of social capital that facilitates channels of cooperation and trust among primary stakeholders. Enhanced social capital at the grassroots improves the chances of project success as defined by norms and good practices of participatory development. Any given stock of social capital frozen in socio-temporal contexts is a benchmark of the community's faith in itself as an exemplar of good urban governance.
13. Lall (ed), *op. cit.*
14. Capacity-building is a dynamic process by which given human entitlements are organically translated into capabilities *vis-à-vis* primary stakeholders. Any given stake is an entitlement that is required to evolve in an enabling environment of sustainable development.
15. Micro-level collectives such as women's water user groups may be established. Self-Help Groups may be formed/facilitated (primarily among women) in order to launch poverty alleviation initiatives and income-generation programs underpinned by short-term vocational training courses (informed by training needs analyses) and forward/backward linkages. IGPs are required to ensure "affordable access" to basic urban amenities such as water supply and sanitation services.
16. The communitarian approach seeks to reorient the collective in terms of operation and maintenance activities during the project and at the post-project stage.

17. See A. Aoki, B. Bruns, M. Drabble, M. Marope, A. Mingat, P. Moock, P. Murphy, P. Paci, H. Patrinos, Jee-Peng Tan, C. Thomas, C. Winter and H. Yang, "Education". http://www.worldbank.org/poverty/strategies/chapters/education/educat.htm
18. Sustainable development is defined as a pattern of social and structured economic transformations (*i.e.* development), which optimizes the economic and societal benefits available in the present, without jeopardizing the likely potential for similar benefits in the future. A primary goal of sustainable development is to achieve a reasonable and equitably distributed level of economic well-being that can be perpetuated continually for many human generations. http://sdnp.delhi.nic.in/
19. http://www.un-habitat.org/govern/
20. See Prasenjit Maiti's Introduction to KR Gupta (ed), *Urban Development Debates in the New Millennium: Studies in Revisited Theories and Redefined Praxes*, Volumes I-IV (New Delhi: Atlantic, 2004).
21. *Ibid.*
22. *Ibid.*
23. Participatory Monitoring and Evaluation: Learning from Change. *Op. Cit.*
24. *Ibid.*
25. http://www.unfpa.org/monitoring/toolkit/tool2a.doc
26. http://www.iclei.org/europe/DISCUS/theory.htm
27. *Ibid.*
28. See *Monitoring and Evaluation: Guidelines for Country Gateway Implementation Grants* (Funded by the Development Gateway Foundation), p. 6.
29. "Sustainable communities are defined as towns and cities that have taken steps to remain healthy over the long-term. Sustainable communities have a strong sense of place. They have a vision that is embraced and actively promoted by all of the key sectors of society, including businesses, disadvantaged groups, environmentalists, civic associations, government agencies, and religious organizations. They are places that build on their assets and dare to be innovative. These communities value healthy ecosystems, use resources efficiently, and actively seek to retain and enhance a locally based economy. There is a pervasive volunteer spirit that is rewarded by concrete results. Partnerships between and among government, the business sector, and non-profit organizations are common. Public debate in these communities is engaging, inclusive, and constructive. Unlike traditional community development approaches, sustainability

strategies emphasize: the whole community (instead of just disadvantaged neighbourhoods); ecosystem protection; meaningful and broad-based citizen participation; and economic self-reliance." http://www.iscvt.org/FAQscdef.html

30. See *Monitoring and Evaluation: Guidelines for Country Gateway Implementation Grants, op. cit.*, p. 27.
31. The mass media serve as a system for communicating messages and symbols to the general populace. It is their function to amuse, entertain, and inform, and to inculcate individuals with the values, beliefs, and codes of behaviour that will integrate them into the institutional structures of the larger society. In a world of concentrated wealth and major conflicts of class interest, to fulfill this role requires systematic propaganda.
http://www.thirdworldtraveler.com/Herman%20/ManufacConsent_Prop_Model.html
32. *Mountain Association for Community Economic Development (MACED):* Hart Environmental Data. http://www.subjectmatters.com/indicators/Sustainability/DefinitionsCommunity.html
33. *Cf.* Gayatri Chakravorty Spivak, "Can the Subaltern Speak?", in Bill Ashcroft, Gareth Griffiths and Helen Tiffin (eds), *The Post-Colonial Studies Reader* (London/New York: Routledge, 1995). This essay was originally published in Cary Nelson and Lawrence Grossberg (eds), *Marxism and The Interpretation of Culture* (London: Macmillan, 1988). Edward W. Said had earlier observed in *Orientalism* (New York: Random House, 1978) that "Orientalism expresses and represents that part culturally and even ideologically as a mode of discourse with supporting institutions, vocabulary, scholarship, imagery, doctrines, even colonial bureaucracies and colonial styles ... Taking the late eighteenth century as a very roughly defined starting point Orientalism can be discussed and analysed as the corporate institution for dealing with the Orient—dealing with it by making statements about it, authorising views of it, describing it, by teaching it, settling it: in short, Orientalism as a western style for dominating, restructuring, and having authority over the Orient. I have found it useful here to employ Michel Foucault's notion of a discourse, as described by him in *The Archaeology of Knowledge* and in *Discipline and Punish*, to identify Orientalism. My contention is that without examining Orientalism as a discourse one cannot possibly understand the enormously systematic discipline by which European culture was able to manage—and even produce—the Orient politically, sociologically, and imaginatively during the post-Enlightenment period. Moreover, so authoritative a position did Orientalism have that I believe no one writing, thinking, or acting on the Orient could do so without taking account of the limitations on thought and action

imposed by Orientalism. In brief, because of Orientalism the Orient was not (and is not) a free subject of thought or action. This is not to say that Orientalism unilaterally determines what can be said about the Orient, but that it is the whole network of interests inevitably brought to bear on (and therefore always involved in) any occasion when the peculiar entity 'the Orient' is in question. How this happens is what this book tries to demonstrate. It also tries to show that European culture gained in strength and identity by setting itself off against the Orient as a sort of surrogate and even underground self." Also see—in this connection—Amartya Sen, "Our Culture, Their Culture", *The New Republic* (1 April 1996).

34. Partner Non-Government Organizations to be involved in urban development projects may be selected according to certain pre-set criteria. NGOs so deployed by the Project Management Unit would liaise with Community-Based Organizations in order to jointly work in the area of community mobilization and participation. Such field facilitation exercises involve rapport-building, designing/ implementing vocational training programs for poverty alleviation and formation as well as facilitation of self-help groups and user groups. Territorial jurisdictions may be earmarked for city-level NGOs in order to streamline their community liaison programs. Such NGOs may be in an advantageous position to identify local-level Community-Based Organizations that are interested in voluntary social work, understand problems specific to urban slums, gauge the mind set of the community and estimate its level of preparedness so far as actual implementation of training and poverty alleviation programs is concerned. Personnel strength of partner NGOs may constitute an indicator to assess its human capital. It may be inferred that partner NGOs are adequately equipped to monitor and evaluate CBOs carrying out their community mobilization and participation activities if they employ suitably trained professional staff. Area(s) of activities of NGOs would help identify their expertise in terms of track record and working experience in the field. NGOs specializing in areas such as community development, vocational training and income-generation programs may be preferred by PMU to liaise with slum-level CBOs in order to carry forward urban projects based on the norms of participatory development. Community-level feedback with regard to the performance of field-level NGOs may constitute a benchmark to assess the perception of primary stakeholders and/or beneficiaries so far as project-related socio-economic interventions are concerned. Feedback from CBOs regarding the performance of their partner NGOs is yet another critical indicator that helps assess their acceptance (or otherwise) of professional development agencies/voluntary organizations.

ANNEXURE-1

Eminent Domain[1]

Prasenjit Maiti
3 June 2006

The recent debate concerning acquisition of agricultural land and properties/structures is now raging violently in West Bengal in general and Kolkata in particular. The Left Front Government has now taken up industrialization as its topmost priority while its developmental agenda is informed by establishment of automobile factories, mini townships, private airports, roads, flyovers and bridges.

The Communist Party of India (Marxist) is now trying its level best to rope in other Left Front allies to support its land acquisition endeavours. This is an extremely sensitive issue that requires careful handling and political management. A broad-based consensual approach is imperative in this regard. The recent fracas at Singur near Hooghly District is a most topical case in point. Irate peasants assembled to protest against acquisition of their land and homestead. State Government officials had gone to visit the site along with representatives from Tata Motors. But the farmers pledged that they would not hand over their land to the administration at any cost. The Opposition in the State has also taken a Janus stand with regard to this issue. While they keep on insisting that they would not stand in the way of economic development they are also urging the State Government to ensure that only barren/fallow land under private ownership should be acquired for the purpose of agriculture.

The Left Front Government's policy stance in this respect is rather disturbing. It is known worldwide since it first came to power in 1977 as a pro-poor administration that carried out historic land reforms known as Operation Barga to ensure security of tenure and socio-economic justice for the cultivator. It had originally popularized the slogan: *Land belongs to the tiller of land*. But now the Left Front Government is trying to champion another political rhetoric: *Agriculture is our base while industry is our future*. It is true that fragmentation of land holdings has led to city-bound migration and reduced profits in agricultural activities. But it is also true that a perspective planning process is yet to be institutionalized by the State Government. For instance: the much talked about model of alternative economic development is yet to be noticed in action in West Bengal.

The State Government had earlier committed historic errors in judgment such as obstructing introduction of computer literacy and removing English Language education at the primary level. These blunders have handicapped an entire generation that is not only unemployed but also unemployable in the job market. Now the Left Front Government is trying to progress in areas such as information technology, food processing, service sector, heavy industries, agribusiness, knowledge process outsourcing and so on and so forth. But it is to be remembered that such thrust areas require an adequate pool of trained manpower and backup resources to effectively merchandize the end products. The shift from labour-intensive to capital-intensive industry is a historic necessity and vindicates Karl Marx's scientific formulation that the relations of production are informed by the mode of production that in turn is guided by the forces of production. But what is rather disquieting in the case of West Bengal is the State Government's apparent inability to institutionalize the best practices of dialogic broadbase interactions in order to broadbase its public consultation exercises with regard to acquisition of land and properties. The New Town project at Rajarhat adjacent to Salt Lake City is an example where compensation packages have not been duly awarded to the peasants whose plots of land were acquired for this township (if media sources are to be believed). This has led to disruption of livelihood of peasants. Owners of land and properties are now reported to be working as domestic helps in the affluent families of Salt Lake City *i.e.* the uprooted families of Rajarhat have been impoverished and compelled to lead a life of indignity and subservience (according to media reports).

Now the Left Front Government has returned to power for a record seventh time and is in the process of emulating former Chief Minister Bidhan Chandra Roy's dream vision of an industrialized West Bengal that can compete with the other Indian States on economic terms. But this vision requires to be seriously informed with the logistics of market, politics and the economy. West Bengal's land map needs to be studied first to identify stretches of barren/fallow land. But the tragedy is that industrialists always want to set up their plants near big metropolitan centers like Kolkata while the land in and around Kolkata at Hooghly, North and South 24 Parganas and Howrah are all fertile where multiple cropping is carried out twice or even thrice a year. Now the State Government has taken serious strides to facilitate establishment of the proposed automobile factory by Tata Motors at Singur. Other important projects that would require land acquisition are the Greenfield International Airport at South 24 Parganas and different new road projects in North and South 24 Parganas. The process of land acquisition is an extremely sensitive issue that requires political management of the highest order. But the State Government, in order to hasten through its project of rapid industrialization, is trying occasionally to bypass the usual channels.

Farmers who stand to lose their land and homestead at Singur have tried to build a platform of protest from where they can negotiate with the administration. What is worse is the fact that the media is coming up with conflicting news stories on this issue. Once we get to hear that the CPI(M)'s mass organization Krishak Samiti is on its way to solve this problem by building a consensus while the very next moment we come across another contradictory news item that the Opposition is trying to mobilize the local farmers not to surrender their land to the State Government. A good practice in this regard can be cited from the ongoing Second Vivekananda Bridge Project where owners of private land have voluntarily given their land to the Project Authority in order to receive attractive compensation packages. This bridge project is a major initiative that would significantly improve West Bengal's rail-road-port-airport connectivity and promote the cause of rapid industrialization in this process.

ANNEXURE-2

Development *versus* Displacement[2]

Prasenjit Maiti
21 April 2006

Kolkata these days is supposed to be in the midst of the election frenzy provoked by the State Legislative Assembly polls 2006. Candidates were allowed to use public address systems recently after conclusion of the examination season. But the tempo is missing all the same. West Bengal is known for its volatile culture of political campaigning on the part of candidates and their supporters who have desperately thrown in their lot in the electoral fray. But this time around both the Election Commission of India and the Calcutta High Court have severely trimmed the wild and exuberant excesses of electoral campaigning in the thick of the quite infamous Indian Summer.

The basic issue of the state polls this year happens to be the critical inquiry about the increase or decrease in the margin of seats of the ruling Left Front Government that is in power since 1977. Nobody is even remotely interested whether there would be any imminent change of guard in West Bengal or not. It is almost fait accompli that the ruling Left Front would again return to power while the Communist Party of India (Marxist) would emerge as the single largest party with an absolute majority status.

Development versus displacement could have surfaced as a major issue during this election. But this was not to be. The Opposition has not really questioned the political agenda of development in a constructive manner. Nobody has yet come up with an alternative model of sustainable development while the Left Front has time and again raised its slogan based on the rhetoric of an improved Left Front. This is a master strategy that has left the Opposition hapless and looking for creative political ideas.

The issues and concerns of this election can be amply noticed in and around Kolkata. Shopping malls, multiplexes, flyovers, coffee shops, night clubs, discos, health clubs, foreign banks, call centers, designer outlets, private clinics, five star hotels and theme restaurants are some of the new identities of this metropolis that also has slums, pavement dwellers, red light districts, inefficient Government Hospitals, infamous Corporation Schools, indifferent Government Offices and inadequate urban services for the poor.

The primary tenets of development have not been questioned before this election. Nobody is bothered why Kolkata should expand by acquiring fertile agricultural land that is the main source of livelihood of farmers on the outskirts of the City. Nobody would question why roads are repaired in a most casual manner just before the elections. Nobody would ask all sorts of uncomfortable questions about child death in Government Hospitals, corruption in public officers, police inaction or excesses, lack of sanitation facilities and drinking water supply, faulty road lighting system, water logging of City streets, frequent power cuts, runaway inflation and the increasing problems of road vendors who have actually appropriated the pavement from everyday pedestrians. The education system, the public health infrastructure, traffic indiscipline, lack of accountability and little transparency in the Government Departments and apathy on the part of the political masters are some of the problems that Kolkata have to live with yet there are a few and scattered voices that protest against the Development is Good Governance type of simplistic prescription recently being championed by the World Bank.

It cannot be denied that Kolkata has improved in terms of its appearance. Anybody visiting the City after about a decade would be vastly surprised at the kind of changes that have taken place. The major credit for such changes must go to the Left Front Government that has exhibited commendable initiative during the middle to late 1990s. An awakening has dawned of late that infrastructural developments are the order of the day and cannot really be substituted by empty populist rhetoric.

But the dissenting voices of democracy have been stifled. The radical left activists in the border districts of West Bengal have to be politically negotiated rather than tackled by the State's repressive agencies. One has to apply one's mind exactly why such extremists have taken recourse to the path of violence. The human rights activist movement of West Bengal in general and Kolkata in particular has not been quite vocal in recent times. Concerns such as the environment, animal rights, pollution, child rights, gender security, poverty and social development are some of the prominent issues that were handled earlier by Non-Government Organizations and Civil Society Organizations. But the intensity of these movement has somewhat ebbed nowadays in and around Kolkata. The socially upwardly mobile youth of Kolkata are not really interested either in politics or in social welfare. They are a set of hedonistic persons whose one and only objective in life appears to be self-preservation in style. The middle class youth have also followed suit. There are automated vendors these days selling contraceptives at outlets near discos and night clubs. So the moral guardians of the City have taken it for granted that the youth would indulge in promiscuity without any trappings of social commitment whatsoever. This is a most disturbing state of affairs, as we are not generally used to such behaviour in our mainstream daily lives.

The community fabric that we are so very proud of would soon be a distant memory of the past in Kolkata. The kind of care that we used to exhibit in public life *vis-à-vis* our fellow citizens is fast on its inevitable way out. There have been recent disquieting incidents where pedestrians have collapsed on the streets of Kolkata to die in full view of thousands of passers-by and shopkeepers. Nobody was interested to help or reach out because of the fear of police harassment. There are also heartening incidents where cab drivers have voluntarily returned money and jewelry and expensive mobile phones to their rightful owners with the help of the police. So all is not yet lost. Convent-educated school children still go to voluntarily serve in the slums. So there is yet hope that Kolkata would still be able to redeem its dignity and humanity and march on against heavy odds.

ANNEXURE-3

Violence of Politics and the Politics of Violence[3]

Prasenjit Maiti

West Bengal is something of an exception in India's contemporary political landscape. Whereas many states have experienced political instability over the past two decades, West Bengal has been relatively well governed since 1977. That stability has been remarkable because it has not been the result of low levels of political mobilization; West Bengal probably was India's most politically mobilized and chaotic state in the 1960s. West Bengal's restoration and maintenance of political order naturally direct our attention to the issue of how growing crises of governability can be reversed.

—Atul Kohli 1991[1]

The above contention no more holds true in absolute terms. West Bengal is about to go to the legislative assembly polls in less than a year (early to mid-2001?), and it is being widely conjectured in the media within and outside the state that this election would be especially violent as there are chances of a change of guard in Left Front ruled West Bengal for the first time since 1977.

Whether incited by such popular speculation or not, the general law and order situation in West Bengal has been adversely affected to create governance problems. The situation has become so critical that the Communist Party of India (Marxist), the LF's Big Brother, has now demanded that the Trinamul Congress supremo, Mamata Banerjee, should be immedia-tely arrested for rabble-rousing while the Opposition has, in its turn, even pressed for imprisonment of the Chief Minister, Jyoti Basu himself—this is indeed a rather disquieting state of affairs.

The CPM has even lashed out against American Consulate officials visiting violence-affected Nanur in Birbhum district while Mamata Banerjee described her rally at Chamkaitala in Midnapore district as the Second War of Independence (9 August 2000) against the state government. General terms of political discourse in West Bengal are changing fundamentally, and civil society in the state has to now interface with a certain language of politics that is bereft of the traditional Bengali cultural baggage.

It is true that the Bengali *bhadralok*[2] had generally helped institutionalize a "tradition of unorthodoxy"[3] since the days of undivided Bengal. This is perceived in the archetypal Bengali *bhadralokian* psyche and lineage of anti-establishment, left-of-centre politics since the days of India's national liberation movement. But whatever is happening in the state today is quite unprecedented in terms of political violence, with the probable exception of the brief Naxalite movement (late 1960s-early 1970s) that was radical (?), iconoclastic and somewhat non-sensitized to its clientele among the tea plantation labourers in North Bengal. This movement, in the course of its excesses, was eventually removed from *bhadralokian* support.

However, it must also be added that progressive public opinion in West Bengal was outraged at the coercive manner in which Siddhartha Shankar Ray's Congress government dealt with this movement. Their (the Naxalites) attempts at making short work of the revolution had the paradoxical impact of strengthening the forces of counter-revolution.[4]

The CPM now alleges that the TMC and its uneasy electoral ally, the Bharatiya Janata Party, are allied with big landowners/*jotedars*—this reactionary class equation is responsible for the disturbing spate of agrarian violence in districts like Midnapore, Bankura, Hooghly and Birbhum, to cite just a few instances. The TMC denies this, however, arguing in turn that it is the ruling party that has its back to the wall, and is desperately fighting a strategic battle of position(s) to continue in office even after the next assembly election in West Bengal.

If the bourgeois print/electronic media reports[5] are to be given any credence and their contents analyzed, one would come to the conclusion that this agrarian violence is, after all, being provoked by the possibility of a change in the Left Front regime in West Bengal. While the ruling party-led coalition is fighting a battle of dispossession the Opposition is intent on proliferation—and everything is happening rather thick and fast in rural Bengal where, according to the West Bengal government, land redistribution since 1977[6] (Operation Barga) has almost reached its logical culmination.

Dwaipayan Bhattacharyya, however, disagrees, and points out that "The CPI(M) excelled in what may be regarded as the 'politics of middleness'... Irrespective of its claims to the contrary, the CPI(M) has brought about a gradual de-radicalisation in the character of redistributive reforms in rural West Bengal over the 1980s."[7]

This is not to suggest, however, that the cities in West Bengal are any more safe. There was a lot of violence during the by-poll in the recent Salt Lake City civic polls (June 2000) in the neighbourhood of Calcutta. The CPM scraped through by a single seat majority here. The Calcutta Municipal Corporation, however, was wrested by the TMC from the Left Front; this election was also marked by 'severe' irregularities, according to the media. Compare this with incidents of violence against newspersons[8] in the Uttarpara civic polls in Hooghly district (August 2000) where the TMC won by a considerable margin. Such incidents of rural and urban violence are indicators of non-governance in the state, and able analyses of such problems of rule are required if the situation is to be somewhat salvaged.

The background to this political violence was in the making quite sometime back. The CPM state committee came out with a draft resolution[9] in the not-so-recent past where it was admitted that the performance of the Left Front had deteriorated during the period 1987-1997 in West Bengal. This document also conceded that a downhill slide in governance was quite evident in West Bengal after the tenure of the first two Left Front governments (1977 and 1982) in the state. This resolution also criticized the lack of coordination in the cabinet as well as in the government.

Apart from the immediate news reports of fresh violence from different areas of West Bengal, another more important issue is at stake. This concerns the state's level of political culture. The Bengali *bhadralok* as a social category was more or less secure in its cocoon of high culture. But the political events of the state are fast proving beyond reasonable doubt that West Bengal is perhaps no more superior, in terms of governance, even to Bihar, the constant reference point of the present Left Front government.

But all this is part of a larger reality. West Bengal is now passing through the doldrums, so to say. Limited employment opportunities, an indecisive pace of industrialization made worse by a much-criticized education policy (leading to a flight of human resource from the state), little or no health infrastructure and, finally, limited visions of a leadership that cannot perhaps problematize and coordinate liberal democratic decentralized governance with the basic tenets of democratic centralism.

"The point that is driven home here is that the self-governing institutions such as panchayats and municipalities, or for that matter, popular participation and self-governance, are incompatible with the omnipotent presence of a hierarchically organised and centralised communist party. One can mobilise others, but cannot become the substitute for others' participation which is an activity valued in itself. The notion of grassroots democracy cannot then, truly be accommodated within the discourse of communist modernity which is dominating."[10]

So West Bengal's history of rule since 1977 till today is largely an account of the CPM's attempts to expand its support base, proliferate its mass organizations and develop the networks of patron-client relationship among the state government employees, trade unions, the intelligentsia and academics, the panchayats and cooperatives, big business (a much later trend), banking and finance institutions and other similar interest/pressure groups. The Left Front governments and the CPM were gradually fused as a monolithic identity in this process.

Harihar Bhattacharyya has interrogated the near absence of democracy at the grassroots in West Bengal and holds both the CPI(M)'s style of local-level governance as well as the "conceptual inadequacy of the masses" responsible for such a state of affairs.[11] Prabir Das Ghosh notes that the Left Front government's attempts at cooperative mobilization coupled with rural development measures are not isolated phenomena from the viewpoint of left politics. Ghosh adds that the Left Front has utilized all the cooperative institutions, politicized panchayats and other left-led peasant organizations as instruments of politics and of rural development.[12]

Subrata K Mitra cautions that "If the wielders of power concede the point to those who challenge established values and norms, they risk losing their legitimacy. On the other hand, the failure to give satisfaction to the discontented might deepen their sense of outrage and alienation which can further reduce their legitimacy."[13]

It cannot possibly be true that West Bengal's rulers are entirely lacking in political goodwill or administrative competence; perhaps they cannot effectively implement their collective vision of progress/stability in the state. Moreover, the Bengali civil society lacks a dynamic public sphere (since the days of the Naxalite Movement that was prematurely aborted and had, in its turn, effected a paradigm shift of sorts in the mainstream Bengali ethos) that could have meaningfully cohered a political dialogue with the state apparatuses.

Nobody can anymore think of a Brave New World in West Bengal; this has, in effect, actively discouraged the evolution of a creative civil society-state interface in the state. Perhaps the reasons are not too difficult to seek; today's political violence reminds one of the last days of the Siddhartha Shankar Ray-led Congress government in West Bengal[14] when Congress absolutism had reached a climax of political perversion.

The Emergency [a brain child of Ray among others (1975-77)] had been imposed, and Opposition in West Bengal was sought to be gagged by press censorship, political violence and police repression. But democracy bounced back with the first ever Left Front government being elected to office in the state.

It was now "politics as usual", informed (at least partially) by an essential *bhadralokian* ethos. In conclusion, this much can be cautioned that those of us who tend to forget history have generally been condemned to repeat it—only time would prove whether history has come a full circle in West Bengal since the "euphoria of deliverance" of 1977.

Acknowledgments

The author is grateful to Dr Harihar Bhattacharyya, Professor of Political Science at the University of Burdwan, India for insights into the Left Front's governance in West Bengal based on field research and the CPM's inner party documents (unattributable). I also wish to thank Dr Pamela G Price, Professor of South Asian History at the University of Oslo, Norway for her kind suggestions regarding how really to go about drafting this article. It was suggested that the focus should not primarily be on formal political institutions in West Bengal, but that informal institutions (like factions) and values, as well as the (implicit) ideologies associated with them, should also be researched. See Sajal Basu, *Factions, Ideology and Politics: Coalition Politics in Bengal*, Minerva, Calcutta, 1990, in this connection.

NOTES AND REFERENCES

1. Atul Kohli, *Democracy and Discontent: India's Growing Crisis of Governability*, Cambridge University Press, Cambridge, 1991, Ch. 10, p. 267.
2. See John H Broomfield, *Elite Conflict in a Plural Society: Twentieth Century Bengal*, University of California Press, Berkeley, 1968, for both conceptual and episodic treatments of the Bengali *bhadralok*.
3. See Marcus F Franda, 'West Bengal', in Myron Weiner (ed), *State Politics in India*, Princeton University Press, Princeton, 1968, p. 249.
4. See Apurba Mukhopadhyay, 'The Left in West Bengal: Government and Movement, 1967-1982', in Rakhahari Chatterji (ed), *Politics in West Bengal: Institutions, Processes and Problems*, World Press, Calcutta, 1985, Ch. 4, p. 95.
5. See newspapers like *Anandabazar Patrika*, *Bartaman* (in Bengali), *The Statesman*, *The Telegraph* and *The Asian Age* in this connection.

6. See, for related insights, Ben Rogally, Barbara Harriss-White and Sugata Bose (eds), *Sonar Bangla? Agricultural Growth and Agrarian Change in West Bengal and Bangladesh*, Sage, New Delhi, 1999.
7. Dwaipayan Bhattacharyya, 'Politics of Middleness: The Changing Character of the Communist Party of India (Marxist) in Rural West Bengal (1977-90)', in *ibid.*, Part 2, Ch. 10, pp. 279-300.
8. This led to debates in the Union Parliament and protest demonstrations in Calcutta.
9. See *Anandabazar Patrika*, 3 December 1997, pp. 1 and 8.
10. See Harihar Bhattacharyya, *Micro Foundations of Bengal Communism*, Ajanta, Delhi, 1998, p. 186.
11. Harihar Bhattacharyya, 'Democracy and Rural Governance in West Bengal Since 1978', in Sobhanlal Datta Gupta (ed), *India—Politics and Society, Today and Tomorrow: Essays in Honour of Professor Amal Kumar Mukhopadhyay*, K.P. Bagchi, Calcutta, 1998, pp. 227-240.
12. See his unpublished doctoral thesis (Burdwan University, 1998), 'Rural Cooperatives, Left Politics and Rural Development in West Bengal Since 1977: A Case Study of the District of Burdwan', p. 268.
13. Subrata K Mitra, 'Legitimacy, Governance and Political Institutions in India After Independence', in Mitra and Dietmar Rothermund (eds), *Legitimacy and Conflict in South Asia*, Manohar, New Delhi, 1997, p. 23.
14. During the first half of the 1970s, the so-called decade of liberation. This was due to the Naxalite Movement.

ANNEXURE-4

Monsoon Music

Prasenjit Maiti[4]
23 July 2006

Heavy showers unleashed by a somewhat delayed monsoon have flooded Kolkata nowadays. The picture is identical almost everywhere. Perhaps one of the worst-hit zones in terms of water-logging is Sector Five of Salt Lake City, the prestigious and elite township situated on the eastern fringes of Kolkata. Ministers, politicians, bureaucrats, doctors, engineers, industrialists, businessmen and professionals reside at Salt Lake City. In fact an address at Salt Lake City is in itself a status symbol.

Sector Five was earlier known as Salt LEC *i.e.* Salt Lake Electronics Complex. Now it has been recently rechristened as *Naba Diganta i.e.* New Horizon. The communist rulers of West Bengal have ostensibly come a long way from 1977 when they first came to power. They had banned the entry of computers in the state, stopped teaching English at the primary level and even contemplated training an entire generation of barefoot doctors (quacks) to complement the mainstream public health system that they considered to be inadequately equipped at that point of time.

The state government has since then reversed its policy priorities. It has reintroduced English teaching at the primary level and is trying its level best to woo the big names in the information technology sector to invest in West Bengal. Infosys is yet to enter while Wipro, IBM, Price Waterhouse Coopers, Cognizant, TCS, Mindtree etc have already established their operations at Sector Five in Salt Lake City.

Salt LEC will soon become a Notified Area. It will no longer be under the jurisdiction of the Bidhan Nagar Municipality. The government authorities have decided to upgrade the civic amenities of Naba Diganta. Improved road connectivity, enhanced condition of roads, better public transport facilities, tightened security, vigilant law and order situation, solid waste management, sewerage and drainage, street lighting, piped drinking water supply etc are the major concerns at the present moment.

The rains this season have exposed the inadequate civic facilities available at Naba Diganta. This is supposed to be the information technology hub of West Bengal where multinational giants have started their operations on a more or less reasonable scale. Call Centers have been set up and software development is taking place simultaneously to cater to growing domestic and international demands.

Kolkata is fast catching up with technopolises like Bangalore and Hyderabad (Cyberabad). Some of the best brains of the country work at Naba Diganta. These whiz kids mint fortunes in terms of their pay packets and are seen jet setting along the new information technology horizons of Kolkata. Formal training in information technology enabled services and business management is the key to open the magical doors of success: a ticket to Silicon Valley and a Green Card along with the Non-Resident Indian status.

But the picture that has emerged this monsoon is indeed a sorry one. All around vehicles have broken down, half submerged in water. Traffic has almost come to a standstill. Dirty and turbid water has entered the wonderful and futuristic office complexes that are architectural marvels of steel and glass. Litter is floating on the water and spreading everywhere. As far as the eyes go there is water, water everywhere but not a drop to drink.

White collar labourers are stuck on the flooded thoroughfares of Sector Five along with their blue collar menials. The streets resemble rivers. People cannot enter or get down from their generally low slung cars for fear of water entering the inside of these vehicles. Cars have broken down, as water has entered their exhaust pipes and choked their silencers.

It is as if all hell has broken loose and the rain gods above have unleashed their pent-up furies against a city that is saturated in sin and senselessness. New cars like the Maruti Swift, Toyota Innova, Maruti Wagon R, Maruti Zen, Tata Indigo, Toyota Qualis, Honda City, Honda Civic, Hyundai Santro, Tata Indica, Tata Sumo Victa, Fiat Uno, Daewoo Matiz etc have generally failed to swim through the waters of hell that are swirling in an angry manner all around Naba Diganta.

Upwardly mobile Kolkata residents had so far read about the Mumbai floods last year or even this year. They have seen pictures flashed across the flat screens of their expensive television sets of film stars and celebrities getting stuck in the rains. They have also read about the erosion of River Ganga elsewhere in the state where poor and hapless people have lost their homes and hearth due to changes in river courses catalyzed by torrential rains. But apocalypse now appears to be the present mood of nature *vis-à-vis* Kolkata, and especially Sector Five of Salt Lake City.

The ineptitude of the civic authorities both in the Kolkata Municipal Corporation as well as in Bidhannagar Municipality is partially responsible for this dismal state of affairs. Drains have not been cleared on a periodic basis. Plastic wastes have clogged the catchpits and drainage outfalls. This has led to choking of drains and obstruction of their free passages. So rains and storm water cause backflow of wastewater onto the city roads and even into private premises.

Kolkata is supposed to be logistic hub centering around which the Government of India's much-hyped Look East Policy will be implemented to promote economic development and better road/rail/water/air connectivity in South and East Asia. New roads, airports, Special Economic Zones, townships, knowledge cities, health cities, food parks, chemical hubs, textile parks, bridges, flyovers, interchanges, automobile factories, software development centers, industrial complexes etc will be designed and constructed in this connection. But the future will not be secured until and unless basic amenities are provided efficiently in and around Kolkata.

ANNEXURE-5

Health Hazards[5]

Prasenjit Maiti
20 August 2006

The public health system of Kolkata and West Bengal are despicable, to say the least. While the Health Minister has retained his portfolio after the latest State Legislative Assembly Elections, his Department is steadily sliding downhill in terms of efficiency and accountability. Cats, dogs and mice frequent the Wards of Government Hospitals and Primary Health Centers. Mice nibbled away the eyes of a patient at a Government Hospital in Kolkata last year. Frequent skirmishes take place between junior doctors and patient parties, following deaths caused by negligence and lack of proper medical attention. The situation is deplorable and made worse by the apparent indifference of the powers that be. Health Minister Dr Surjyakanta Mishra is famous for his rebuttals to the media and lack of adequate sensitivity to public health issues. Dr Mishra is disengaged, so to say, and immune to criticism from the Press and even from Chief Minister Buddhadeb Bhattacharjee, who has on more than one occasion (even during the recent electoral campaign) expressed his serious displeasure and grave concern about the state of the public health service delivery system in West Bengal.

The public health system of West Bengal suffers from certain critical limitations such as inadequate government funds, shortage of skilled manpower, equipment, medicines, infrastructural resources etc. Add to that the enormous pressure of patients on the system. Even today the hapless majority visit Government Hospitals and Primary Health Centres for treatment. But there is yet another aspect of this story. Doctors generally do not want to serve in the remote districts that are not well-connected with urban metropolitan centers. Nurses more often than not are found wanting in proper execution of their professional duties. Expensive medical equipment is not used properly and breaks down as a result. Poor patients are thus compelled to visit private pathological clinics for different types of expensive examinations. Their food is often sold in the open market (according to media reports). A class of persons calling themselves attendants are found in Government Hospitals. They can arrange for extra medical care and special attention, nutritious food and proper treatment supported by the presence of personal nurses. This is yet again an entirely illegal system that (according to the media) thrives in the public health system of West Bengal.

Global initiatives that focus on health system strengthening work with country-level stakeholders must concentrate on priority-ranking the multicultural issues that inform the dynamics of health sectors in developing countries like India. Public health is often a context-bound concern that is underpinned by the specifics of ground-level realities. Inputs provided by country-level stakeholders are identity-driven, as the choice of inputs itself is a value-loaded exercise. So the construct of health issues in the public sphere is occasionally an expression of social reflexes. This is especially noticed in the general response patterns of society to incidence of HIV/AIDS, leprosy, Sexually Transmitted Diseases, Multiple Personality Disorders etc. Global initiatives have not yet comprehensively addressed priorities like augmentation of social capital and facilitation of civil societal resources that constitute the core of health systems among related concerns. No meaningful progress can be achieved in developing countries regarding health issues without first cohering an empowered civil society that is based on networks of mutual trust and cooperation and at least a working notion of human rights. A Health Systems Action Network can effectively contribute in terms of accountability, transparency and efficiency to ensure good governance in terms of medical care for those primary stakeholders who happen to be the so-called beneficiaries of health systems in developing countries. Past funding in the health sector by the World Bank and present prospective funding for health sector reforms by the

Department for International Development of United Kingdom are topical examples of bilateral support to build local capacities for globalized efforts.

One such worldwide public health initiative is the Pulse Polio Program of the World Health Organization that is implemented by the Government of India in association with the state governments. Global initiatives to eradicate small pox and tackle tuberculosis have been successful in India. But diseases like plague, malaria and dengue still visit India, especially West Bengal. This indicates serious lacunae in our health system. A certain section of society is convinced that if male children were allowed to take polio drops they would be rendered impotent in their adolescence. This widespread conviction has often led to the defeat of this program. On the other hand, several cases of child mortality have occurred in West Bengal due to defective polio drops. This is criminal negligence and cannot be tolerated. Chief Minister Buddhadeb Bhattacharjee keeps on harping on certain fundamental issues of good governance such as transparency, accountability, efficiency, honesty and promptitude. His famous Do It Now slogan has by now entered the folklore of Bengal and found a permanent place in the country's political rhetoric like the late Sanjay Gandhi's Talk Less Work More slogan. But Bhattacharjee's repeated exhortations have failed to evoke any public spiritedness on the part of the state government's health department staff members and health workers. The popular imagination of the poor in West Bengal has realized only too well that all is not in proper order in the state in terms of public health.

Media reports keep on pointing out that workers at Swasthya Bhavan at Sector Five of Salt Lake City arrive at office around 11:00 AM and leave around 3:00 PM whereas the official working hours are 10:00 AM till 5:30 PM. This callous and indifferent attitude towards a most critical public service (funded by Government Agencies and International Donor Organizations) that can make or break lives cannot be lightly treated. Even Government Hospitals at Kolkata are nothing short of living hell. Several patients littered across one bed, others writhing in agony on the floor, eating food not fit for human consumption, lying prostrate at the mercy of junior doctors and nurses, often victim to wrong treatment ... the sordid list relentlessly goes on and on and on. A pro-poor and pro-people government (that the Left Front claims itself to be) cannot really afford to indulge in such casual toying with poor people's lives. We are talking about real persons here and not just issues and concerns of development that happen to impact all of us in an uneven manner during the course of the politics of our everyday lives.

Public health is a most critical issue that requires proper planning and comprehensive execution at the administrative levels in order to ensure sensitive handling of cases that are all unique. It is true that extra care and attention cannot be practically ensured in all the cases but at least patients expect a humane approach from doctors and nurses and health workers. The Hippocratic Oath should be upheld at all times to ensure the human face of public health.

ANNEXURE-6

Populist Governance[6]

Prasenjit Maiti
6 August 2006

The case of West Bengal is a classical study that indicates how copybook communists conforming to different shades of ideologies ranging from pink socialism to hardcore Marxism-Leninism have grappled with the realities of Statecraft in order to continue in office for close to three decades since 1977 when they first came to power following the conclusion of the infamous Emergency (1975-77).

The Communist Party of India (Marxist) has always led the successive Left Front Governments that have ruled West Bengal since 1977 when the first Left Front Government came to power by riding the wave of the historic socialist movement led by veteran leader Jayaprakash (JP) Narayan. Prominent Left Front allies have been the Communist Party of India (that joined later), the Forward Bloc and the Revolutionary Socialist Party. Other smaller parties are also part of this ruling coalition.

We would concentrate exclusively on the evolution of the CPI (M) as the leading party in power that has effectively tackled the demerits of incumbency to institutionalize a series of stints in government that has redefined the meaning of regime in order to identify it with the more value-loaded term of hegemony. The party has effectively reconciled the apparently divergent trends of movement and government so as to evolve as a unique practical political outfit that depends on organization, entrenchment, networks, patron-client relationships and a pragmatic pro-people/pro-poor image that can radically declass itself as and when required.

The first ever Left Front Government adopted certain important policy decisions. These were relevant in the volatile political context of the mid-1970s when the single party dominant rule of the monolithic Indian National Congress led by Indira Gandhi was effectively challenged by the upsurge of an alternative politics that was supposed to have emerged from the grassroots and supported by local as well as regional long-term aims and aspirations.

Such new political ambitions were not entirely unexpected. A long and sustained period of Congress rule had led to a profound sense of relative deprivation on the part of the local political actors that were eager to play in the multicultural and pluralist political arena of the Indian liberal democratic system. Another critical factor that was operational in this regard in West Bengal was the misgovernance factor.

West Bengal was not properly governed during the decade of 1967-77 that has been described by various political scientists and social historians as the critical and disturbed period of *interregnum* that was provoked by successive Union Front Governments led by Ajoy Mukerjee of Bangla Congress that was a breakaway splinter from the ruling Congress Party led by Prafulla Chandra Sen. Profound cabinet instability marked both the Union Front Governments that were formed in 1967 and 1969.

Jyoti Basu of the CPI (M) happened to be the Deputy Chief Minister in Ajoy Mukherjee's Cabinet. This was an ideological dichotomy of the Union Front Governments that experimented with strange bedfellows like the communists (who were more radical in their political outlook at this point of time) and the mainstream Bangla Congress leadership that was more comfortable with the centrist mode of politics informed by the norms and conventions of the parliamentary democratic system.

Radical firebrand leaders such as Harekrishna Konar and Subodh Banerjee led the land grab and *gherao* movements to ensure social justice in the state. But the fact that they themselves were part of the Establishment during this period confused their political agenda further and subsequently led to a period of total anarchy and misrule against a most volatile political background that ultimately facilitated growth of the well-known Naxalite Movement during the late 1960s till the early 1970s.

The incidents of armed insurgency led by the Maoist outfits (that maintain liaison with their counterparts in Nepal) in West Bengal during the present decade point to the fact that the basic tenets of organized protest are still very much present in the state. Poverty, inadequate development, unemployment etc continue to haunt the communists in office.

Even starvation deaths have been reported widely in the popular media. Security forces have cracked down upon the militants while the rebels themselves have inflicted heavy casualties on the police personnel deployed in the arid and generally backward districts such as Purulia, Bankura and West Midnapore.

The Maoist rebels who frequent the forest areas of these districts are heavily armed and use remote-controlled explosives and anti-personnel landmines to challenge the police forces. Their communication networks are well-maintained and the local villagers act as their conduits of information either for fear or favour.

These rebels are also located in states like Andhra Pradesh and Bihar where they fight bloody wars with the security forces and illegal private armies of feudal landlords. Maoist rebels are gradually trying to establish a regional alliance in South Asia. They have already influenced the course of history in neighbouring Nepal where the King has been forced to usher in an era of parliamentary constitutional reforms led by the democratic parties.

Indian communist leaders have even taken part in deliberations with the Maoist leaders of Nepal to initiate this process of a historic transfer of power. This indicates a steady understanding between the CPM and the Maoists in the international context while the picture is entirely different in the case of West Bengal.

ANNEXURE-7

Ideological Insurgency[7]

Prasenjit Maiti
30 July 2006

The Naxalite Movement signified the end of values and ideology for an entire generation. Subsequent generations did not feel enthused to follow the path of armed struggle for liberation. This end of a dream actually spelt out the onset of degeneration for the children of an abortive revolution.

This agrarian movement was ideologically located well within the tradition of the Tebhaga and Telengana Movements that emerged due to agrarian injustice and oppression exercised on the part of the unduly privileged classes who were a product of the Permanent Settlement introduced by Lord Cornwallis way back in 1793 in Undivided Bengal. The landless agricultural labourers, the share-croppers and the tenant farmers were the worst affected classes under this land revenue system that created a category of absentee landlords who stayed in their estates in Kolkata (erstwhile Calcutta) and elsewhere and depended upon their managerial staff to collect revenue. The Zamindari Abolition Act and the Land Ceiling Act were passed in the 1950s to secure agrarian justice but land reforms in the objective sense of the term were not carried out till 1977 in West Bengal.

Student intellectuals of Kolkata were inspired by the revolutionary teachings of Mao Ze Dong (Chairman of the Chinese Communist Party). These student activists mainly joined the Naxalite Movement from the famous Presidency College of Kolkata that was established as the Hindu College way back in 1817 even before Calcutta University was founded in 1857.

Naxalite leaders believed in radical doctrines such as the source of power lies in the barrel of the gun and that the

Parliament is a pigsty where revisionists and reactionaries conspire with the bourgeoisie to relentlessly oppress the proletarian classes by institutionalizing a mode of production whose productive forces adversely condition the uneven relations of production by hoarding any surplus value created by the labourers.

But the essential problem with the Naxalite Movement was that it was organized by city-bred young intellectuals who cherished a noble dream without being equipped with the resources that were required to transform their vision of egalitarian social change into reality. Student leaders had no organic intellectual or even psychological connection whatsoever with the grassroots represented by the tea garden workers for whom they first took up arms against the police and state authorities at Naxalbari Village in North Bengal.

It is worthwhile to note at this point that more prominent Naxalite leaders like Charu Mazumdar, Kanu Sanyal and Jangal Santal had formed a new political outfit called the Communist Party of India (Marxist-Leninist) by breaking away from the CPI(M) that had itself broken away from the Communist Party of India in 1964 due to differences in perception about the bourgeois democratic revolution and the people's democratic revolution among other related ideological concerns.

Naxalite leaders subsequently championed the politics of assassination that soon degenerated into the politics of vendetta led by the lumpen proletariat. The high point of this period of misgovernance was reached during the infamous Baranagar-Cossipore Killings in North Kolkata when allegedly CPI(M) and Congress activists rounded up and massacred several Naxal supporters (with the help of the police authorities) during one single night.

Failures of the Naxalite Movement point to certain political lessons. This was an early attempt to conjoin the issue of economic development with the ethics of governance but the movement still was destined not to succeed because it was not supported by a mass base, perspective planning, organizational strength, visionary leadership and essential resources. The type of urban guerilla warfare that the Naxalite activists had started practicing ultimately backfired when stiff resistance was offered by their political opponents and the police forces (who were reported to have engaged in a series of fake encounters to liquidate Naxal leaders and their followers).

This aborted movement signified virtually the end of a revolutionary dream and the end of the so-called project of emancipation. One must remember that this period also witnessed the Liberation War in East Pakistan that culminated in the creation of Bangladesh just across the international border. Refugee influx into West Bengal was a critical problem during this period. This problem in fact continued right from the Partition of India and Independence at 1947. The communists promptly utilized the refugees as a political weapon to agitate against the ruling Congress Party during the 1950s and 1960s.

The 1950s and 1960s constituted the disturbed period when several communist-led agitations took place, including the food movements that were organized to protest against the public distribution system policies of the Congress Government. The infamous War for a Pice also occurred at this juncture to protest against the fair hike in public trams.

The communists did not allow the refugees to resettle in the Andaman and Nicobar Islands and Dandakaranya. But it was an irony of history that the first Left Front Government unleashed police repression against the refugees at Marichjhanpi in 1978.

ANNEXURE-8

Terror and Trauma[8]

Prasenjit Maiti
16 July 2006

This week Kolkata had to share the trauma of terrorist attacks against Mumbai, India's commercial capital. A red alert was declared throughout the state of West Bengal, and this included the city of Kolkata, India's cultural capital. Railway stations and airports and major industrial centers along with public offices were put under strict surveillance.

The authorities even carried out large-scale evictions of illegal encroachers along the Eastern Metropolitan Bypass on the fringes of Kolkata in order to carry out the road widening works of this important thoroughfare. Security was cited as a sensitive issue to dismantle the illegal structures along a sizable section of this road. Widespread speculation was fanned by the incident of an explosion inside a parked car at Jadavpur in South Kolkata. Apparently the reason for this explosion was the presence of a carbon dioxide gas cylinder that was inside the vehicle. But the police arrested the owner of the car and have started investigations in this regard.

It is a well-documented fact that insurgents from Pakistan and Bangladesh have been using Kolkata as a safe haven for quite sometime now. We keep on reading about incidents where police forces from outside West Bengal have nabbed wanted criminals from Kolkata without soliciting any intelligence backup or logistic support from the local authorities, anticipating information leaks at strategic levels. Even shootouts and encounters have taken place in the heart of Kolkata without the local police authorities having any advance information on the same.

The long and insecure international border that West Bengal shares with Bangladesh is porous, to say the least.

Smuggling of cows, rice, narcotics and gold and trafficking in women and children are among the several illegal activities that take place in the border area. Coupled with this is the constant terror of crossfire between the Border Security Force and Bangladesh Rifles. While the BSF tries to pushback illegal immigrants, the BDR ensures that the Indian security forces' actions and attempts are thwarted, according to Press and Media sources.

Some years back there was this infamous terrorist attack against security personnel stationed in front of American Center at Kolkata. The gang responsible for this daredevil attack in broad daylight was later identified as an inter-state criminal organization that also specializes in kidnapping of celebrities. Terror is a mind game that is targeted to numb the citizens' morale and emasculate the State's repressive apparatuses. It is an intellectual resource whose physical deployment is a constant reminder of forces that operate within and without national boundaries for ulterior purposes of evil.

Security preparedness of the local police authorities needs to be upgraded at all levels. This is also true for combating the radical left activists in the state. Even the Chief Minister's residence is apparently not quite safe. It is true that inadequate economic development and growth of militant radical left politics are complementary forces, but it is also relevant to explore the ways and means to strengthen the State's vigil so that the lives and properties of peace-loving and innocent civilians are safeguarded.

Gory incidents like the Mumbai explosions prove how insecure we all are in this age when terror has been globalized in its philosophy, impacts and application. Kolkata should be always alert to avert such incidents in the future. But the cosmopolitan character of Kolkata is a hindrance to locate strangers. The assassin of Phulan Devi (Bandit Queen turned Member of Parliament) was recently arrested from Kolkata by the police force of another state. This indicates the lack of confidence in Kolkata Police on the part of other police forces.

West Bengal is under constant threat from insurgents of terrorist organizations located in Pakistan, Bangladesh and even Nepal, where the Maoist rebels have recently succeeded to topple the last Hindu King from his throne and have entered the constitutional arena of parliamentary politics.

India's muddle and meddle foreign policy is largely responsible for this sorry state of affairs. We have failed to exhibit the iron hand in the velvet glove whenever and wherever required. Kicks and kisses were required to maintain a viable balance of power in South Asia, but we have constantly toyed with the morale of our military forces and have chosen the wrong allies at historically wrong junctures.

India should have consolidated her military gains during the series of wars it had fought since Independence. But she had squandered the military advantages in the name of *Panchasheel* policy that propagates non-aggression, non-interference, mutually peaceful existence and regional cooperation etc. But critical issues like Kashmir and Siachen cannot be simply solved on the basis of goodwill. Confidence-building measures also fail in the face of transborder terrorism.

So tough measures short of actual warfare appear to be the only solution. Riding piggyback on Big Brother United States will not actually help India, as the USA will never ever allow India to emerge as a regional superpower in South Asia. So strategic alliance with China and Russia would appear to be the short-term tactical policy that India should adopt in order to fight terrorism in Kashmir and elsewhere in the country.

The lessons for Kolkata in this context are to tighten community vigil and citizen watch in all public and private places that have sensitive value or strategic importance. Terrorists are cowards in the final estimation, so community policing is an essential requirement at this hour of crisis when the security of the state is in grave question.

ANNEXURE-9

Gender Violence in Contemporary West Bengal[9]

Prasenjit Maiti
18 June 2006

We would argue that gender violence is more often than not a statement of the dominant male political discourse over and above the "other" female self, and in this sense it is an exercise in critical negotiations with the androgynous heterogeneity of the masculine psyche. This is the initial position we adopt while discoursing on gender violence irrespective of ethnicity, class, religion or even culture. We cannot afford to discuss sexual violence without addressing a statement of power like penetration that has been offset in the feminist vocabulary with a term of discourse like engulfment.

Much of today's feminist movement began with the ontology of equal rights with men but even this metaphor could not quite carve out the niche of women as the "otherness" of men over and above the discrete culture paradigms of the male ego.

The problem appears much more compounded in the context of India's melting pot of civilization where values, ethos and perceptions have been exposed to different systems of belief and politics of everyday life since time immemorial. So the problem of gender violence in India (and especially in a highly mobilized state like West Bengal) is predicated upon analyses that are much more complicated than the black/white scenario informed by mutually exclusive categories of understanding.

The Problem

India's National Commission for Women was established in January 1992 as a statutory body under the National Commission for Women Act 1990 (Act No. 20 of 1990 of the Government of India) to review the constitutional and legal safeguards for women, recommend remedial legislative measures, facilitate redress of grievances and advise the Government on all policy matters that affect women.

The NCW has adopted a multi-directional strategy to tackle the problem of gender violence. The Commission works toward spread of legal awareness among women, building as well as developing their capacities to use their rights. It helps women redress their grievances by way of pre-litigation services. Parivarik Mahila Lok Adalats are organized in different parts of the country to expedite the delivery of justice, review the existing provisions of the Constitution and other laws affecting women and recommend necessary amendments in this connection.

The Complaints and Counseling Cell of the Commission processes complaints related to domestic violence, dowry-related torture, desertion, bigamy, rape, refusal to register FIR, cruelty/deprivation by husband, gender discrimination and sexual harassment at work place.

West Bengal: Myth and Reality

There is a general civil societal perception in the state and elsewhere that the Bengali Hindu middle class *bhadralokian* ethos serves to prevent reduce gender violence. Bengal has always had "a tradition of unorthodoxy" conjoined by a higher degree of political mobilization than most other regions of the country that are more often not identified with male chauvinistic values whose historical roots may well be traced back to the feudal mores.

Such systems of dominant male belief never really addressed women as the essential other but considered the feminine from within a construction moored in sexist and discriminatory perceptions. The woman is not really an actor but an agenda that caters to requirements like libido, comforts like housekeeping and necessities like male off-springs.

Despite remarkable progress made in the Nineteenth Century by social reformers during the controversial Bengal Renaissance, it appears that "mainstream" society has only been able to make superficial strides while the deep text of this most problematic discourse as yet remains to be effectively interrogated.

Eve teasing is on the rise in Calcutta and Salt Lake City, witch hunting continues unabated in tribal belts of Midnapore and Purulia, incidents of gang rape are reported from South 24 Parganas, dowry deaths happen in Bengal's cities and villages, instigation to suicide and actual bride burning are not entirely unknown, underprivileged girl children are either smuggled out across the international border to Bangladesh from districts like Malda and Murshidabad, domestic violence is a reality while rape in police custody takes place along with infamous incidents like Bantala and Birati.

Question is: why has gender violence escalated in Bengal since 1994? Is it due to an expanding consumer culture that tends to influence the manner in which a society reacts to mis-governance, gender violence and conventional values? Or is it due to problems of urbanization, unemployment and population explosion that facilitate anomie, indifference/antipathy and erosion of social capital (networks of trust and cooperation within the communitarian discourse) among faceless and "unknown citizens"?

ANNEXURE-10

Women and War[10]

Prasenjit Maiti
30 April 2006

Worst Victims

Among the worst victims of any war are women as, they have been traditionally picked out by the dominant male power as the most vulnerable civilian enemy targets during military engagements. You actually succeed in subverting the very basis of your enemy's virile power if you succeed in violating the enemy's women. Then rape becomes disguised military destruction, as you also inevitably destroy the enemy's morale and legitimacy and his masculine, fighting qualities in this process. Any war necessarily leaves behind a trail of devastation in its bloody wake as noticed in widows and mothers who have lost their sons and sisters who have lost their brothers and daughters who have lost their fathers in action. We read about such feminine suffering in the epics and war novels and watch movies, admire paintings and listen to music that focus on related themes. But reality is perhaps always more disturbing than art. Prisoner of War camps, the handling and exploitation of comfort women by soldiers in combat, Nazi atrocities against women during the Second World War, the collective memory and killing fields of Vietnam: they all bear grim testimony to the fact that woman, being a most ordinary civilian and, therefore, a non-military subject, nevertheless becomes a most prominent military target during invasions. War times are insane moments in human history when the exercise and passage of civilized law and order and governance (let alone good governance) are temporarily suspended to encourage widespread plunder, inhuman brutalities and mayhem.

Impact of Mass Violence

We have to look into the possible impact of mass violence against women and the violence this triggers off as a dangerous chain reaction with mind-blowing consequences. Children suffer, dependents suffer, the service sector of the economy suffers and the entire domestic ethos of a given people may even be destroyed with the destruction of women (not necessarily in the physical sense) and their sanctity in war. Woman has always been the weaker, fairer other in the context of both martial and masculine hegemony. It becomes convenient, therefore, on the part of fighting men to attack and appropriate the women first and, in this logical process of culmination, to eventually appropriate the otherness of the enemy's territoriality with a kind of xenophobic frenzy because the woman in the final assessment is a man's property and nothing much else (according to the dominating male discourse). The enemy is not only then brought to his humble, submissive knees but the very core of his dignity and sanctimonious moral values is also simultaneously ripped out and violated in public. Just recall the Court Scene in the Mahabharata when Queen Draupadi, who was even menstruating at that point of time, was manhandled (without any effective protest whatsoever) before her famous and macho husbands and all the royal elders. Lord Rama fought with Ravana and ultimately killed him over the issue of a single woman: however, Rama also asked his wife Sita to prove her (unspoiled) chastity by entering into a circle of fire once the war was over. Therefore, Rama had fought the war not to prove his affection for Sita but to prove his unfaltering machismo.

Double Jeopardy

It is true that wars have been declared because of women (recall Helen of Troy) and wars have been instigated by women like Cleopatra. But it is an even greater truth that women have always been exploited and finally destroyed during combat. A woman faces a double jeopardy during war: she has to suffer as a woman and she has also to suffer as the symbol of pride, prestige and property of her man. Invading armies have been traditionally given the license to gang rape women, often before their helpless men at gunpoint: this not only results in distorted sexual gratification for the invaders but also effectively breaks down the enemy's final vestiges of any meaningful resistance. So the Women and War interface would come across as both a gender and a humanitarian issue to which global bodies and Non-Government Organizations should accord immediate and topmost priority. They must help formulate agreements like the historic Geneva and Berne Conventions. This would at least constitute the first faltering step towards a better human civilization and a Brave New World in this most insecure new millennium.

Quo Vadis?

But the disturbing question remains: is woman simply a construct that has to be effectively destroyed during warfare or is woman a human category that has to be addressed critically by the discourse of violence and the violence of politics? An opposite trend has emerged in recent times after the invasion of Iraq by the United States of America. Male prisoners of war at the infamous Abu Ghraib Prison have been sexually assaulted and harassed by American security forces that included women personnel. This is a pathetic twist that indicates history making one full turn where human nature tends to avenge human nature by equating sexual domination with power games. Our original position about Women and War thus takes on a different existential stance in the light of recent military engagements worldwide. Abu Ghraib happens to be an exception when one recalls military excesses committed against women in North-East India and (reportedly) in Jammu and Kashmir. Such atrocities are the logical fallout of protracted army presence in civilian areas on the pretext of battling terrorism. Manhunts without any warrant, disrespect to human rights and disregard for the Rule of Law in disturbed times lead to the subversion of moral fabric of any civil society. So much so that the aged women in North-East India protested against the brutality of security forces by parading naked in public.

Reconciliation and Reprieve

There cannot be any conceivable reconciliation between the forces of violence and the subjects of war at such a critical juncture. The only reprieve that one may construe long after the effects of violence have somewhat subsided lies in the core of civil society and social capital that may help conjoin the sanity of the collective with the goodwill of the State. For often it is the State and its array of repressive apparatuses that are responsible for sponsoring violence against women during anti-terrorism military exercises. But the State unleashes its own brand of sexual violence and widespread terror in this process.

Conclusion

There cannot be any convenient conclusion with regard to this most critical discourse on Women and War. But Civil Society Organizations, Voluntary Organizations, human rights activists, peace workers and academic institutions may deliberate upon such disturbing issues in order to explore practical solutions to this problem. Sensitization workshops should be held to train the security forces worldwide so that they may read notions of human rights into military manoeuvres and tactics, and learn to respect the dignity and sovereignty of the human body. It becomes a sort of body politic treatise in this process that teaches one to respect the human body and its sanctity. Force may not always be deployed in a sanitized manner but at least its aftershocks may be restricted to military and not civilian (and therefore vulnerable) soft (?) targets like women.

ANNEXURE-11

Participation as Development[11]

Prasenjit Maiti
18 June 2006

Participation may be defined as purposive interaction that helps primary stakeholders at the grassroots level gain access to decision-making processes either directly or through legitimate institutionalized bodies such as Community-Based Organizations and/or Non-Government Organizations that happen to represent their interests and define their stakes in development projects. The Stakeholders' Consultative Process that emerges as a result of participatory development contends that community involvement is imperative

1. to identify the needs and perceptions of primary stakeholders;
2. to sustain and maintain civic amenities after withdrawal of implementing agencies;
3. to monitor and evaluate the facilities and services created during the project;
4. to institutionalize community-based mechanisms; and
5. to develop trusteeship among the community *vis-à-vis* their civic facilities.

Rapport at the community-level may be achieved by organizing events that mobilize primary stakeholders to share a common platform from where their concerns may be voiced. Such events serve as an entry point to address the community psyche and streamline an interactive process, utilizing which identified Representative Groups may adopt a proactive role in the overall decision-making process and micro-planning of project activities and their implementation.

Rapport-building would also depend on the formal and informal groups capable of impacting the community in terms of interventions. Activities undertaken for initial rapport-building should also be gender-specific, and depend on the willingness to organize such programs on the part of primary stakeholders. Follow-up of the events by way of community-level feedback would help reassess needs and reorient future intervention strategies.

Community mobilization also seeks to cohere social capital at the community-level that would facilitate Monitoring and Evaluation of physical works undertaken during the project. Social capital would also ensure that the community continues to look after its collective assets even after completion of the project. Community participation strategies operate at

1. the communitarian level where the community is brought back into developmental focus in order to sustain a proprietary sense among primary stakeholders, and
2. the neo institutional level where actors and institutions are transformed into actors in institutions *i.e.* end-users of institutionalized civic services are mobilized to identify their personal agenda with community interests.

These are in effect utilitarian tools to motivate the community to become proactive and safeguard collective concerns at the corporate level. Community participation programs may be strategized to streamline developmental interventions and facilitate an interactive dialogue process between primary and secondary stakeholders. Such programs serve to build empathy at the stakeholders' level and facilitate dialogic rather than pedagogic interfaces at the project implementation, monitoring and evaluation levels.

Community mobilization is not an end but a means to secure rapport-building that, in its turn, ensures acceptance of interventions at the community level. This acceptance would finally serve

1. to assess needs with regard to civic services/assets and

physical works, vocational training programs and income-generation,

2. to spread awareness with regard to health and hygiene and safe community practices, and
3. to monitor and evaluate progress of physical works by the community itself.

The Energy and Resources Institute is an NGO consultant to the Asian Development Bank-sponsored Kolkata Environmental Improvement Project (2002-07) jointly implemented by the Kolkata Municipal Corporation and the Irrigation and Waterways Department of the Government of West Bengal in association with the West Bengal Pollution Control Board. TERI is mandated under KEIP to implement the Stakeholders' Consultative Process that is expected to serve as the defining axis of the project during needs assessment exercises with regard to physical infrastructure (such as water supply and sanitation services) as perceived and prioritized by the primary stakeholders.

KEIP aims to upgrade basic urban services and ensure "affordable access" to the same on the part of Project Affected Persons by enhancing their livelihood and raising the material quality of their everyday life. This requires interventions on the part of TERI and its project partner Bharat Sevashram Sangha in terms of community mobilization and participation programs and awareness-generation activities related to health and hygiene, solid waste management, sewerage and drainage and poverty alleviation initiatives (such as short-term vocational training, microfinance networking and income-generation programs).

TERI and BSS have staged street theatre productions and puppet shows as part of its creative communication strategy. These combine mime as well as mass theatre techniques in a participatory manner of performance to disseminate information pertaining to safe waste disposal measures and best practices of urban good governance in the context of overall community development.

TERI and BSS also held sit-and-draw competitions for school children in slums selected under KEIP and subsequently organized community meetings with local women to discuss their specific needs with regard to water supply, sanitation and basic urban services. Vocational training needs analyses were also carried out during such exercises. TERI was able to form the first ever women's Self-Help Group under KEIP at 99 Suren Sarkar Road (a selected slum in East Kolkata) where a short-term vocational training course sponsored by the Community Polytechnic Cell of the Government of India was launched during November 2003. Other SHGs have since then been formed in the project area.

Creative communication strategies will be efficacious during Participatory Monitoring and Evaluation of ongoing physical works. TERI and BSS' field facilitation endeavours with regard to progress of physical works at Pyarabagan Nagarpalli (KEIP's pilot project) and elsewhere helped streamline different ground-level angularities that emerged due to differences in perception between primary and secondary stakeholders with regard to priorities, designs and implementation of physical works.

Creative communication techniques such as street theatre, nature trail events, video displays, wall painting exhibitions and sit-and-draw competitions serve to underpin TERI-BSS' SCP exercises that are generally planned in accordance with the NGO's Social Action Plan. Upscaling of urban infrastructure is more often than not located in the tension between development and displacement: this is particularly reflected in KEIP's Rehabilitation and Resettlement Component. TERI-BSS' creative communication activities seek to resolve such field-level discontent in the most effective manner possible by defining development in a participatory and pro-people mode. Project Affected Persons are conveyed the message with the help of static and dynamic tools that KEIP's development interventions are "for the people, by the people and of the people".

ANNEXURE-12

Reservations and Rebellions[12]

Prasenjit Maiti
28 May 2006

This week in Kolkata the reservation riots are continuing in our health sector. Junior doctors of state-run government hospitals are on the rampage, paralyzing the traffic of downtown Kolkata, refusing to attend to patients in the general wards and even maintaining skeleton staff at the emergency departments although the Honourable Supreme Court of India has passed orders that no patient in a critical condition can be refused medical attention in the emergency departments.

We would not enter into the polemics of the reservation debate in this week's column but would like to attract the attention of our readers to the fact that the public heath sector is still very much vulnerable in a developing country like India where substantial pockets of citizens are yet to uniformly access basic amenities of life such as safe drinking water, sanitation, electricity, roads, safe housing, nutritious food, primary education and emergency medical services.

The Press has recently published multiple lead stories on the reservation issue but a couple of human interest items have merited our attention for obvious reasons. One story dealt with the death of a young boy in the hands of a young girl when the latter hit the former during a scuffle to grab leftover items of food from a wedding ceremony.

The girl even inquired about the health of the boy when she was being taken to the juvenile corrective home the next morning to do time there and finally develop into a professional criminal. A monk wrote a letter to a vernacular newspaper reacting to this incident, and wondered about the country's progress since Independence in 1947.

Such incidents have to be studied in perspective in order to arrive at certain concrete lessons about our life and times. An old man has single-handedly dug a pond in his village during the last seven years, using only a hand-held digging equipment. His motivation was his son's death seven years back when the young man was shot dead during a crossfire involving rival criminal gangs of the locality.

The old man's son died while begging for water to quench his thirst but nobody helped him. The father was not informed in time and it was too late when he arrived at the scene. This led him to dig the pond alone while braving the blazing Indian sun and the torrential rains. The news story described his act as the elevation of a common man to the greatness of human achievement.

These incidents open our eyes and awake us to the realities of everyday life. We can better relate to the crisis concerning reservations for Scheduled Castes, Scheduled Tribes and Other Backward Classes to be introduced in our institutions like IITs and IIMs and Medical Colleges. Medical students and others have formed an interest group called the Youth for Equality to bring pressure upon the United Progressive Alliance at New Delhi.

It is a fact that political parties do not ordinarily advocate for reservation on economic grounds alone. No political outfit has yet come up with any concerted plan of action to support reservations based upon economic considerations. The Jawaharlal Nehru University at New Delhi used to provide students with merit-cum-means scholarships in order to encourage meritorious young men and women from an underprivileged background to pursue higher education.

Political masters should realize that pursuing vote bank politics is not always a wise course of action in the greater interests of the country as a whole and students in particular. All this rhetoric about correcting historical wrongs committed by the higher castes against the lower castes (who were often considered to be the untouchable sections of society) and ensuring social justice is nothing but expanding and institutionalizing pockets of political influence.

The Government of India should first come up with a sound social development policy to introduce reservations in jobs and educational institutions on merit-cum-means basis. Otherwise caste divisions would continue to deepen and threaten the very community fabric of our social institutions. This is a Pandora's Box that should not be toyed with by short-sighted politicians.

Kolkata has also been a part of all this organized lawlessness that is continuing in reaction against reservations in medical colleges and institutions of higher education. The anomaly in India is that our priorities of development are tragically lopsided. The State is hell bent upon sponsoring free and easily available higher education to all and sundry while nobody seems to care about the state of primary education.

Higher education is not for all. Students with inadequate merit may be guided early in their careers to opt for vocational or technical education that would create a rich pool of well-trained professional resources in the country. It is perhaps a fact that the minister who has supported reservation for medical students would think twice before allowing himself to be treated by an SC or ST doctor simply because it may play upon his mind that such a physician has studied medicine on the basis of his or her social background and not on merit.

The above cannot be misconstrued as our lack of sympathy for the backward sections of society. What we are advocating in this week's column is the need for a level playing field where everyone should have equal opportunities and resources. This can only happen by introducing economic reservations and financial support at the level of primary education so that young men and women can compete on the basis of their merit later on in their careers.

The relative advantages and disadvantages of background can be corrected to some extent by financial sponsorship. We should not read about students who cannot pursue medical careers due to lack of money. But the debate should continue to explore better ideas.

ANNEXURE-13

Police Story[13]

Prasenjit Maiti
21 May 2006

This week in Kolkata the police have risen to the occasion repeatedly to make major headlines in the leading City newspapers. Ordinarily the citizens of Kolkata associate the police force with inaction, inefficiency, corruption and atrocities. But in these latest examples of a concerned and conscientious police force in action one must admit that the Kolkata Police have come across in a most shining and commendable manner.

Let us recount the incidents one by one. Traffic sergeants have helped ill passers-by on the streets of Kolkata to regain strength and revive in the custody and care of clinics. One young sergeant even signaled a crowded public bus to enter the Seth Sukhlal Memorial Karnani Hospital (better known as PG Hospital) in downtown Kolkata in order to help an aged passenger who had fallen sick in the bus itself.

This sergeant ensured that the passenger received adequate medical attention by networking with the medical and support staff of this busy City hospital where getting admission and proper treatment is a complicated affair due to excessive bureaucratization, pockets of vested interest and enormous pressure of patients coming daily for referral treatment from elsewhere in the City and adjoining Districts.

Another police constable was stationed near the Nandan complex (the cultural hub of Kolkata) when he saw that a labourer working in the vicinity got injured due to an accident. The other workers promptly fled the scene of accident but the constable was successful to retain two workers. They went to hospital where the constable busied himself in the formalities and paperwork regarding admission of the patient.

He returned only to find that the two remaining labourers have also escaped. It then became his single-handed responsibility to admit the critically injured labourer and attend to all the necessary details. He modestly told the Press that it was his duty as a policeman to help a man in need of urgent medical attention.

A traffic constable found a large sum of money lying on the street. He deposited it in the nearest police station for safe custody. He thought that he was only performing his duty as the keeper of law and order in doing so.

These are our silent heroes who are not always recognized in the public eye but who nevertheless go on performing their duties at busy street junctions while a merciless sun beats down upon them and thunder showers drench them to their bones. We do not always remember their sterling role in keeping our City habitable and safe. It is true that Kolkata (like most other metropolitan cities of the world) suffer from occasional bouts of lawlessness and crimes against women. But one can take courage from these selfless acts of devotion to duty on the part of our law keepers.

It is a fact that usually the interaction between the police and the civil society in a highly volatile city like Kolkata is problematic simply due to the fact that the police force more often than not serves as the Repressive State Apparatus in the hands of the ruling party that forms the State Government. This was amply borne out by the fact that the Election Commission of India recently decided to dissociate the police force under the State Government from the just-concluded Legislative Assembly Election in West Bengal. There was widespread apprehension that the police force would act in a partisan manner to serve the interests of the ruling Left Front. So paramilitary forces were brought in from outside the State to secure the law and order situation in the State. Incidentally the Left Front Government takes oath this week in Kolkata for a record seventh time and it remains a fact that the West Bengal Police and Kolkata Police have played an important role to keep the rulers in power at Writers' Buildings in the heart of the City.

The Left Front Government has even allowed policemen to practise trade unionism. This is most unprecedented, as ordinarily regimented forces are not permitted to form unions of their own. These recent exemplary acts of public service have nevertheless glorified the image of the pölice force in the public eye. Citizens now feel somewhat confident to approach policemen for help and direction during an emergency. The State Government in the recent past had introduced football tournaments where ordinary citizens would play with policemen in order to promote public relations exercises of the Home Department.

The Chief Minister of West Bengal, himself a leading intellectual and a visionary in his own right, is also the Home Minister. He also happens to lead the Cultural Affairs Informantion and Department. It would be indeed unique if he can uplift the rather tarnished image of his police force in the eyes of the citizens of Kolkata in particular and West Bengal in general. It is a fact that more empathy is required between the police force and the ordinary citizens so that their mutual problems are negotiated from common platforms. Policemen are social human beings and they have to relate more to the mainstream aims and aspirations as well as anxieties and apprehensions of the society all around them.

Commoners also have to realize that policemen are fellow citizens who should be readily approached during moments of genuine need so that solutions to grave or even everyday problems can be explored across the table in terms of coherent and meaningful dialogues. For instance, the police did not use force to disperse protesting medical students when they paralyzed a busy street intersection at Dorina Crossing near the Governor's House but tried to reason with them instead. It is not always easy to converse with the administration, especially policemen, whom we traditionally view with awe and fear because of their background of legitimate and organized violence sanctioned by the State.

But at least an initial step towards this challenging direction may be taken to institutionalize a better civic life for the City of Kolkata. This may reduce the incidence of crime and lawlessness in the City in the near future while the police and public may finally join hands to make Kolkata a better place to live and prosper in the context of the State Government's liberal pro-industry policy that is increasingly attracting Foreign Direct Investments to West Bengal.

ANNEXURE-14

Emotions and Elections[14]

Prasenjit Maiti
14 May 2006

This week Kolkata has witnessed certain acts of high drama that apparently do not happen to touch our everyday lives but are disturbing nevertheless. A middle class housewife attempted to immolate herself at a busy street intersection by drenching herself liberally with kerosene oil. A sizable crowd had gathered to watch this scene in silent horror but nobody actually could muster the guts to step forward and save the lady.

Another lower middle class housewife was returning home with her husband at that time after having offered her homage to the Goddess Mother at the famous Kalighat Temple in South Kolkata. It was her marriage anniversary and she had gone to the Goddess Kali to pray and offer her respect in order to ensure a happy and fruitful conjugal life.

She happened to be one of the crowd that had gathered near the Rashbehari Crossing to watch the distracted lady burn herself to death. Her opportunity arrived when the box of matches in the hands of the suicidal lady fell to the ground in the pool of kerosene. She rushed forward to grab the lady about to commit self-immolation and dragged her away from imminent death.

The savior lady even went to the police station to give her statement and offer her solace to the woman she had just saved from the jaws of a horrendous death in public. Her act would be remembered by us because she had saved us from yet another ignominy, another scandal that we the citizens of Kolkata can pass our days and ways in gay abandon while our fellow sufferers rot in their private hells of silent agony.

She has set a rare public example of selflessness and self-effacement during a moment of intense crisis when able bodied men and women were tongue-tied and frozen in their collective act of inaction. The lady about to commit suicide was suffering from bouts of depression due to her mother's illness and subsequent death some days earlier. Even her family members could not gauge her depths of frustration and apparent failure to relate with the daily rhythms of life that continue all around us, unnoticed and perhaps uncelebrated.

Another young man committed suicide around the same time in Kolkata. His father is suffering from terminal illness, and he simply could not survive the impact of this news. He was an aspiring modern executive in a City office when he killed himself, and was also a musician in a Bengali Band. But his life was not destined for any material success or intangible happiness as his emotions got the better of him and destroyed him in a frenzied moment of desperate helplessness.

Can we really judge the depths of people's frustrations and private sorrows before passing comments on their apparent lack of responsibility or acts of inanity that cause grief and trouble to others close to them? Are we competent enough to analyze the sufferings of our fellow citizens and their anxiety and hopelessness? A young man was run over in New Town the other day while returning from his boy's school. Police officers have given statements that it was the man's fault that he was crossing the road casually enough to invite trouble. But nobody talks about inadequate traffic safety and lack of road facilities such as the provision of underpasses, traffic signal systems, service roads, flyovers, interchanges, rotaries etc.

The communists have again returned to power in West Bengal. This time around the allegation of electoral malpractice was not raised so much by the Opposition, as the Election Commission of India had ensured free and fair polls in the state. Kolkata as such did not witness the mindless electoral tempo, as restrictions on campaigning were observed in a stringent manner in the City. This should be the hallmark of a mature liberal democratic political system. People know who perform and who do not, and they accordingly cast their vote. There is no need for any additional fanfare before the election to make people aware of policies and performance.

The Election Commission of India must be congratulated for the commendable measures taken before, during and after the polls in West Bengal. Even an ordinarily volatile metropolitan city like Kolkata did not have the faintest opportunity to erupt in pre-poll or post-poll violence despite the explosive and provocative comments made by some leftist political leaders. The Rule of Law has been established firmly in the state, and one hopes that this newly entrenched tradition of stable political ethos continues in the City in the future as well.

The presence of Opposition politics in Kolkata in particular and West Bengal in general is limited to fanfare and more often than not ineffective slogan campaigns, processions and demonstrations and sit-ins. One must admit that the Opposition parties have been found wanting in terms of their political resources and wisdom while the Left Front Government has been able to successfully formulate its own political rhetoric couched in the appropriate ideological idiom.

Cricket fans of Kolkata continue to be despondent at the exclusion of Saurav Gangopadhyay from the Indian national cricket team bound for the West Indies where both test match and one day international series would be played against the Caribbean team led by Brian Lara. The announcement made by Sachin Tendulkar about his fitness has impeded the inclusion of Saurav Gangopadhyay further in the national squad.

East Bengal's hopes of winning the National Football League has been dashed to the ground after the party's series of defeats in its away matches played at Goa and Mumbai. Dissent among East Bengal players has mounted against their Belgian coach, the first foreign coach at Kolkata. The East Bengal cricket team has finally won the Kolkata First Division League. This happens to be the only trophy the club has managed to win during this season.

The Football World Cup is expected to rock the City later this year when the giants of international soccer would hold all and sundry hypnotic with their magic spell cast on football lovers around the world. Kolkata is expected to go exuberantly crazy during this tournament. People would spend sleepless nights watching football while each and every Kolkata citizen would overnight turn into a soccer expert of no mean value! This is fiesta time in Kolkata and it is great fun soaking in all the youthful excitement and joy of life while knowledgeable citizens holler themselves hoarse for either Brazil or Argentina or Germany or France.

The City's blood banks are running short of blood supply during the summer months. This is a most common trend that repeats itself each and every year. The scorching heat occasionally gets reduced to bursts of late afternoon showers and storms. But the health infrastructure of the City is currently poised at perilous crossroads due to the inadequacy of blood. The electronic media has also highlighted this problem of late. Let us hope for a speedy redress of this grave problem during this summer so that our fellow citizens may get well soon.

ANNEXURE-15

An Indian Summer[15]

Prasenjit Maiti
7 May 2006

Kolkata is currently in the throes of the infamous Indian Summer when day temperatures reach around 42°C shade and evenings are just as stifling and sultry. People really do not know what to do and what not in this most stifling heat and humidity that sap them of any available energy and the willingness to do any physical or even intellectual work.

The fortunate few have air-conditioned offices, houses and cars but the suffering majority toil on almost silently, equipped with the knowledge base that Kolkata cannot have any other climate pattern during April (the so-called cruelest month following poet and banker TS Eliot) and May (when they happen to crown the May Queen in London).

The state polls are continuing on top of everything. This time around West Bengal has had its State Legislative Assembly elections in as many as five phases, an unprecedented state of affairs in this country that habitually boasts itself as the largest functioning democracy of the world that is also characterized by its ethos of functioning anarchy (following John Kenneth Galbraith).

The elections took place only recently in Kolkata when people queued up in this most scorching heat to cast their vote. The Opposition did not have any opportunity this time to raise their voices of dissent against electoral irregularities and political violence, as paramilitary forces such as the CISF, CRPF and the ITBP were on duty during the polls.

Even VVIPs such as the Chief Minister, the former Chief Minister and the Mayor etc were not allowed to enter the polling booths with their bodyguards. The Mayor even had to face challenge from the election personnel as he was not carrying his voter's identity card. A state minister was not allowed to enter the booth by a security force guard. This led to a lot of brouhaha that was eventually managed by all and sundry.

The communists are most likely to return to power in the state, and it must be added that they have been able to achieve considerably in real terms in the last five years or so in terms of urban infrastructure development. Though the uncomfortable questions remain: development for whom and at what price?

The media has added a lot of muscle to its repertoire in and around Kolkata these days. Any illegal construction, filling of wetlands, defacing of heritage buildings, public corruption, irregularity in high offices etc are highlighted by the media. Newspersons are constantly on the move, trying to gather and garner news like busy ants.

Certain incidents have taken place at Kolkata during the last week or so that display the wonderful character of this metropolis. A young taxi driver found a large amount of unclaimed money and jewelry in his car some days back but ensured that the same was retuned to its rightful owners. Perfect strangers have helped a sick man on the streets of Kolkata while the Kolkata Police have helped a young woman return to her native village located some distance away from the City.

The above incidents are not major enough to attract news headlines but they still exhibit the human content of Kolkata in a simple enough manner. Great acts do not always require much fanfare but can be executed in silent but noble ways. This is the humane core of Kolkata that may not always be noticed due to the many problems that face the everyday life of the City but that nevertheless comes shining through at critical and more often than not difficult junctures.

Joints such as the City Center at Salt Lake are thriving with people who do not always buy but rather go on window shopping sprees. Expensive restaurants and multiplexes cater to the tastes of the young and upwardly mobile pretty young things who stroll at ease along Park Street and other happening spots of the City.

The night clubs and discos are doing brisk business these days. Contraceptive vending machines may soon be installed at these places to promote the concept of safe sex. The aggressive campaigns being carried out of late by the National AIDS Commission (NACO) have raised a lot of distraught eyebrows. Letters have been published in local newspapers where concerned parents have voiced their discomfort against such open information and education exercises that lead to considerable embarrassment before their children.

Indians in general and the citizens of Kolkata in particular are not quite famous for their sense of propriety and proportion. So incidents happen in public life that are not always desirable. We have simulated the promiscuity of the West but we have not yet been able to entirely emulate the Protestant Ethic and honesty and civic integrity of the West. The West is not always the Best but at least we should make conscious efforts to glean the exemplary lessons from other civilizations and cultures.

Culture is what we do and civilization is what we are. So it is not perhaps difficult to gauge the ways and means in which people ordinarily behave and react in and around Kolkata. The Metro Railways happens to be an example: people do not normally spit underground but they start spitting merrily on the streets once they have surfaced from the Metro. Does this really indicate that Kolkata has two cultures? One above the ground while another underground? This is a most disturbing question that may be addressed by social scientists. It was recently suggested that the unemployed youth could be engaged in the election process. This was a hotly debated issue in the local media. Such a controversy proves that Kolkata is still intellectually alive. It simply requires a culture boost so that politics and society can engage with one another to begin to answer some disquieting questions.

ANNEXURE-16

Spectrality of Kashmir in Indo-Pak Relationship: A Discursive Analysis of Ghost and Host

Key Words

Civil Liberties, Foreign Policy, Ghost, Hospitality, Host, Human Rights, National Interest, Specter.

Executive Summary

This paper briefly discusses the issue of Kashmir that more often than not tends to inform the dynamics and future of Indo-Pak relationship in the methodological context of Jacques Derrida's hospitality theory. We argue in this context that the Spectrality of Kashmir can be creatively utilized to resolve the tension in South Asia by negotiating in terms of spatio-temporal pockets and geostrategic capsules limited by specific issues and concerns of bilateral importance rather than trying to solve the problem by adopting a perspective approach. Short histories and brief time modules may be more suitable than grand narratives and comprehensive solutions.

Introduction

The problems that highlight Indo-Pak relationship can be studied from the angle of Derrida's hospitality theory that presupposes the interplay between defined sets of actors.[16] This theory assumes all the more critical importance in the light of Track Two diplomacy and the different types of Confidence Building Measures that both India and Pakistan tend to pursue in order to maintain the communication channels between these two State-Nations of South Asia. Hospitality as a methodological device may be focused upon to analyze the dimensions of the most critical Kashmir problem from a psychoanalytic as well as deconstructive angle.

Historical Context

The history of the Indian Subcontinent itself has dictated the course of political affairs in Kashmir. Partition at 1947 was based on the principle of Mohhamed Ali Jinnah's erroneous Two Nation Theory, the folly of which was perceived as well as established during the Bangladesh War of 1971. The Radcliffe Line was drawn on the basis of Hindu dominated and Muslim dominated territories, and that was how Bengal and Punjab were divided. But Kashmir was a different issue, as Maharaja Hari Singh signed an Instrument of Accession with India to voluntarily opt for inclusion of Kashmir within sovereign Indian territory. His act incited Pakistan to send *hanadars* backed by the Pakistani Army to invade Kashmir. And so India was compelled to fight the first ever Indo-Pak War of 1948. As such the ethnographic and demographic composition of Kashmir is rather complicated. The Hindu Pandits used to stay in Jammu, the Muslims in the Kashmir Valley and the Buddhists in Ladakh. So the political inclination of the Kashmiris has always remained a wide open question. The political blunder that Prime Minister Jawaharlal Nehru committed during the military engagement of 1948 was to issue orders asking the advancing Indian Army to stop short of Lahore. Nehru then referred this issue to the Security Council of the United Nations and paved the way to convert a bilateral regional issue into an international agenda of South Asian peace and security. This prompted both the United States of America and the hitherto Union of Soviet Socialist Republics to take an active interest in the Kashmir issue.

Global Focus

Kashmir soon became an international hotspot like Palestine where everyone with open or concealed national interest could afford to play important or insinuating roles, depending on the military potentialities involved. So the Pandora's Box has been finally opened in Kashmir, and the series of military engagements of 1948, 1965, 1971 and Kargil has only remained as a historic vindication of the blunders committed during Independence and Partition in 1947. Those who do not learn from history are most likely condemned to repeat it, and this is noticed in today's proxy wars between these two South Asian neighbours who have not yet been able to entirely resolve the fundamental problems of poverty, food security, basic amenities of life, primary education, population explosion, literacy, nutrition, human rights, gender empowerment, child rights, civil liberties and participatory democracy. It is clear by now that the USA will never step out to support India unconditionally in its war against terror, as it requires Pakistan to maintain the geostrategic balance of power in South Asia. And India's foreign policy in this region has always been informed by both muddle and meddle.

Foreign Policy

While India wanted to support lesser neighbours like Bangladesh, Sri Lanka, Nepal and Maldives, the charge of Big Brother-like political interference has been levelled against the largest democracy of the world. Even Bangladesh, whose Independence was earned by India by defeating the Pakistani Army, has started campaigning against India by sponsoring cross-border terrorism in tandem with Pakistan's Inter-Services Intelligence. The tragedy is that India, by trying to please everybody in South Asia, has ended up by pleasing nobody. Pandit Nehru's Pancha Sheel doctrine of foreign policy built upon non-interference and peaceful coexistence has led to the image of India as the regional bully who behaves in an irresponsible manner strengthened by her nuclear capability. It is clear by now that India's foreign policy stance should be independent of the issue of Pakistan. Indian diplomacy at the global level should be informed by the country's status as a major economic power that is developing fast on the basis of superior technology and skilled manpower. Global respect for

India's resources has to be consolidated in the country's pursuit for lasting peace in South Asia.

Hospitality Theory

Jacques Derrida's theory of hospitality has emerged in recent times as a comparatively new organon to understand and project existing realities and innovative models of international relations theory. Derrida has proposed that in this post-postmodern world there are no fixed ideologies, movements, meanings or even theories. Everything is in a state of constant and dynamic flux when signifiers and signifieds continuously proceed in a continuum of *difference* that tries to resolve the uncoordinated tension between actions and their implications or interpretations. So the Ghost is actually a construct of undefined potentialities that needs to be accommodated and assimilated by the Host in order to derive insights into the unknown and unmapped eventualities of future relationships. The Host has to negotiate with the Ghost in the context of an unknown regime of discourse that would in turn be informed by meanings and implications and actions of situation-specific and context-driven imperatives. The Ghost is the Specter, and Derrida has invoked the ghost metaphor from William Shakespeare's *Hamlet, Prince of Denmark* to institutionalize the beginning assumptions of his critical theory. The Specter is known or not known for its quality of Spectrality that again is an arrangement of exciting possibilities for which the Host has to be prepared in order to establish an interactive dialogic culture *vis-à-vis* the Ghost.

Ghost and Host

We now propose to read the basic tenets of Derrida's fascinating theory into the tragic history of Indo-Pak relationship from which neither country has benefited but has suffered considerably on so many counts. Each country is a classic example of a State Nation *i.e.* the State was politically and legally created first before the Nation could muster around itself the psychological and cultural baggage of oneness cohered by collective memories and concerted intellectual efforts and actions. India and Pakistan are the Ghost and Host and vice versa *i.e.* each country approaches the other as an unknown quantity that has to be negotiated in the light of new polemics and revised pedagogy. The historic blunder of Jinnah's Two Nation Theory was exposed during 1971 when the Indian Army had to enter East Pakistan (now Bangladesh) to liberate it from the torture and atrocities of the Khan Sena or the West Pakistani Army. What is to be noticed in this context is that the Pathans and Punjabi Muslims of West Pakistan had raped and butchered Bengali Muslims of East Pakistan though the oppressor and the oppressed shared the same religion and identical citizenship. So religion cannot possibly unite all the while. The next possibilities are religion, ethnicity and culture. West Bengal and Bangladesh generally speak the same language, read the same literature and listen to the same music. But debates about distribution of river water and infiltration of insurgents working in tandem with Pakistan continue to be irksome realities. Inbound and outbound illegal migrations across the porous international border is yet another contentious issue.

Criticality of Trust

So the dialectics and dialogues between the Ghost-Host and Host-Ghost are rather critical in order to pinpoint areas of common concern that may be resolved by exercising working modalities of consensus. More trade and commerce, more rail and road and air and water traffic, more cultural missions, more Hindi films made in Bollywood, more cricket diplomacy, more areas of common interest where people converge out of their own compulsions and predatory market instincts and so on and so forth ... These are only the first faltering steps towards that great bone of contention called Kashmir. President Bhutto had reportedly declared that Pakistanis would even eat grass for one thousand years if they have to reclaim Kashmir! And consider the history of uneven diplomacy and lack of trust between the two neighbours. Bhutto returned from the Simla Agreement (2 July 1972) with Prime Minister Indira Gandhi only to start eating fire even when India had released the Pakistani Prisoners of War and returned the Pak territories captured during the Bangladesh War. President Nawaz Sharif was smiling with Prime Minister Atal Behari Vajpayee even when General Parvez Musharraf (himself a Mohajir) was planning the Kargil campaign. Pakistan is still licking the wounds of the Bangladesh War. So it has to smuggle nuclear technology illegally from a rogue state like North Korea to make indigenous missiles like Ghauri. Pakistan still maintains links with international terrorist outfits like Al Qaeda and harbours wanted criminals like Dawood Ibrahim. Its single agenda foreign policy initiative is to capture Kashmir and humiliate India.

Spectrality of Kashmir

So Kashmir emerges as the specter in Indo-Pak relationship that has to be ably negotiated with in order to ensure lasting peace in the Subcontinent. The Line of Control that separates Pak Occupied Kashmir (Azad Kashmir) from the remaining Indian territory of Kashmir can be recognized as the new international border between India and Pakistan. This is the only realistic solution that is left, as neither India nor Pakistan can claim the whole of Kashmir. But Pakistan has to first discontinue its clandestine war against India sponsored by the ISI in terms of sabotage and terrorists attacks on innocent civilians. It is useless on the part of General Musharraf to declare that he has no control over the fundamentalist sections of the ISI who follow the philosophy of the Taliban and the ideology of Al Qaeda.[17] So the unique spectral quality of Kashmir has to be duly acknowledged by both India and Pakistan while trying honestly to resolve this imbroglio. Both regional powers have to duly admit the fact that the Kashmir issue can only be resolved by sharing almost equal portions of the cake.

Capital as Specter

Even the local economy of Kashmir is in ruins. The tourism industry has rapidly dwindled, threatened by the fear of terrorist attacks. And tourism was the principal motivator of the Kashmiri economy. The woollen trade has also been adversely affected. The other revenue earning sectors are fruits and dry fruits. But the Valley of Gods has now become the Valley of Fear. So the circulation of capital has also slackened. Shooting of Hindi films no more take place in Kashmir. Allegations of military excesses and violation of human rights are raised occasionally against the Indian Army while the security forces allege that the local people extend shelter to the terrorists who come from across the international border. A lot of problems resulting from relative deprivation can be solved by enhanced well-being. Kashmir has always enjoyed a special legal status. But now it has fallen upon evil times. So development of the local economy can restore its prosperity and address its grievances and discontent. But peace has to be restored first in order to ensure economic prosperity of Kashmir.* The free flow and wide circulation of capital in the form of foreign exchange earned through international tourism can ensure widespread and lasting peace in the Valley.

Spectrality and Development

The agenda of development may defeat the Spectrality of Kashmir in the sense that basic issues like food, clothing, housing, roads, drinking water, electricity, education and security can always find precedence in the domestic policy agenda of both India and Pakistan. Both countries spend sinfully for their military expenditures while they could have perhaps partially resolved certain basic problems of human development with that money. The Spectrality of Kashmir may take a backseat once the rhetoric of development is entrenched in the political idiom of both the countries. Regrettably enough, democratic India and dictatorial Pakistan are similar when it

* 'God's Own Country' is Kerala. 'Is Kashmir also referred to as such or 'Paradise on Earth?'

comes to high political drama. But one has to remember that you cannot fool all the people all the time although you may fool some of the people some of the time!

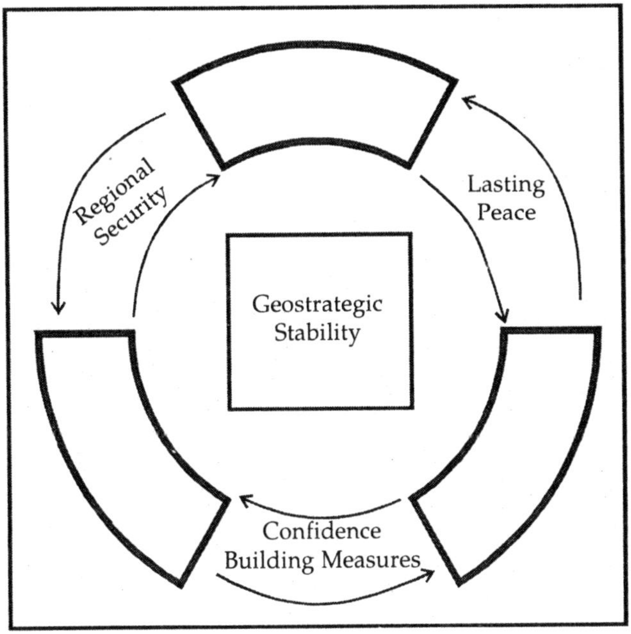

Model 1: Balance of Power Model in South Asia

Regional Development

The above model indicates the possible dynamics that may guide the process of regional development and political stability in South Asia in general and the Indian Subcontinent in particular. Development through regional platforms such as the South Asian Association for Regional Cooperation and South Asia Free Trade Agreement should gain prominence during global dialogues initiated by the World Trade Organization and the International Monetary Fund in association with the World Bank. The Asian Development Bank should actively sponsor infrastructure development projects in this region to promote well-being and combat poverty. Such sensible approaches may always initiate States to work towards common goals rather than fight in a futile manner. Most

Favoured Nation statuses have to be extended, and regional trade and investment should be encouraged to ensure profits and better standards of living. Public opinion in favour of peace and stability will be formed automatically.

Policy Dialogues

Continuous policy dialogues at the levels of Heads of State and Government, Foreign Secretaries, Diplomats, Bureaucrats, Industrialists, Scientists, Technocrats, Political Analysts and Media Personalities should take place in order to keep open the functional channels of both formal as well as informal communication. Two way traffic and dialogues are essential to understand the Other's points of view. Derrida has repeatedly insisted on Openness to the Other and respecting the Otherness of the Other, without which meaning and symbiotic relationships cannot develop. India and Pakistan need to interact predicated upon the dynamics of Openness and Otherness *i.e.* while it is true that a polyphony of voices would be heard it is also imperative to cohere a carnival of choices that would be influenced by the marketplace of regional politics.

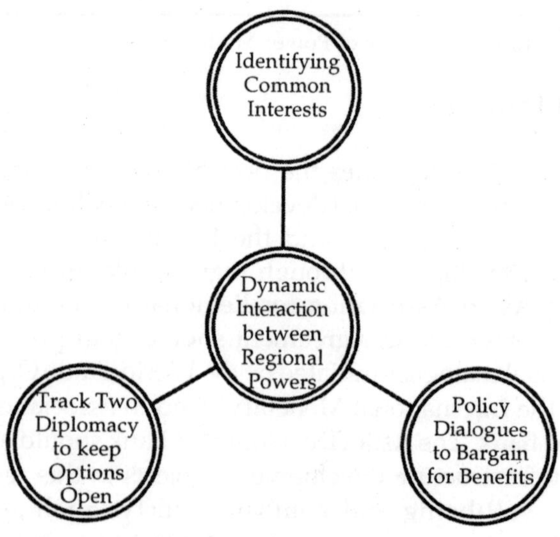

Model 2: Policy Dialogue Model

Conclusion

So we conclude that Kashmir as one of the most critical defining factors of Indo-Pak relationship should be ideally divided along the Line of Control in order to ensure a harmonious relationship between these two South Asian neighbours, both of whom now happen to possess nuclear capability. Otherwise Kashmir will worsen as an international flash point like Palestine. It is difficult to implement this decision to recognize the Line of Control as the new international boundary between India and Pakistan, as for India it would imply surrendering its territorial integrity and sovereignty and for Pakistan it would mean winning only half the coveted prize. But both these countries should realize that it is useless to protract the Kashmir issue. It is high time precise answers are given to historic questions in order to progress along the path of future. Neither India nor Pakistan can afford to lengthen this conflict for long. The new millennium has arrived with a lot of potentialities that have to be tapped in order to survive in the period of critical globalization that has almost effaced the realities of time and space from the discourses of international relations. So it is either now or never. Democracy should be restored in Pakistan so that India can find a suitable counterpart to continue its dialogue of peace, progress and security in the Subcontinent. Democracy is a flawed political system, but a better system is yet to develop. So Indo-Pak Relationship will now have to wait for an ambience of hospitality underpinned by democracy in the near future.

ANNEXURE-17

Clash of Civilizations[18]

Prasenjit Maiti
23 April 2006

American political scientist Samuel Huntington had expressed apprehension way back in 1996 that the 21st Century would be marked by conflicts between Islam and the West—a throwback to the Crusades of the Middle Ages. This projection was described in Western scholarship as the jihad-versus-McWorld scenario, an eventuality that would test the resilience of the Free World against the forces of religious fundamentalism and terrorist insurgency.

But it is rather disturbing that all such doomsday prophecies came true on 11 September 2001, with terrorist attacks on the World Trade Center in New York City and the Pentagon in Washington, D.C. Such mindless acts of violence against the civilian population provoke certain questions.

First, are the basic tenets of Islam incompatible with other world religions? We know it is the religiously assigned duty of Muslims to wage war against non-Muslims in order to transform the world into an acceptable and exclusivist *dar-ul-Islam* (World of Islam) from an unacceptable *dar-ul-harb* (World of Infidels). Islam as an organized world religion should come to terms with the realities of the new millennium and should re-socialize itself, so to speak, to cohabit with the emergent ethos of pluralist and multicultural societies.

Second, does violence beget violence? It obviously does. But the United States at this time should also appreciate the exact nature of cross-border terrorism in flashpoints like Kashmir in India and help both the other NATO members, as well as willing countries in the developing world (like India), to destroy pockets of insurgency, especially those drawing ideological, military and financial support from Islam's thoroughly discredited thesis of the jihad (holy war). U.S. citizens should now realize the kind of trauma that Indian Hindu pandits suffer daily in Jammu and Kashmir—this former Valley of the Gods has now been tragically reduced to a valley of fear and death by Muslim terrorists trained and equipped by rogue states like Afghanistan, Pakistan and even Libya. Pakistan's army-chief-turned-president even had the insufferable audacity to describe these insurgents as freedom fighters during his visit to India.

Third, are human rights and democracy Eurocentric constructs? They most certainly aren't, but the United States should stop acting as the moral guardian of a unipolar world and instead effectively build bridges, underpinned by trust and a common agenda of human development, to reach across to potential regional partners in the developing world like India—a country that, despite poverty, malnutrition and hunger, has sustained its liberal democracy (unlike Pakistan) since its independence from Great Britain in 1947.

U.S. policymakers should realize that it is high time they begin dismantling the United States' strategy of cultural isolation and indifference. It is a disquieting fact that an average urban student of the developing world knows more about the United States than an average U.S. undergraduate knows about other people and cultures. Dissemination of multicultural knowledge should be facilitated both within and outside U.S. academia, industry and social service sectors.

Familiarity can also breed understanding and help expand worldviews of an entire people. The logic of globalization, more often than not, has worked in a one-sided manner, provoking even Western scholars to come up with insightful expressions like *McDonaldization* and *Coca-Colonization* and The U.S. is us!

America's war against terror has provoked sharp reactions and animated protests worldwide. It has long been established that the battle to topple Saddam Hussein was fought on the most flimsiest of grounds. No weapon of mass destruction was discovered in Iraq. The military exercise in Afghanistan is another example in this regard. America is almost certain to attack Iran in the near future to destroy the so-called axes of evil. It is as if the U.S. has decided that those who are not with us are against us in accordance with the McCarthy Doctrine.

It does not suit the United States to flaunt ideals such as democracy, human rights, development and peace. Till date America is the only country to have used atomic weapons in war and that too at such a juncture when such an action was not at all tenable in military terms. Japan was already at the receiving end when the nuclear holocausts took place at Hiroshima and Nagasaki. Even then America decided to go ahead with its atomic bomb project in order to avenge the Pearl Harbour incident.

Democracy and human rights for the United States mean safeguarding American Democracy and American Human Rights. The World is America for all practical purpose now. Even God is an American! So the interpretations of independence, freedom, good governance, social capital and nuclear non-proliferation are essentially American definitions that exclude multicultural or pluralist worldviews. This attitude to global politics has tempted America to make situational friends and long-term enemies worldwide. The search for oil and the boost to domestic weapons and construction industries are overriding concerns that have prompted America now and again to wage war in the Persian Gulf.

This profiteering attitude has also compelled the United States to forge new alliances with India and China in order to expand business and capture markets and utilize cheap but highly skilled labour power trained in the English language and information technology. Even President Bush has warned American school children of the competition from their Indian and Chinese counterparts whose seniors are bagging lucrative jobs increasingly in the BPO and IT sectors of the American economy. Market, politics, society and culture have all become muddled in the eyes of the isolationist American foreign policy that has to realize that resources need to be shared if these are to be optimally utilized. Mutually Assured Destruction is the only other conceivable alternative.

ANNEXURE-18

Dilemma of India's Distance Education System[19]

Prasenjit Maiti
28 May 2006

The concept of distance education has taken a while to be accepted in the popular imagination in India where it has been traditionally accepted since Independence that the State will pay for higher education irrespective of the market, merit or even financial status. But the pinch is now being increasingly felt in the job market where virtually "unemployable human resources" equipped with almost useless graduate or postgraduate degrees are being churned out year after year by our colleges and Universities. India is a welfare country where subsidies (non-merit public expenditures) more or less benefit the privileged middle classes and higher education is considered to be a tool that facilitates proliferation of democracy. But *"democratization of education"* (read proletarianization of meritocracy) can never be a solution to the problem of unemployment and a stagnant job market.

Add unemployment and youth discontent to a serious population growth scenario and you get an explosive combination where the entire nation happens to sit on the top of a dormant volcano, apparently idling away time watching cricket, while permanent employment and social security are fast becoming obsolete in a society where a job is supposed to be like your mother in terms of security and sustenance.

However, the open school or University system can address this simmering tension and disturbing state of affairs in an effective manner only if more professional courses are designed by specialists to accommodate our educated generalists, that is students with degrees in the humanities, literature and social sciences. One such option can be social work where the catchment area may cater to students from sociology, history, political science, anthropology, public administration and the like. The job market here is specific: the NGOs who sponsor third actor intervention, public action and civil societal advocacy.

Science and commerce graduates may even be taught entrepreneurial and microcredit financing skills so that they may also contribute to the nation's self-help movement in the professional services sector. Netaji Subhas Open University, Calcutta is one of the foremost Indian educational institutions in this area, according to Professor Asish Guha, Director of Study Centres, NSOU.

The University Grants Commission's sponsored teachers' training programs like refresher and orientation courses for college and University lecturers are more or less like academic picnics where precious public money is wasted in a meaningless manner over a period of three weeks or so. As such our generalist colleges and Universities produce manpower that is often not employable without any further skill enhancement in areas like computer literacy, management or any other technical training. But India's tax payers have to still bear the brunt of an expensive higher education system that almost entirely runs on subsidies and without any material returns whatsoever. Doctors and engineers and management professionals join the country's bureaucracy after their professional attainments, thus resulting in huge losses in terms of human resource management.

The UGC should seriously rethink its system of awarding scholarships, funding seminars, symposia, workshops, travel grants, book and equipment purchase and so on and so forth. Refresher and orientation courses are almost entirely useless, as after completion of these programs the only people who happen to benefit are the teachers themselves so far as their Career Advancement Scheme is concerned and nobody else. High theory is flaunted at these programs with no regard to the UGC's guidelines that undergraduate courses should primarily be brought into focus. Let's face it: the commonplace and average student doesn't really need to read about Plato or Aristotle—he or she is much better off studying how commodities are produced for and exchanged in the market. This may sound unduly harsh but students or trained human resources are, in the final analysis, commodities in the job market to be bought and sold against a value defined and determined by forces of demand and supply.

ANNEXURE-19

Failure Slur on Self-Help Project[20]

Prasenjit Maiti
5 November 2002

A prominent NGO today said Bengal's venture into micro-credit for the rural poor has failed to make any headway, but the government contests the claim. Amalendu Halder, project co-ordinator of the Loknath Divine Life Mission, a Calcutta-based NGO, claimed the failure was evident in "the many loopholes" in the below-poverty-line and the above-poverty-line estimates. "The venture has dismally failed," he said.

But government officials were quick to shoot it down, saying the Loknath Mission and other NGOs operating in micro-credit had not adequately familiarised themselves with the working of the various schemes.

"Loopholes or problems are situation-specific; at times they do vary widely but we try to sort these out as thoroughly as practicable by way of government supervision," said Bhaskar Pal, a senior official in Bishnupur. Broadly, the Swarna Jayanti Gram Swarojgar Yojana, a rural self-employment project jointly launched by the Centre and the state government, has been in operation for two years.

Potential beneficiaries either directly approach the district rural development cells manned by West Bengal Civil Service officers for approval or their cases are forwarded by NGOs. Haldar said the project faces subsidy and incentive-related financial irregularities that also bedevil many other schemes of the panchayats. BPL groups receive subsidies ranging from Rs 7,500-10,000 per Rs 1-lakh loan granted by banks.

There are complaints that bank loans so extended to self-help groups under this project are not free from irregularities. However, Pal said only nationalised, cooperative and gramin banks are authorised to extend loans and so far no reports of irregularities have reached the government.

Sources in the State Institute of Panchayats and Rural Development confirmed there are widespread irregularities in implementation of the scheme. "It's a fact that there are serious grievances among self-help groups regarding APL and BPL estimates although there exist clear-cut Planning Commission guidelines in this regard. Anomalies have distorted the lists, thanks to vested vote bank interests of rural politicians," said an SIPRD official on condition of anonymity.

ANNEXURE-20

School Children are Hungry in India[21]

Prasenjit Maiti
2 March 2003

"Fifty per cent of the world's hungry live in five countries: India, Bangladesh, Nigeria, Pakistan and Indonesia. Though we have heard these facts many times over, most of us can neither fathom the sufferings of the underprivileged, nor can we grasp the difficulties faced by millions of such people, barely clinging on to their lives. One of the most neglected forms of human deprivation is malnutrition, particularly among children. Scientific evidence suggests that the risk of death from common childhood diseases is doubled for a mildly malnourished child, tripled for a moderately malnourished child, and may be even as high as eight times for a severely malnourished child, when compared with the risks faced by a well-nourished child."

—Ronald Anil Fernandes, Paramount Welfare Educational Trust, Bangalore

"The Calcutta High Court has ordered the Government of West Bengal to file a criminal law suit against the Inspector of Schools of Midnapore District on charges of selling mid-day meal rice in the open market in collusion with a local Block Development Officer and a private supply agency.

— Anandabazar Patrika, Calcutta, 20 February 2003

A few state governments in India have of late waged a war of attrition with the Union Government over the contentious issue of providing cooked mid-day meals to underprivileged primary school children. This is primarily a central government-funded public welfare scheme where the center provides uncooked cereals (and transportation of foodgrains) free of cost. However, "cash-strapped" state governments plead inability to provide cooked meals to children in the Below Poverty Level category, and seek to provide uncooked cereals instead (that too on an irregular basis), although it costs about INR 1 per child per day to provide cooked meals for the stipulated 200 days a year.

The Supreme Court of India, the country's apex federal court, in an interim judgment, has recently ordered these State Governments to immediately comply with the Union Government's regulations or else the Center's aid to the States will be diverted to sponsor the mid-day meals project in primary schools. NGOs like the *Right to Food and Work Network, Campaign against Child Labour, West Bengal Education Network* and the *Calcutta NGO Forum of Street and Working Children* organized demonstrations by underprivileged children on 14 November 2002 (Children's Day) in Calcutta and across West Bengal to protest against the State Government's inability to provide mid-day meals to primary school students.

Children mobilized a symbolic fund-raising drive with banners stating: "Our State Government claims it doesn't have the necessary money to provide us with food in our schools, so we're begging for money from the common people. We shall send this money to Chief Minister Buddhadeb Bhattacharjee so that he can provide cooked meals to hungry children." However, the West Bengal Government, citing financial stringency, hasn't yet sanctioned INR 190 crore to provide cooked meals to about 95 lakh students in the state. The West Bengal Government, in response to a Supreme Court ruling that States should not compromise with children's food, had earlier petitioned that it was unable to implement the Central Government-funded mid-day meals project due to severe funds crunch. But the apex court rejected the petition and cautioned on 3 September 2002 that Central aid to the States would be diverted for the meals project if cooked meals were not duly provided in schools.

The *People's Union for Civil Liberties* (Rajasthan) filed a petition in May 2001 in connection with the "right to food" in the Supreme Court, demanding that the country's food stock should be used without delay to prevent hunger. The Supreme Court, in its "interim order" passed on 28 November 2001, converted the benefits of eight nutrition-related federal schemes into legal entitlements and directed the State Governments to provide cooked mid-day meals for all children in Government and Government-assisted schools:

- "It is the case of the Union of India that there has been full compliance with regard to the Mid-Day Meal Scheme. However, if any of the States gives a specific instance of non-compliance, the Union of India will do the needful within the framework of the Scheme.
- "We direct the State Governments to implement the Mid-Day Meal Scheme by providing every child in every Government and Government-assisted Primary Schools with a prepared mid-day meal with a minimum content of 300 calories and 8-12 grams of protein each day of school for a minimum of 200 days. Those Governments providing dry rations instead of cooked meals must within three months (28 February 2002) start providing cooked meals in all Government and Government-aided Primary Schools in half of the Districts of the State (in order of poverty) and must within a further period of three months (28 May 2002) extend the provision of cooked meals to the remaining parts of the State.
- "We direct the Union of India and the Food Corporation of India to ensure provision of fair average quality grain for the Scheme on time.
- "The States and the FCI are directed to do joint inspection of foodgrains. If the foodgrain is found, on joint inspection, not to be of fair average quality, it will be replaced by the FCI prior to lifting."

This judgment revised the earlier arrangement under which primary school students were to be provided with 100 gm of wheat or rice for a minimum of 200 days in a year free of cost. However, States like Bihar, Uttar Pradesh and

Jharkhand have violated the order of the Supreme Court by not implementing the project. Manipur also plans not to introduce the scheme. It has even submitted an interim application to the Supreme Court to this effect. Both Manipur and Mizoram have argued that mid-day meals are not part of the eating habit of the people, and that children do not like to eat in the middle of the day, according to the Voice of the Asia-Pacific Human Rights Network.

The Tribune reported on 29 September 2002 that "The States did not have the money and the Center did not assist. The matter was taken up by the States with the Prime Minister and the Ministry of Human Resource Development leading to delay in filing affidavits by States, including Punjab." The mid-day meal scheme happens to be one of the most resisted Central schemes in federal India. This happens to be a Central Government scheme, but the states have to bear the costs of implementing it. This is one of the prime reasons for stiff resistance by the States.

The Hindu reported on 13 September 2002 that "Since the start of the new academic session a few months ago, the mid-day meal scheme is not being adequately implemented for nearly nine lakh children studying in 1800 primary schools of the Municipal Corporation of Delhi. Whatever is being given to the students is unhygienic and sub-standard, the Opposition Bharatiya Janata Party has alleged, a charge denied by the ruling Congress. Further, services of private contractors are being taken for distributing fresh fruits to the students."

The *Jan Swasthya Abhiyan*, an NGO, has reported that the Maharashtra Government has issued an order to the effect that contributions for the scheme will come "voluntarily" from the villages themselves. Local bodies have even been cautioned that they will not receive the benefits of other Central Government schemes if they do not contribute to the mid-day meal scheme.

The Times of India, a national daily, reported on 8 July 2002 that "The Maharashtra Government has decided to wash its hands off the mid-day meal scheme for primary schools, claiming that it has no funds to provide cooked meals to students. The onus of running the scheme has been passed on to the gram panchayats (village-level institutions of decentralized governance).

Jean Drèze, Visiting Professor at the Delhi School of Economics and associate of Noble Laureate Amartya Sen, argues that "60 million tonnes of grain are lying idle in public warehouses. These food mountains have become a resilient national embarrassment. Grain withdrawn from these warehouses is effectively costless, since the procurement expenses have already been borne. In fact, using idle food stocks for school meals would save money, by reducing storage costs" (The Hindu, 21 May 2002).

Collective demands for mid-day meals were raised in more than a hundred districts of the country by way of public hearings, protest demonstrations, hunger rallies and the like on 9 April 2002. The unwilling States, however, are yet to comply. Demonstrations were held in each and every district of Bihar. Thousands of children clamoured for mid-day meals in Patna, the capital city, with empty plates.

"One might have expected State Governments to welcome the school-meal program as an opportunity to win votes at relatively low cost. Indeed, the scheme is likely to be quite popular, and it is not very expensive for the State Governments, given that the Central Government is supplying the grain for free. In most States, however, there is no sign of such enthusiasm. There is something deeply defective about a democracy where people's basic needs count for so little in electoral politics," adds Dreze.

Mid-day meals as a public welfare concept in India date back to 1925 when such a project was launched for underprivileged children in the Madras Corporation area. The Keshav Academy of Calcutta introduced compulsory mid-day refreshments for school children in 1928 (on a subsidized payments basis). A school lunch program was started in parts of Kerala in 1941, followed by Bombay implementing a free mid-day meal scheme in 1942. Another project was launched in Bangalore city in 1946. The Uttar Pradesh government introduced a program in 1953 (on a voluntary basis) to provide cooked mid-day meals to school children. Several States introduced such schemes during the 1950s, aided by international agencies like the UNICEF, FAO and WHO.

The Catholic Relief Service, Church World Service and Meals for Million also lent their assistance to these programs. An Expanded Nutrition Program launched jointly by the FAO, WHO, UNICEF and the Government of India was launched during 1958-59. This subsequently developed into the Applied Nutrition Program.

NOTES

1. http://www.boloji.com/diary/kolkata/006.htm
2. http://www.boloji.com/diary/kolkata/001.htm
3. http://www.india-seminar.com/2000/493/493%20comment.htm
4. http://www.boloji.com/diary/kolkata/011.htm
5. http://www.boloji.com/diary/kolkata/015.htm
6. http://www.boloji.com/diary/kolkata/013.htm
7. http://www.boloji.com/diary/kolkata/012.htm
8. http://www.boloji.com/diary/kolkata/010.htm
9. http://www.boloji.com/diary/kolkata/009.htm
10. http://www.boloji.com/perspective/171.htm
11. http://www.boloji.com/diary/kolkata/008.htm
12. http://www.boloji.com/diary/kolkata/005.htm
13. http://www.boloji.com/diary/kolkata/004.htm
14. http://www.boloji.com/diary/kolkata/003.htm
15. ttp://www.boloji.com/diary/kolkata/002.htm
16. *Cf.* Prasenjit Maiti, Indo-Pak Relations: The Need for Hospitality. *Asian Studies,* Vol. 17, No. 1 (January-June 1999, Netaji Institute for Asian Studies, Calcutta), pp. 89-93; Maiti and Panchanan Chattopadhyay, On Derrida, Marx and Hospitality. *Socialist Perspective* Vol. 25, Nos. 3-4 (December 1997-March 1998), pp. 93-8; and Maiti, Underscoring Peace as Hospitality in Indo-Pak Relations: Toward Alternatives of Conflict Resolution in South Asia. *Journal of Social Sciences,* Vol. 5, Nos. 1-2 (January-April 2001; Delhi), pp. 39-46.
17. Kashmir is critical in the international war against terror, as at present it qualifies as a benchmark against which to assess issues related to escalated international terrorism. The 9/11 tragedy is inhuman but it does not justify civilian casualties in Iraq and Afghanistan caused by Allied military exercises. The United States of America has openly favoured Pakistan on more than one occasion and has repeatedly asked India to exercise military

constraint along its international border! Such double standards only jeopardize the cause of any war lauched against terror on a global scale. Kashmir is not a black-and-white problem, and the USA has to acknowledge the gray areas. India is a more democratic partner for the USA than Pakistan. *Cf.* Maiti, Clash of Civilizations? *The Humanist*. (Washington DC: American Humanist Association, November/December 2001); and Maiti, Human Rights Violation in Kashmir, *Peace Magazine*, January-March 2002.

18. http://www.boloji.com/opinion/0187.htm
19. http://www.boloji.com/perspective/175.htm
20. http://www.telegraphindia.com/1021106/asp/bengal/story_1359043.asp
21. http://www.boloji.com/analysis/063.htm

Select Readings

Civil Society[1]

A. Clayton, ed., *NGOs, Civil Society and the State: Building Democracies in Transitional Countries*, INTRAC, 1996.

A. Fowler, *Striking a Balance: A Guide to Enhancing the Effectiveness of NGOs in International Development*, Earthscan, London, 1997.

A. Seligman, *The Idea of Civil Society*, Free Press, New York, 1992.

B. Shearer, *The Emerging Role of Civil Society: A Force for Social Development*, Synergos Institute, New York, 1995.

E. Gellner, *Conditions of Liberty: Civil Society and its Rivals*, Penguin, London, 1994.

J. A. Hall, *Civil Society: Theory, History, Comparison*, Polity Press, Cambridge, UK, 1995.

J. Burbridge, *Beyond Prince and Merchant: Citizen Participation and the Rise of Civil Society*, Pact Publications, 1997.

R. Holloway, *Civil Society Toolbox*, Pact Publications, New York, 1997.

L. Salamon *et al.*, *Global Civil Society: Dimensions of the Non-profit Sector*, The Institute for Policy Studies, Johns Hopkins University, Baltimore, 1999.

L. Salamon and H. Anheier, *Defining the Non-profit Sector: A Cross-National Analysis*, The Institute for Policy Studies, Johns Hopkins University, Baltimore, 1997.

R. Tandon and M. D. de Oliveira, ed., *Citizens: Strengthening Global Civil Society*, CIVICUS, 1994.

V. Perez-Diaz, *The Return of Civil Society*, Harvard University Press, Cambridge, Mass., 1993.

Community Networks[2]

Robert Putnam, "The Prosperous Community: Social Capital and Public Life," *The American Prospect* 13 (Spring 1993), 35-42;

Robert Putnam, "Bowling Alone: America's Declining Social Capital," *Journal of Democracy* 6:1 (January 1995), 65-78;

Robert Putnam, "The Strange Disappearance of Civic America," *The American Prospect* 24 (Winter 1996).

Francis Fukuyama, *Trust: The Social Virtues and the Creation of Prosperity*. New York: Free Press, 1995.

Sidney Verba, Kay Schlozman, and Henry Brady, *Voice and Equality: Civic Voluntarism in American Politics*. Cambridge: Harvard University Press, 1995

James Coleman, *Foundations of Social Theory*. Cambridge: Harvard University Press, 1990.

Mark Russell Warren, *Social Capital and Community Empowerment: Religion and Political Organization in the Texas Industrial Areas Foundation*. Ph.D. dissertation, Harvard University, 1995

Carmen Sirianni and Lewis Friedland, "Social Capital and Civic Innovation: Learning and Capacity-Building from the 1960s to the 1990s."

Development Ethics[3]

Bull, B (2005), El papel de la sociedad civil en el desarrollo económico y democrático en Noruega: Experiencias relevantes para América Latina? Paper prepared for *Seminario Internacional: Capital Social en Acción*, Universidad Metropolitana, Caracas, Venezuela, 6 April, 2005.

Bull, B (2004), La responsabilidad social de las empresas: Una solución para el desarrollo en América Latina?, *Revista Venezolana de Gestión* (Venezuela) (28).

Bull, B (2004), Empresas responsables: Donde la ganancia no es lo único, *Cuarto intermedio* (Bolivia) (70):44-57.

Bull, B (2003), *Responsabilidad Social Empresarial: Una perspectiva Nórdica*, Paper prepared for the meeting: Encuentro Internacional: Movilizando el Captial Social y el

Voluntariado de America Latina, Santiago, Chile, 22.05.2003-23.05.2003.

Bull, B (2003), The IDB's Ethics and Development Initiative: A Step Forward for the Development Ethics Debate? *IDEA Newsletter* 2003(2).

McNeill, D. 2001. *Ethics and Economics*. Paper prepared for the Annual Meeting of the IDB, March 15th, 2001, Santiago, Chile.

Bull, B. 2001. *Liberalization and Privatization of Telecommunications: Ethical Questions*. Paper to IDB Conference in Honduras 1-3 September, 2001.

McNeill, D. 2000. 'Statistics—the Development Researcher's Guilty Secret', *Forum for Development Studies,* Vol. 27, No. 1, pp. 145-150.

McNeill, D. 1999. 'Market Ethics and Global Ethics', *Forum for Development Studies,* Vol. 26, No. 1, pp. 59-76.

Human Rights[4]

Dworkin, Ronald. *Taking Rights Seriously*, (London: Duckworth, 1978).

Freeman, Michael. *Human Rights: An Interdisciplinary Approach,* (Cambridge: Polity, 2002).

Finnis, John. *Natural Law and Natural Rights*, (Oxford; Clarendon Press, 1980).

Gewirth, Alan. *Reason and Morality*, (Chicago: Chicago University Press, 1978).

Gewirth, Alan. *Human Rights: Essays on Justification and Applications*, (Chicago; University of Chicago Press, 1982).

Jones, Peter. *Rights*, (Basingstoke; Macmillan, 1994).

Mackie, J.L. *Ethics: Inventing Right and Wrong*, (Harmondsworth; Penguin, 1977).

Nickel, James. *Making Sense of Human Rights: Philosophical Reflections on the Universal Declaration of Human Rights*, (Berkeley; University of California Press, 1987).

Rorty, Richard. "Human rights, rationality, and sentimentality". In S. Shute and S. Hurley (eds.), *On Human Rights: the Oxford Amnesty Lectures 1993*, (New York; Basic Books, 1993).

Waldron, Jeremy. *Theories of Rights*, (Oxford; Oxford University Press, 1984) Chapters by Ronald Dworkin, Alan Gewirth, and H.L.A. Hart.

Inequality and Poverty[5]

Gottschalk, Peter and Timothy M. Smeeding. 2000. "Empirical Evidence on Income Inequality in Industrialized Countries," In A. B. Atkinson and F. Bourguignon (eds.), *Handbook of Income Distribution, Volume 1.* New York: Elsevier-North Holland Publishers, pp. 261-307.

Gottschalk, Peter and Timothy M. Smeeding. 1997. "Cross-National Comparisons of Earnings and Income Inequality." *Journal of Economic Literature,* Vol. XXXV (June), pp. 633-687.

Jenkins, Stephen. 1991. "The Measurement of Income Inequality." In Lars Osberg (ed.) *Economic Inequality and Poverty International Perspectives.* ME Sharpe. (Chapter 1) pp 3-38.

Smeeding, Timothy M. 2005. "Public Policy, Economic Inequality, and Poverty: The United States in Comparative Perspective." *Social Science Quarterly* 86(5):955-983.

Garfinkel, Irwin, Lee Rainwater and Timothy M. Smeeding. 2005. "Welfare State Expenditures and the Redistribution of Well-Being: Children, Elders, and Others in Comparative Perspective." Luxembourg Income Study Working Paper No. 387. Center for Policy Research, Syracuse University. October.

Kenworthy, Lane. 2004. "Welfare States, Real Income and Poverty." Chapter 6 in Lane Kenworthy, *Egalitarian Capitalism.* New York: Russell Sage Foundation.

Smeeding, Timothy M. 2006. "Poor People in Rich Nations: The United States in Comparative Perspective," *Journal of Economic Perspective* 20 (1): 69-90.

Jäntti, Markus. 1997. "Inequality in Five Countries in the 1980s: The Role of Demographic Shifts, Markets and Government Policies," *Economica* 65(255): 415-440.

NGOs and Laws

Handbook on Global Standards and Best Practices for Laws Governing NGOs, The International Center for Not-for-Profit Law, World Bank, Washington D. C., 1997.
Legal Principles for Citizen Participation: Toward a Legal Framework for Civil Society Organizations, CIVICUS, Washington D. C., 1997.

NGOs and Business

S. Heap, *NGOs and the Private Sector: Potentials for Partnership,* INTRAC, 1998.
D. Logan, D. Roy and L. Regelbrugge, *Global Corporate Citizenship: Rationale and Strategies,* Hitachi Foundation, Washington D. C., 1997.
J. Nelson, Business as Partners in Development: *Creating Wealth for Countries, Companies, and Communities, Prince of Wales Business Leaders Forum, World Bank,* UNDP, 1996.

Poverty and Well-Being[6]

Rainwater, L., and T.M. Smeeding. 2003. *Poor Kids in a Rich Country.* New York, NY: Russell Sage Foundation.
Bardasi, Elena. 2004. "The Luxembourg Income Study and the Luxembourg Employment Study as a resource for labour market research," *Socio-Economic Review* v2 n2 p239-261.
Allegrezza, Serge, Georges Heinrich, and David Jesuit. 2004. "The contribution of LIS to understanding the situation of Luxembourg," *Socio-Economic Review* v2 n2 p263-283.
Gonzalez, Libertad. 2004. "Single mothers and work," *Socio-Economic Review* v2 n2 p285-313.
Todd Bronchetti, Erin and Dennis Sullivan. 2004. "Income packages of households with children: A crossnational correlation analysis," *Socio-Economic Review* v2 n2 p315-339.

Poverty Reduction Strategies

Bigman, David , and Hippolyte Fofack. *Geographical targeting for poverty alleviation: methodology and applications,* World

Bank Regional and Sectoral Studies. Washington, D.C.: The World Bank, 2000.

Bigman, David *et al.* "Community targeting for poverty reduction in Burkina Faso." *The World Bank Economic Review 14*, no. 1 (2000): 167-193.

Bigman, David, and Hippolyte Fofack. "Geographical targeting for poverty alleviation: an introduction to the special issue." *The World Bank Economic Review 14, no. 1*(2000):*129-145.*

Evans, Allison. *Poverty reduction in the 1990s: an evaluation of strategy and performance.* Edited by World Bank Operations Evaluation Department. Washington, DC: The World Bank, 2000.

Social Capital[7]

Briggs, Xavier de Souza. "Social Capital and the Cities: Advice to Change Agents." *National Civic Review* 86, No. 2 (Summer 1997): 111-118.

Berry, Jeffrey M., Kent E. Portney and Ken Thomson. *The Rebirth of Urban Democracy*. Washington, DC: Brookings Institution, 1993.

Ehrenhalt, Alan. *The Lost City: Discovering the Forgotten Virtues of Community in the Chicago of the 1950s*. New York: Basic Books, 1995.

Lemann, Nicholas "Kicking in Groups." *Atlantic Monthly* (April 1996): 22-24.

Loury, Glenn "The Social Capital Deficit." *The New Democrat* (May-June 1995): 28-29.

Loury, Glenn, "The Divided Society and the Democratic Ideal." Boston University's University Lecture, 1996.

Portes, Alejandro and Patricia Landolt, "The Downside of Social Capital." *The American Prospect* 26 (May-June 1996): 18-21, 94.

Potapchuk, William R., Jarle P. Crocker and William H. Schecter, Jr. "Building Community with Social Capital: Chits and Chums or Chats with Change." *National Civic Review* 86, No. 2 (Summer 1997): 129-140.

Putnam, Robert D. *Making Democracy Work*. Princeton, NJ: Princeton University Press, 1993.

Schambra, William and Michael S. Joyce. "A New Citizenship, A New Civic Life." The Hudson Institute: 139-163.

Skocpol, Theda. "The Tocqueville Problem." Address to Annual Meeting of the Social Science History Association, New Orleans, October 12, 1996.

Vanourek, Gregg, Scott Hamilton, and Chester Finn. "Is There Life After Big Government?: The Potential of Civil Society." The Hudson Institute.

Verba, Sidney, Kay Lehman Schlozman, and Henry E. Brady. *Voice and Equality: Civic Voluntarism in American Politics.* Cambridge, MA: Harvard University Press, 1995.

Walzer, Michael, "Civility and Civic Virtue in Contemporary America." In Radical Principles: Reflections of an Unreconstructed Democrat. New York: Basic Books, 1980.

Walzer, Michael. "Idea of Civil Society." *Dissent* (Spring 1991): 293-304.

Wilson, William Julius. *When Work Disappears: The World of the New Urban Poor.* New York: Knopf, 1996.

NOTES

1. http://www.mihancivilsociety.org/suggested.html
2. http://www.cpn.org/tools/dictionary/capital.html
3. http://www.sum.uio.no/research/global_governance/ethics/index.html
4. http://www.iep.utm.edu/h/hum-rts.htm#top
5. www.lisproject.org/workshop/06readinglist.pdf
6. *Ibid.*
7. http://www.bowlingalone.com/socialcapital.php3

Author Biography

Dr Prasenjit Maiti (1971-) began his academic career as a Senior Lecturer in Political Science at the University of Burdwan, West Bengal. He obtained his Bachelor's and Master's Degrees from Presidency College (University of Calcutta) and Jawaharlal Nehru University, New Delhi respectively. Dr Maiti topped his Graduation Class at Presidency College and was awarded the National Merit Scholarship of the Government of India for this achievement. He later specialized in comparative federal theory and the politics of Third World societies during his postgraduate studies at JNU.

The Institute of Federalism (University of Fribourg, Switzerland) awarded him a fellowship in 1999 to pursue his Doctoral Research on India's problems of governance since Independence. He originally began working on this problem while associated with a research project funded by the South Asia Institute of the University of Heidelberg, Germany. This study was subsequently revised and published in 2002. He attended the International Conference on Federalism at the University of St Gallen upon being invited by the Swiss Government.

Dr Maiti later joined the Development Sector in 2003 when he started working as a staff member of The Energy and Resources Institute, New Delhi on the Kolkata Environmental Improvement Project funded by the Department for International Development, United Kingdom and Asian Development Bank. He was a member of the Resettlement Plan Implementation Working Group of KEIP while professionally associated with TERI (NGO Consultants to the Project). He worked briefly for the Forum of Federations, a Non-Government Organization based at Ottawa, Canada. He later served as an Evaluation Consultant to TERI while working on the National Green Corps Project funded by the Ministry of Environment and Forests, Government of India.

Dr Maiti also worked for the Consumer Unity and Trust Society, Jaipur as a Consultant on a livelihood perception study in the context of the World Trade Organization's policies in the agriculture and textiles sectors. He worked briefly with the Council for Development Studies, West Bengal Pollution Control Board, ActionAid and *The Telegraph*, Kolkata. His second book, *Development Discourses*, was published in 2005. Dr Maiti edited the multi-volume book series, *Development Studies*, and also coordinated publication of another series of volumes on Urban Development Debates.

Dr Maiti served as a Reviewer for *Policing: An International Journal of Police Strategies and Management* (College of Education, Division of Criminal Justice, University of Cincinnati) in 2001. He is also Referee for *Environment and Development Economics* (University of York, Heslington) published by the Cambridge University Press and *Crime Prevention and Community Safety* (Perpetuity Press, Leicester) as well as Reviewer for *Globalization and Health*.

Dr Maiti has written more than fifty papers in professional journals worldwide. His present research interests include the politics of development, civil society and political ecology. He has contributed his expertise in the urban development sector to the Kolkata Urban Services for the Poor Project sponsored by DFID. He presently serves as a Project Manager with Consulting Engineering Services (India), Kolkata where his professional inputs are utilized for social impact assessment studies of infrastructure development projects. He was invited as a Guest Professor to the University of Southern Denmark, Esbjerg in 2007.

Terms of Discourse

Capacity-Building
Civil Society Organizations
Communist Party of India (Marxist)
Communist Party of India (Marxist-Leninist)
Community Participation
Community-Based Organizations
Corridor of Impact
Culture Root Paradigms
Democratic Decentralization
Development
Development Alternatives
Development Ethics
Dialectical Materialism
Ecology
Empowerment
Entitlement Matrix
Environment
Freedom
Gender
Globalization
Grassroots
Ideology
Information Technology
Infrastructure Development
Land Acquisition
Land Reforms
Land Rights
Left Front Government
Livelihood Restoration
Monitoring and Evaluation
Non-Government Organizations
Operation and Maintenance
Operation Barga
People's Democratic Revolution
Progress
Project Affected Persons
Resettlement Action Plan
Resettlement and Rehabilitation
Right of Way
Security of Tenure
Social Development
Stakeholders
Structural Adjustment Programs

Index